KEY IDEAS in POLITICS

Moyra Grant

Published in 2003 by:
Nelson Thornes Ltd
Delta Place
27 Bath Road
CHELTENHAM
GL53 7TH
United Kingdom

03 04 05 06 07 / 10 9 8 7 6 5 4 3 2 1

A catalogue record for this book is available from the British Library

ISBN 0 7487 7096 8

Page make-up by Florence Production Ltd

Printed and bound in Spain by GraphyCems

Contents

Introduction

Politics has been shaped by a range of key ideas, some of them comprehensive ideologies, others specific concepts, and yet others institutions or processes. The aim of this book is to review a selection of these key ideas in a way that is more comprehensive than a standard dictionary, but which is sufficiently concise to provide the reader with quick and easy-to-read summaries of the key ideas, as a basis for understanding important political issues and events. The ideas are presented in alphabetical order for ease of reference.

The book covers key ideologies (such as conservatism, liberalism, socialism), core political concepts (such as equality, freedom, justice), topical issues (such as the European Union, 'new' Labour, globalisation), and concepts central to the UK political system (such as devolution and parliamentary government). Some, such as the concept of human nature, are as old as politics itself but still form the bedrocks of contemporary political thought; others, such as globalisation, are relatively new but are having a real impact on all of our lives.

Each section is divided into three sub-sections: 'The Idea' – a very short introduction and core definition; 'Development of the Idea' – an outline of the origin, background and development of the concept, with relevant names and related concepts; and 'Evaluation of the Idea' – an analysis of diverse usages (and misusages), and of the validity and applicability of the idea to the UK and politics today. *Key Ideas in Politics* is a handbook, intended mainly for students on AS/A2 Level courses, but also useful for the general reader who wants to gain some insight into a subject which profoundly shapes our daily lives.

Acknowledgements

❖

The author and publishers would like to thank the following for permission to reproduce photographs:

- Associated Press, AP (p.124)
- Corel 654 (NT) (p.7, 129)
- Diamar 14 (NT) (p.53)
- Digital Vision BP (NT) (p.134)
- Illustrated London News VI (NT) (p.60, 119)
- Illustrated London News V2 (NT) (p.110)
- Stockpix 7 (NT) (p.55)
- The National Portrait Gallery, London (p.28, 107)
- Topham Picture Point (p.2, 65, 79, 92)

Anarchism

A PHILOSOPHY WHICH REJECTS ALL FORMS OF COERCION, ESPECIALLY STATE AND government. The term derives from the ancient Greek meaning, literally 'no rule', and is often used negatively to imply chaos and disorder. The nineteenth-century anarchist Pierre-Joseph Proudhon (1809–65) was the first to announce proudly, in 1840, 'I am an anarchist' – as an advocate of direct self-government, personal freedom and rejection of all forms of power.

A LTHOUGH THERE ARE PRE-NINETEENTH-CENTURY ANARCHISTIC MOVEMENTS AND thinkers – for example, the Diggers of the 1640s (a group of rural egalitarians), and William Godwin (1756–1836) who proposed a free-market economy with a minimal state – anarchism largely developed in the nineteenth century as an alternative revolutionary theory to Marxism.

There are many diverse schools of anarchist thought, and they agree on only a few basic points. They all reject any form of coercive power as well as most forms of authority based upon consent – including the law, politics, police, penal system, armed forces, education and religion – because anarchists believe that such consent is not genuine but a product of socialisation and manipulation by the power-holders.

Political socialisation is the process by which political beliefs and attitudes are acquired and instilled. Every individual has to learn to adapt to the system in which they are living and every system, if it is to survive, must encourage this process of adaptation. Thus everyone from a relatively early age holds some sort of ideology or political belief system, even if it is usually only a very vague and unthinking acceptance of the status quo or of one's parents' beliefs. We do not pop out of the womb as little flag-waving fascists or liberal democrats – we learn what we are to become. All individuals, in all countries, are subject to the process of socialisation – sometimes by open and crude indoctrination, usually by more subtle, less honest and often more effective methods. The most important agencies of socialisation are the family, mass media, school and work, peer group (friends and colleagues) and religion. For example, it is through such socialisation that most people in the UK come to define the concept of 'democracy' purely in terms of the British, electoral, parliamentary model, which is in fact only one, quite limited, form or variant of democracy. Equally, most Americans dislike 'communism' though few know or understand the theory. Such restriction or distortion of knowledge about competing ideologies is, itself, often an important part of the socialisation process. Anarchists believe that socialisation creates false support and consent for political systems which are inherently oppressive and coercive.

All anarchists also, above all, reject state and government. (They point out that, until some six thousand years ago, all humans lived in stateless societies and, therefore, could readily do so again.) They all have a highly optimistic view of human nature. One of the earliest anarchistic thinkers, Godwin (1793), went so far as to say that *'Perfectibility is the most unequivocal characteristic of the human species'*. Where humans are bad, say anarchists, this is due to the corrupting influence of state, police and church power and exploitation – hence it is a product of nurture, not nature. They all, therefore, share the common philosophical goal of freedom as a primary objective. They all reject orthodox forms of representative democracy, dismissing them as a sham and a facade where voters surrender their personal autonomy and thus collude in their own oppression. Finally, since they all seek a fundamental transformation of society, they are all revolutionary. Beyond these few points, however, anarchists agree on very little.

As befits the very nature of the philosophy, there are almost as many different theories of anarchism as there are anarchist thinkers and writers. Very broadly, anarchism can be subdivided into two schools: left-wing, collectivist, 'ultra-socialist' varieties, and right-wing, individualist, 'ultra-liberal' varieties.

The original, and still predominant, body of anarchist thought is left-wing and collectivist, favouring collective economic ownership, equality and small, self-governing, directly democratic communes and other collective organisations. Many of them, like the Russian Peter Kropotkin (1842–1921), are 'anarcho-communists'. This is a philos-

ophy which is very similar to the communist theories of nineteenth-century writers such as Karl Marx, but which rejects the idea of any state, even a workers' state. Anarcho-communists believe that human nature is essentially social and altruistic and that society should be based upon mutual cooperation and voluntary associations. Laws imposed from above should be replaced by genuinely democratic contracts – voluntary and cooperative agreements – within and between communes.

Other left-wing anarchists, like James Guillaume, are 'anarcho-syndicalists', advocating a form of revolutionary trade unionism which would overthrow the

Peter Kropotkin

state and collectivise the economy via the tactic of a general strike (but which, unlike pure syndicalism, would not set up a workers' state).

These strands of anarchism clearly derive from revolutionary socialist ideas and share goals very similar to those of Marxism. However, they disagree profoundly on how to achieve those goals: Marx scathingly described contemporary anarchists like Proudhon as 'utopian socialists' in contrast with his own objective, materialist theory of 'scientific socialism'; by this he meant that their theories were based upon emotion and moralistic value judgements (for example, Proudhon's famous statement that *'Property is theft'*) rather than upon hard, factual analysis. Collectivist anarchists, in their turn, wholly reject Marx's transitionary phase of a *'dictatorship of the proletariat'*, that is, a temporary workers' state, after the revolution. As the Russian anarchist Mikhail Bakunin (1814–76) put it – with prescience, some would say – *'Equality without freedom is the despotism of the state. The most fatal combination that could possibly be formed, would be to unite socialism to absolutism; to unite the aspiration of the people for material well-being with the dictatorship or the concentration of all political and social power in the state'* (Bakunin 1990). Critics of the oppressive nature of twentieth-century 'communism' in countries such as the former Soviet Union might suggest that Bakunin foresaw the future accurately.

Whereas collectivist anarchists derive their ideas from socialism, individualist anarchists derive their ideas largely from classical liberal thinking. Max Stirner (1843) developed a theory of 'egoism': a concept of complete personal authority and autonomy where the individual is the centre of his own moral universe, with no obligation to accept the rules or restraints of others – a sort of 'anarchism of the mind'. Anarcho-capitalism, by contrast, is a form of extreme libertarianism which takes free market, laissez-faire economic theory to its logical conclusion and argues for absolutely minimal government intervention – that is, private police and courts, no compulsory taxation or education, no state regulation of health and safety at work or of the content of foods or medicines etc. – thus the 'invisible hand' of free market forces, as opposed to the 'dead hand' of state regulation (as the eighteenth-century liberal Adam Smith put it), would truly reign supreme.

The methods of political action and social transition advocated by anarchists are also many and varied. Anarchism was originally, and logically, pacifist (e.g. Proudhon, Kropotkin and the writer Leo Tolstoy). Since anarchists reject coercion in all its forms, and since violence is the ultimate form of coercion, most anarchists naturally reject it. Some anarchists, however, have turned to violence, either in the form of terrorism (e.g. Bakunin) or the potentially violent general strike (Guillaume) due to frustration at their lack of success, a belief in the nihilistic virtue of destruction, the need to counter a violent state or simply the desire to expose the inherently violent nature of the state by provoking it. This tactical divide between pacifist and violent anarchism is found mainly within the left-wing, collectivist strand of the philosophy. Thus, the range of methods employed by anarchists includes peaceful education and persuasion; mass, passive resistance to the state; non-payment of taxes; boycotts of key institutions, products and companies; strikes and other forms of industrial action; meetings, marches and demonstrations; committing 'acts of senseless beauty' such as painting the lampposts green; civil disobedience, that is, forms of peaceful law-breaking as political protest (associated particularly with the American libertarian Henry Thoreau); riots and insurrection; and acts of violence and terrorism, particularly against politicians, judges and military leaders. What anarchists philosophically cannot do is participate in mainstream, orthodox, ballot box and party politics, since that would be subscribing to the politics of the state.

Evaluation of the Idea

'ANARCHISM' AND THE WORD 'ANARCHY' ARE WIDELY MISUNDERSTOOD – OR deliberately misused – to imply chaos and disorder. Even when anarchism is understood as a philosophy of human betterment and progress, it is widely condemned as 'utopian' in the negative sense of over-optimistic, unattainable fantasy. Much depends on whether commentators share anarchists' faith in human nature. Anarchists themselves, of course, would say that scepticism about human nature is the product of socialisation and of the corrupting state and power systems which they seek to overthrow.

Philosophies such as traditional conservatism, liberalism and fascism argue that it is both impossible and undesirable to construct a stateless society. Toryism and fascism do not favour freedom; but even liberals, whose primary doctrine is freedom, argue that the state and its laws are necessary to guarantee genuine freedom, and that representation through the ballot box is necessary to ensure democracy rather than 'mobocracy'. Liberal critics of anarchism fear that, in a lawless society, a tyranny of majority public opinion would prevail which could be deeply intolerant of minority rights and views. They point to the apparent need for state legislation against sexual and racial discrimination, apparent public support for capital punishment and so on.

A quotation from the Russian anarcho-communist Peter Kropotkin (1842–1921) may lend support to this view. In anarcho-communism, work would be voluntary and most people would have sufficient sense of common interest to participate willingly. But what of those who would not work? *'If you are absolutely incapable of producing anything useful, or if you refuse to do it, then you live like an isolated man or like an invalid. If we are rich enough to give you the necessities of life we shall be delighted to give them to you. You are a man, and you have the right to live. But as you wish to live under special conditions, and leave the ranks, it is more probable that you will suffer for it in daily relations with other citizens. You will be looked upon as a ghost of bourgeois society, unless friends of yours, discovering you to be a talent, kindly free you from all moral obligations by doing all the necessary work for you'* (Kropotkin 1902). This suggests a punitive form of social exclusion that could be crueller than most forms of retribution imposed by the state and its laws.

Even Marxists, who share the anarchist goal of the stateless society, point out that, while anarchists are very good at condemning the state, they are not very good at explaining the state. If human nature is potentially so good and the state is so intrinsically evil, oppressive and corrupting, how and why did it come into being in the first place, why is it so persistent and pervasive, and why do most people not see through its consensual facade and reject it more readily?

Does anarchism have any relevance to modern, industrialised societies? Some philosophies such as Toryism and fascism, of course, would argue that it was never relevant, desirable or possible, largely because they do not share anarchists' faith in human nature. Other writers, notably twentieth-century neo-Marxist Herbert Marcuse (1964), have argued that modern, industrialised, mass societies – whether capitalist or communist – are tending almost universally towards totalitarianism, that is, in the opposite direction from anarchism.

Advocates of anarchism, however, would say that the reality of present-day society presented by Marcuse makes anarchism all the more necessary and desirable today. Right-wing anarchism (invigorated by the rise of New Right conservatism) blossomed in America in the 1970s and 1980s, with writers like Robert Nozick (1974) and Murray Rothbard (1978) arguing for a minimalist state and a self-regulating market economy. Left-wing anarchism has real practical relevance in modern politics, from the Spanish anarchists of the 1930s, through violent groups in post-war Europe such as the Red Brigade in Italy and Class War in Britain, to incidents like the assassination of Italian Prime Minister Aldo Moro in the 1980s, the anti-poll tax riot in London in 1990 and the current 'Stop the City' and anti-capitalist demonstrations throughout Europe. Pacifist anarchism, too, has had strong influence within the anti-nuclear, environmentalist and (again) anti-capitalist movements of the last two decades.

Weaknesses of anarchism therefore include its utopian view of human nature, its rejection of traditional forms of political organisation, its philosophical diversity and divisions and its tendency to violence which critics perceive as counter-productive.

As an uplifting philosophy of potential human goodness and social progress or even perfectibility, anarchism cannot be bettered. As a philosophy of rational, realistic explanation and analysis, it is often doubted.

Authority

❖

The Idea

THE ABILITY TO ACT, OR TO MAKE OTHERS ACT, BECAUSE THEY BELIEVE THAT THE decision maker has the right to do so – that is, legitimate power based upon consent and respect. Authority may derive, not only from election, but also from tradition, knowledge and experience, rules and principles or sheer personality. It should be distinguished from power, that is, the capacity to coerce and compel obedience, regardless of consent.

Development of the Idea

THE PRIMARY POLITICAL INTERPRETATION OF 'AUTHORITY' IS 'THE RIGHT TO RULE' – TO BE 'in authority'. Political authority implies government by consent – or at least compliance – based on the acceptance that the decision makers have the legitimate right to fulfil that role, even if their decisions are not always popular ('assent without credence', as the philosopher Spinoza put it). It can mean, for example, the right to pass a law, to instruct soldiers to fire upon a crowd, to confer an honour or title or to impose the death sentence. A secondary interpretation – to be 'an authority' – is expertise. Both interpretations imply the subordination of one person's will or judgement to another's.

To say that a decision maker or leader has authority is not, nowadays, to describe any single form of rule, but rather to describe the attitude of the people who are subject to that rule, and their acceptance of it. Authority is therefore a relational concept which may attach to a wide range of forms of rule. Perhaps, like beauty, it is in the eye of the beholder.

De jure authority implies legitimate power in theory, that is, according to the laws and rules, as opposed to practice – *de facto* authority. For example, the UK monarch has extensive theoretical authority under the law; her royal prerogative powers include the right to appoint all ministers, declare war and choose the date of the general election. *De facto* – by convention or tradition – these powers have passed to the prime minister of the day in order to grant them democratic legitimacy.

Political authority involves a claim to the consent, respect and obedience of its subjects, and attempts to justify it have been at the core of political philosophy for centuries. The idea of a social contract as the basis of legitimacy was introduced by Plato and taken up by many philosophers since, notably Hobbes, Locke and Rousseau. Social contract theory asserts that legitimate government is the product of voluntary agreements between free agents, hence political power is legitimised through consent. This contrasts with, for example, sixteenth-century theories of the 'divine right of kings' which asserted that the unlimited authority of monarchs was ordained by God, regardless of the consent of their subjects. It also contrasts with notions that 'might is right' – that coercive power dictates its own legitimacy.

The German sociologist Max Weber (1864–1920) was, you might say, a leading authority upon the subject. He distinguished three types or sources of authority: first, *traditional* authority deriving from sheer longevity (e.g. the House of Lords or monarchy). This is the basis of the traditional conservative view of authority – deriving, at root, from the divine right of kings – but it is sometimes perceived as increasingly anachronistic in the modern day, associated more with 'primitive' tribal societies and their 'elders' than with modern democratic regimes. Secondly, said Weber, there is *charismatic* authority, deriving from intense personal magnetism and character (e.g. Christ, Churchill, Gandhi or Hitler). This is often associated with dictatorships and may often be *de facto* rather than *de jure* – for example, the popular support granted to a rebel guerrilla leader due to sheer force of personality. Finally, there is *legal-rational* authority, deriving from the office rather than the character of the individual, that is, from due process, training, rules, laws and principles (e.g. the police or civil service, doctors or teachers). The office-holder may, of course, have personal charm in abundance, but the authority of the office is transferred whenever there is a change of personnel. This is widely perceived as the most relevant and accepted source of authority today, especially in liberal democratic societies. However, even there, the media-oriented nature of modern election campaigns has fostered a growing emphasis on personality politics and the electoral advantages of charisma.

Weber was actually attempting to develop a theory of social change, by explaining how one type of authority – e.g. traditional – can be successfully challenged by another – usually charismatic – to generate radical or revolutionary change, but thereafter, how the 'routinisation of charisma' must ensue (because charisma is a highly unstable basis for authority) and legal-rational authority must be established to endow secondary power-holders – notably bureaucrats – with long-term legitimacy. Even if this analysis is perceived as less relevant now than then, his typology of sources of authority remains one of the most useful.

Other, often related, sources of authority include expertise and, of course, election. Clearly, however, authority need not depend upon election – monarchs, peers, judges and civil servants may all have authority without election – although in the modern age of mass democracy it is now one of the most widely recognised and accepted sources of legitimacy and rightful power.

It is, of course, possible – indeed, common – to combine these various types and sources of authority. Islamic religious leaders, for example, derive their legitimacy both from their traditional social status and their implementation of Islamic religious law, which has legal-rational undertones. Political leaders in the UK have, essentially, legal-rational authority deriving from due electoral processes, but some (perhaps Thatcher?) have also had personal charisma, and Conservative leaders especially often used to claim traditional authority based upon birth, social status and the process of prime ministerial appointment by the monarch. Indeed, it was only since the 1960s that the Conservative party deigned to introduce a process of leadership election, and only since 2001 that all Conservative members (rather than just MPs) were allowed to participate in such elections.

In summary, authority may derive from constitutions, laws, conventions or other rules, from tradition, birth, heredity or social status, from election, expertise or superior factual access, from personal character and aura, faith, doctrine and religious belief, from the legitimacy attached to formal office or even from familial love and trust (e.g. parental authority).

Finally, authority alone is not a sufficient basis for rule. The authority granted to a prime minister or a police officer must confer power, so that a prime minister may sack an inadequate minister or a policeman may forcibly arrest a criminal. However, in a democracy it is a necessary basis for rule, and the loss of authority should result in the loss of power – Margaret Thatcher's removal from office by her party in 1990 being one obvious example.

Evaluation of the Idea

E ARLY CONCEPTS OF AUTHORITY USUALLY ASSERTED AN UNQUESTIONABLE MORAL legitimacy deriving, not from the people, but from the source of power itself – for example, the divine right of kings. Similarly, the French philosopher Auguste Comte (1798–1857) argued that authority requires the abandonment of critical thought on the part of those subject to it; that is, the commitment demanded by authority does not allow for legitimate disapproval of whatever is prescribed. This may still be a valid contention where authority is perceived to derive from the superior factual awareness, knowledge or expertise of the decision maker. Otherwise, however, most writers – such as Spinoza – disagree; one can dislike and disapprove of the decisions made by those in authority while still accepting – on the basis of other criteria – their right to decide and also one's obligation to abide by those decisions. Contemporary concepts of authority thus stress its basis in popular endorsement – i.e. it is given, not taken, and it does not disallow independent judgement by the people.

Equally – and contrary to philosophers such as Hobbes – law alone is not, now, generally held to be a sufficient basis of legitimate authority. For example, Nazi law allowed an ss officer to dictate life or death. However, the Nuremberg War Crimes Tribunal decided that such rules of state did not accord with higher precepts of justice or morality.

The utility of making a distinction between legitimate authority and naked power may be increasingly futile in the modern day, in that it is difficult to envisage any contemporary system of rule lasting long without some basis of consent and popular support. The sheer cost, resources, energy and inefficiency necessarily expended upon a regime of naked power would make its long-term survival unlikely. Today's political power-holders increasingly seek, and have the capacity to create, authority based upon popular consent.

How that consent is generated therefore becomes a central question. The common understanding of democracy is that authority generates power; conversely, however, power may be used to generate authority. Especially in the modern age of 'mass society' with mass media and communications, consent and mass support can be artificially created by power-holders through persuasion, propaganda and indoctrination.

'Totalitarian' regimes (a concept which, itself, was only created in the twentieth-century era of mass democratic society) are said to differ from 'authoritarian' dictatorships in that they demand mass, active – indeed, downright fanatical – consent and support. The chief examples were the fascist and Nazi regimes of the 1920s and 30s. This was not the kind of democracy that would be recognised by today's liberal regimes. All fascist movements used a combination of propaganda and terror to create and, indeed, coerce mass consent or compliance. The control and use of the mass media – newspapers and especially radio and film – were crucial to the rising popularity of fascism and confirmed it as a specifically twentieth-century phenomenon. However, once in power, fascist parties eliminated their rivals and manipulated the legal and judicial systems to legitimise their activities. They despised the division and diversity of liberal democracy and sought absolute unity under absolute leadership within the total power of the supremely organic state – 'strength through unity'. Nevertheless, in so far as fascism involved mass consent, participation and authority, it has often been labelled 'totalitarian democracy'. However, such consent is widely perceived by liberal critics to be the product of intensive indoctrination and therefore not to be genuine. This poses problems about authority and consent as criteria of democracy, because the most 'totalitarian' systems may be the most active in creating consent through indoctrination, and therefore in this sense presumably the most 'democratic'.

A prominent contributor to the Cold War School of writers on totalitarianism, Hannah Arendt (1968), countered this thesis by saying, '*If authority is to be defined at all, it must be in contradistinction to both coercion and persuasion by argument*'. However, this argument chooses to discount the pervasive power of socialisation, perhaps from an early age, which may render us incapable of distinguishing legitimate government based upon genuine consent, from government artificially legitimised through indoctrination.

An increasingly fashionable contention is that the very idea of authority is being eroded or discredited in the modern world because of growing scepticism about the legitimacy of today's political power-holders – whether due to perceptions of sleaze, corruption, political self-interest, flawed processes of democracy or anachronistic claims to authority such as tradition. For example, the election of George W. Bush as

American president in 2000 was widely seen as a flawed process to the extent of substantially discrediting the result. (Even President Mugabe of Zimbabwe cheekily offered to send observers to oversee the election.) A growing concern in the UK is that the present Labour government's obsession with image and hence with 'spin' – their desire to manufacture public consent and authority – is precisely one reason why voters are increasingly dubious or disillusioned about the government's underlying, legal-rational authority, that is, basic honesty and competence. This may account for declining turnouts at elections (a mere 59 per cent in the general election of 2001) and increasing civil disobedience, direct action or sheer apathy. Nevertheless, this analysis seems unduly negative. If authority was really so eroded, the extent of public disorder and reversion to purely coercive political power would surely be greater than it is.

From most political perspectives, this highlights the main justification of authority, that, whatever its source, it is a necessary basis of legitimate power and hence of social order, peace and harmony. That said, whether any or all of the concepts and sources of authority outlined above can really justify the extent of power demanded by modern states is much disputed – most notably by anarchism.

Capitalism

The Idea

A N ECONOMIC SYSTEM BASED UPON PRIVATE OWNERSHIP OF PRODUCTIVE PROPERTY for private profit. It may involve a very strong state system of regulation and planning (e.g. fascism), or a very limited state and a free market with minimal compulsory taxation, education, health and welfare, regulations on the content of food or medicines etc. (e.g. anarcho-capitalism).

Development of the Idea

C APITALISM IS AN ECONOMIC SYSTEM BASED UPON PRODUCTION FOR SALE RATHER than for personal use, and based upon the predominant existence of capital – accumulation in the hands of competing, non-government owners (whether individuals, corporations or joint stock companies etc.) for private profit, in conjunction with a system of wage labour, with money as a medium of exchange. Profit maximisation and material gain are the primary motives for investment, enterprise and effort on the part of both capitalists and labourers. The capitalist or his managerial agent is also the 'boss', in control of hiring and firing, buying and selling, production techniques and the work environment. Capitalism therefore differs from, for example, simple commodity production, barter, slavery, serfdom, cooperatives and worker-managed companies. Industrial capitalism first developed in eighteenth-century Europe, but the word 'capitalism' is rarely used by non-Marxist economists. Moreover, (according to the *Oxford English Dictionary*) the word was first used only in 1854, by Thackeray, and even Marx did not use it in writing until 1877.

The left/right divide (see later) is essentially an economic, rather than a political, schism between the opponents and the defenders of capitalism.

Capitalism may, in theory, involve almost any degree of state intervention and power, from none at all, through weak or moderate, to strong or absolute. (In practice, there is no example of a capitalist economy without some degree of state involvement.)

At one extreme, anarcho-capitalism favours an economic system of private ownership for private profit with minimal or no state involvement. This is libertarianism, with a desire to maximise negative freedom, that is, non-interference by the state, whether in the form of help or hindrance. Murray Rothbard (1978), for example, argued that private property is an absolute right for all, taxation is legalised robbery and that advances in modern technology make market sovereignty increasingly feasible and the state increasingly redundant. He therefore argued for '*the dissolution of the state into social and market arrangements*'.

Classical liberalism did not perceive quite such a minimalist role for the state, but nevertheless argued that it should perform only a 'nightwatchman' role; as former US president (1801–1809) Thomas Jefferson said, '*That government is best which governs least*'. At the heart of classical liberalism was a belief in the rationality of human nature and therefore, again, in negative freedom from state interference. The state was seen as inherently oppressive and hence as 'a realm of coercion', whereas private or civil society was 'a realm of freedom'. The state was a necessary evil to safeguard law, order and security, but its role should be limited. It should exist to protect the three basic, natural or inalienable rights of life, liberty and property (said John Locke). Above all, classical liberalism believed in laissez-faire (literally meaning 'leave be'): free market, private enterprise capitalism and the absolute right of the individual to enter and to succeed or fail in the market on his own merits, without state help or hindrance. Thus it advocated a free market economy controlled only by the forces of supply and demand (Adam Smith's 'invisible hand') and not by the 'dead hand' of state regulation or direction. In England, the ideological battle for laissez-faire was won – if only temporarily – in 1846 with the repeal of the Corn Laws which had fixed the price of corn at high rates to benefit the farmers at the expense of the consumers.

After a long period of substantial state intervention in the US and UK capitalist economies, New Right conservatism of the 1980s and 1990s sought to 'roll back the frontiers' of the state in the economy through privatisation, deregulation and curbs on trade union rights and activities; it perceived both the state and the trade unions as preventing market forces from operating freely and efficiently. (However, in contrast with anarcho-capitalism, the New Right demands strong – even authoritarian – state intervention in non-economic spheres.)

Modern liberalism favours a mixed economy with private ownership where possible but state intervention, regulation or provision where necessary to curb private monopolies, to promote positive – actualised – individual freedom and to ensure choice and diversity of goods and services.

Social democracy seeks (or does not object to) yet more state ownership of major industries and services in the form of nationalisation, coupled with significant state welfare provision and, where necessary, state regulation of private enterprise to protect consumers' health and safety as well as workers' pay and conditions, to promote employment and to collect business taxes for social redistribution.

Fascism (e.g. Italy in the 1920s and 1930s) sought a private enterprise economy combined with *lo stato totalitario*: an all-powerful state in both the public and private spheres. It endeavoured to construct 'corporatism': a tripartite economic system – i.e. consisting of three parts – involving representatives of the state, the employers and the workers (firmly in that descending order of power) in economic planning and policy-making. The aim was to eliminate or deny any conflict of class interests and to maximise productivity and profit in pursuit of the national interest. This form of capitalism was therefore intensely state-regulated.

Thus the private economy can range from free market capitalism, through welfare capitalism, to state capitalism.

Evaluation of the Idea

ONE QUESTION IS, HOW MUCH STATE INTERVENTION CAN OCCUR BEFORE A SYSTEM CAN cease to be described as capitalist? The original concept of capitalism – the 'perfect competition' model – was of a wholly free market of individual, relatively small-scale entrepreneurs hiring individual workers at minimum cost to produce maximum output at the cheapest possible price. This was never a true picture, and it has become less true since the early twentieth century. State intervention has been substantial even in the most 'free market' economies such as the USA. From the 1930s on, many writers perceived the rise of shareholding as a new form of capitalism characterised by the separation of ownership and control. This was sometimes even characterised as 'post-capitalism' by those who mistakenly defined capitalism only in terms of the laissez-faire or perfect competition model.

Conversely, the neologism 'state capitalism' has been employed to describe, variously, the controlled economies of the great powers during the World War I, the fascist and Nazi economies of the 1930s, and even (by some Trotskyists) the post-war Soviet economy – on the grounds that, while the Soviet state owned the means of production, it exploited the workers just as private ownership did. This last is an imprecise and clearly ideological usage of the concept of 'capitalism'. The key issue is whether the state owns, or merely regulates, the economic centres of production, and whether private ownership for private profit remains the predominant feature of the economy – in which case, the economy is capitalist, regardless of the extent of state intervention and regulation.

As capitalist economies evolved and state intervention increased in the twentieth century, political and social struggles simultaneously modified the legislative and administrative framework of those economies – for example, gradually extending the electoral franchise and civil rights beyond male property-holders to all adult men and eventually even to all adult women. Although capitalism can take a variety of political forms – monarchical, republican, fascist, authoritarian, anarchic (at least in theory) etc. – most contemporary capitalist systems currently characterise themselves as liberal democracies.

This raises another obvious question: whether, on balance, capitalism is beneficial to the few or to the many, economically and politically.

The case for the defence of capitalism is that private property is a natural right (John Locke), socially necessary (according to the German philosopher Hegel), and a mechanism which limits and disperses economic power. A capitalist economy is said to maximise wealth and production, promote technological development and ensure a rational – even optimal – distribution of resources, thereby enhancing the living standards and freedoms of the many. It secures equality of opportunity as well as basic political liberties. The concept of social justice at the heart of capitalism is the assertion that inequalities of wealth and income fairly reflect the unequal merits, efforts and contributions of those who participate in the economy.

The contemporary writer Francis Fukuyama (1989) has therefore argued that, with the collapse of most of the 'communist' regimes by the 1990s, the 'universalisation' of liberal democratic capitalism marked the 'end of history' and the triumph of the best of all possible worlds. (He has since admitted that he was wrong about the universalisation of liberal democracy – see later under 'consensus politics' – but his ideological enthusiasm for capitalism remains undimmed.)

Eighteenth-century liberal theorists such as John Locke and Adam Smith were staunch defenders of private property – indeed, Adam Smith was the earliest exponent of the 'invisible hand' of the free market forces of supply and demand – but, ironically, by utilising their theories, nineteenth-century anarchists such as Proudhon advanced the argument that 'Property is theft', and Marx developed his anti-capitalist theory of class exploitation. According to Marx, the capitalists – the bourgeoisie – exploit the working class – that is, they buy their labour and use it to create and extract surplus value in the process of production; this is the source of profit in capitalism. There is therefore an inescapable conflict of interests between the two main classes in capitalism which will culminate ultimately in working class revolution and the abolition of capitalism in favour of collective ownership. Theories such as these argue that capitalism is fundamentally unjust, inequitable, unbalanced and undemocratic, since it benefits and empowers only the few.

Lenin – the Marxist who led the Soviet Union after its 1917 revolution – perceived the early twentieth-century age of imperialism as the 'highest stage of capitalism' – the final phase which would generate devastating wars between competing capitalist states and bring about the final downfall of capitalism itself. As Marx had previously said, '*Capitalism contains within itself the seeds of its own destruction*' (Marx and Engels 1848).

However, capitalism has, so far, defied all predictions of its imminent death and is the base element of contemporary globalisation. In the second half of the twentieth century, the sheer size and economic muscle of some multinational companies became the most notable feature of the world economy: of the top 100 economic units in terms of size by 2002, 51 were private companies and 49 were states. This, in turn, has stimulated the rise of increasingly large and active anti-capitalist protest movements and demonstrations, in particular against the deep and persistent inequalities both within developed capitalist economies and between the developed and the less developed economies. The case for the defence of capitalism – and, perhaps, even the very survival of capitalism – remains dubious.

Citizenship

NARROWLY, CITIZENSHIP IS AN INDIVIDUAL'S LEGAL MEMBERSHIP OF, AND RECOGNITION by, a state which grants mutual rights and obligations between state and citizen. Broadly, a citizen is an individual with rights in relation to the state – dating from the Enlightenment mood of republicanism – as distinct from the concept of a 'subject' subservient to the state and the monarchy.

IN A NARROW, LEGALISTIC SENSE, CITIZENSHIP MEANS FORMAL MEMBERSHIP OF, AND recognition and protection by, a state (that is, a formal, sovereign political power over a given territory) of an individual. This legal definition does not apply to everyone who resides within the state; indeed, one current controversy is the growing number of people who live in, for example, the UK but who are denied legal citizenship. So-called 'aliens' are not granted the same rights to live, work and vote within the state as are British citizens. A succession of nationality and asylum laws since the 1960s have restricted rights of legal citizenship in the face of the UK's post-imperial heritage of immigration, unemployment and racialism. In this sense, the idea of 'citizenship' excludes as much as it includes; and this mode of use goes back centuries, as far back as ancient Athenian democracy where citizenship was granted only to some adult males and not to resident foreigners, women, slaves or children.

This formal concept of citizenship, as again for example in ancient Greece, grants both the right to participate in political decision-making within the community and imposes some concept of duty such as the obligation to hold public office if chosen. (The Latin root of the word for citizen, *civis*, is derived from the verb 'to summon', *cieo*.)

In the Athenian city-state of the fifth century BC, citizens – the political decision makers – in return had a duty to the state to undertake military service, attend festivals and act as jurors in the courts. Similarly, in the UK today, an individual who is on the voting register may be called up for compulsory jury service as a civic responsibility. The concept of citizenship, therefore, implies both rights and duties. Insofar as citizenship is defined primarily by the right to participate in the political process, citizenship theory is widely viewed as an extension of democratic theory. Democratic theory focuses on political institutions and procedures; citizenship theory focuses on the rights and obligations of individual participants.

An obligation is a duty or requirement. Obligation may be seen as the 'other side of the coin' – the concomitant or corollary – of the rights of citizenship. For example, in ancient Greece, the right of political participation was also seen as a duty. Today, one person's demand for freedom or privacy implies his or her duty to respect others' freedom or privacy equally. Welfare rights imply the obligation of being taxed to pay for them. Some countries today – e.g. Belgium and Australia – regard voting not only as a right but as a legal and civic obligation.

Individualist philosophies such as liberalism lay the most stress upon the concept of citizenship and corresponding individual rights. The modern 'liberal democratic' concept of citizenship has its origins in the French Revolution of 1789 which first asserted that the king must be the servant, rather than the sovereign, of his people, and which then overthrew the monarchy to establish a citizens' republic. This concept of citizenship lays more stress upon individual rights than upon obligations, at least in theory; and it also hinges on the assertion that such rights should be equally available to all (unlike, for example, the ancient Athenian concept – or, indeed, the theories of classical liberal philosophers such as John Locke, who supported slavery and a limited electoral suffrage despite his talk of 'natural rights'). Organic philosophies such as traditional conservatism and fascism lay the least stress upon the concept of citizenship rights, instead emphasising the duties and obligations of the individual to the sovereign state.

A broader, more abstract concept of citizenship is rooted in a sense of identity and belonging associated with feelings of nationalism and patriotism – thus some people may feel as if they belong to a country even if that country is not a sovereign state (e.g. Scotland or Wales), or even if they are denied legal citizenship by the state which they claim as their own. This more subjective sense of citizenship poses obvious possible conflicts: for example, republican sympathisers in Northern Ireland would rarely identify themselves as British citizens, despite their legal status; whereas many residents of Hong Kong may proudly have claimed British citizenship (at least until 1997) but were denied even the legal right of entry into Britain. Here in the UK, too, the idea of the citizen is complicated by the fact that each individual is also a subject of the Crown, implying subservience and duty over rights and freedoms – concepts which republics such as America and France have rejected since their respective revolutions.

Evaluation of the Idea

THE ATHENIAN CONCEPT OF CITIZENSHIP CENTRED ON THE RIGHT, AS WELL AS THE DUTY, of political participation. The gradual extension of the franchise in Western states such as the UK in the nineteenth and twentieth centuries meant that formal citizenship was granted, eventually, to men who were not property holders, and then even to women. As formal citizenship became universalised but widespread economic poverty and dependency continued to prevail, the nature and very concept of citizenship came under growing scrutiny. Philosophers such as Marx argued that a social revolution was necessary to reconcile the Greek ideal of civic participation with genuine social equality and economic well-being for all. Others looked instead to reform and a growing role for the state.

The concept of 'social citizenship' was first introduced in Britain by modern liberal thinkers such as Hobhouse, Tawney and Beveridge and was developed by the sociologist T.H. Marshall (1950). He identified three types of rights: civil rights which, he asserted, developed in the eighteenth century; political rights which emerged and expanded in the nineteenth century; and social rights such as employment, education, health, welfare and social security which developed in the twentieth century. The modern – especially post-war – emphasis on social rights implies a positive role for the state in enhancing individual and collective rights and, from the socialist perspective, equal rights for all; for the radical socialist, this means equality not just of opportunity but of outcome. Socialists also stress workers' collective rights in the workplace, whether in respect of health and safety provisions or in demands for workers' participation in the running of the company. They also emphasise trade union rights of association, assembly and action which both liberals and conservatives would query, qualify or reject out of hand.

The post war development of the welfare state embodied the modern liberal concept of social citizenship and was intended to extend the social and economic rights of citizenship – such as a job, and access to comprehensive health and welfare entitlements – to all. However, this liberal or social democratic version of citizenship in practice came to be seen, by the late 1970s, as excessively statist and bureaucratic, as well as paternalist and often downright patronising; more about care, compassion and control from on high than about genuine entitlements and empowerment for all. Hence the alternative New Right interpretation of citizenship which emerged in the 1980s.

According to the ideology of the New Right, the 'good citizen' is an individual who makes an active and responsible contribution to the community, whether by joining their local Neighbourhood Watch, by 'walking with purpose' (to quote former UK Home Secretary Michael Howard's much-derided description of voluntary street patrols), by picking up litter, looking after the young, the old and the sick through family or 'care in the community', by becoming a school governor or by running a profitable business. This concept of the active citizen is actually more about civil obligations than about civil rights, and is ideologically at odds with the notion that the state has a duty to provide for the citizen in terms of welfare and protection against need or deprivation.

This New Right approach perceives the active citizen as a possessive market individual rather than as a participant in the political and social community and, according to liberal and socialist critics, it is implicitly divisive with its not always unspoken disapproval of the passive, dependent and needy.

The concept of an 'underclass' was widely deployed in the late 1980s and early 1990s to describe those excluded from the economic advantages of the free market. Critics of the New Right blamed Conservative government policies for generating structural unemployment and inequality. Supporters of the New Right, however, depicted the underclass in cultural terms as people whose own immoral and illegitimate behaviour was to blame for their plight – behaviour which had been sanctioned by previous Labour and traditional Tory governments' policies which had fostered a 'culture of dependency'.

The election of the first 'new' Labour government in the UK in 1997 marked the rejection of the rampant market individualism and exclusive concept of citizenship of the New Right in favour of a more communitarian approach which, nevertheless, stressed both rights and responsibilities and rejected the egalitarianism of previous Labour governments.

Meanwhile, many groups in society – ethnic minorities, women, homosexuals, the disabled, the elderly, the poor and unemployed – are still fighting for equal rights in a whole range of different areas, especially work, legal equality and social acceptance. They may still perceive themselves to be – and are often described as – 'second class citizens'.

The concept of citizenship also has an increasingly international as well as a domestic dimension. For some, Europe is a common home. Article 8 of the Maastricht Treaty establishes 'citizenship of the European Union' for every legal citizen and worker of a member state.

Finally, a growing perception of, and concern about, looming ecological crisis on the world scale has given impetus to the rise of green politics with an emphasis on our citizenship of Planet Earth, with universal, environmental rights and obligations which transcend geographical and political boundaries.

Except, perhaps, in the latter sense of the word, anarchists and libertarians entirely reject the concept of citizenship. They regard it as a bogus assertion of democratic rights in relation to states which, by their very nature, are coercive power institutions that deny genuine 'people power' and freedom to the individuals under them. Marxism also rejects the idea of citizenship in the context of statehood and anticipates the 'withering away' of the state in classless communism.

Continuing economic and social inequalities and the contemporary controversies in Western European states over immigrants, refugees and asylum-seekers highlight the fact that citizenship, both as a legal and as a normative concept, even today remains an exclusive and divisive categorisation far removed, as yet, from genuine equity.

Collectivism

A BELIEF THAT SOME KIND OF GROUP OR COLLECTIVE IS THE MOST IMPORTANT UNIT IN the social structure and that people function better, both ethically and efficiently, in cooperative groups rather than as selfish or self-seeking, competitive individuals. Collectivism includes both 'left-wing' concepts of communitarian equality and 'right-wing' concepts of organic hierarchy.

C OLLECTIVISM IS SOMETIMES CONTRASTED WITH BOTH INDIVIDUALISM AND WITH statism to mean the advocacy of voluntary, cooperative and non-coercive groups and associations pursuing a common purpose; but it is more commonly understood to include statist theories and systems such as fascism and Stalinism.

Narrowly, collectivism implies left-wing theories of common economic ownership and equality of outcome – more precisely defined as 'collectivisation'. These include philosophies such as Marxism and collectivist anarchism which reject the state in favour of direct democracy, collective ownership vested in the people and various forms of communal living. However, left-wing collectivism also includes very statist philosophies such as democratic socialism, which advocates a high level of state nationalisation of the economy and substantial state taxation, redistribution and regulation. It even includes so-called 'totalitarian communist' systems such as Stalinism which constructed a command economy, entirely owned, planned and directed by a highly centralised and oppressive state. All of these left-wing forms of collectivism may also be labelled economic 'collectivisation'.

Where such left-wing theories refer to rights, they are collective rights: for example, the right of the working class to freedom from exploitation and oppression, or the collective rights of trade unions to freedom of association and assembly, and the mass rights of workers to picket and strike.

More broadly, however, collectivism embraces any philosophy which perceives any group, society or state as more important than the individual. It therefore also includes some right-wing philosophies such as traditional Toryism and fascism, with their organic theory of the state as an integrated whole with a common interest which far outweighs the importance of any individual. However, these organic theories do not have faith in human goodness or rationality and do not advocate equality in any form. They do both advocate a strong or even – for fascism – a 'totalitarian' state.

Collectivism also includes group philosophies such as racism (invariably a theory of hierarchy, therefore also generally characterised as right wing) and nationalism (a very flexible doctrine which can attach itself to many wider ideologies of left, right or centre).

Certain early collectivist theories may transcend the left/right divide: for example, Rousseau's theory of the 'general will' as the indivisible will of the sovereign collective people in pursuit of the common good – which, he argued, was not simply the aggregate of individual wills, that is, the 'will of all', nor the aggregate of group or 'partial wills'. This was an idealistic vision of 'people power' or direct democracy in action. Rousseau (1712–78) was writing in the eighteenth century before the left/right model of politics had been developed. Another example of early collectivism is the work of the French sociologist Emile Durkheim (1858–1917). He argued that, prior to industrialisation, there existed a 'collective consciousness' which united society around a system of common norms and values. This had been broken down by economic 'progress' and the increased division of labour, which had fragmented society and generated anomie – a lack of social norms and standards – and undesirable individualism. One consequence was the rise in pathological conditions of society illustrated, for example, by changing suicide rates. His writings fused theory with empirical research in an attempt to prove that there were social facts and causal relations which were not reducible to individualist explanations. He is widely regarded as one of the founding fathers of modern sociological study.

Collectivism can therefore be left wing or right wing or perhaps neither, optimistic or pessimistic about human nature, and it may advocate a strong state or the complete abolition of state.

Evaluation of the Idea

COLLECTIVISM IS WIDELY PERCEIVED AS THE OPPOSITE OF INDIVIDUALISM: IT PUTS THE group (whether class, nation, race, society, or state) before the individual. However, collectivist theories are much more diverse and wide-ranging than are individualist theories, at least in terms of the left/right spectrum and the criterion of self-identity. The *Blackwell Encyclopaedia of Political Thought* (Miller et al. 1991) devotes a mere ten lines to the concept of collectivism, as opposed to approximately 200 lines to the concept of individualism, saying that collectivism '*is not normally employed as a term of self-description and hence is not used with the analytical or prescriptive intention associated with the term individualism*'. Perhaps this is because of the greater diversity of the concept of collectivism; for example, no communist wants to be associated with fascism, nor vice versa.

Individualists raise a variety of objections to collectivism. One is that the very concept is an illusion: any collective is no more than the construct and aggregate of the individuals who compose it. No collective therefore has any meaningful identity, rights or decision-making capacity except as defined by the individuals who make it up. Rousseau's distinction between the general will and the will of all, for example, is philosophically and practically untenable. This is the point Margaret Thatcher was making when she famously said, '*There is no such thing as society – only individuals and families*'.

Another objection to collectivism – whether left wing or right wing – is that it neglects or actively threatens the rights and freedoms of the individual.

Left-wing collectivism, for example, ranks equality over freedom. It believes that social justice can never be achieved as long as economic inequality prevails, and therefore a more equal distribution of property, wealth and income is necessary, even where that may entail constraints on individuals' freedom to acquire property, wealth or higher income on personal 'merit' as individualists advocate. The Stalinist regime in the Soviet Union of the 1930s forcibly collectivised the economy, killing thousands of land-owning kulaks (rich peasants) in the process. Parliamentary socialists have sought high taxation and redistribution of income for extensive welfare provision, thus – from the individualist perspective – denying high income earners the right and freedom to keep and spend their hard-earned money as they choose. Such democratic socialists also advocate the abolition of private health and education in order to safeguard equal opportunity and access, thus denying freedom of choice.

Right-wing collectivism is organic, hierarchical and statist; it stresses the individual's duty and subservience to the state. Fascism takes this furthest with its philosophy of '*Everything for the state; nothing against the state; nothing outside the state*' (as stated by the 1920s' Italian fascist ideologue, Giovanni Gentile) – or, as Mussolini put it, '*The keystone of fascist doctrine is the conception of the state . . . For fascism the state is an absolute before which individuals and groups are relative . . . The fascist conception of the state is all-embracing; outside it no human or spiritual values can exist, much less have value . . . Thus understood, fascism is totalitarian. . .*'. Here, the individual has no importance or even identity except as a loyal servant of the state. For Nazism, by contrast, the race was prior to the state. As Hitler put it in *Mein Kampf* (1969), '*The state is a means to an end. Its end lies in the preservation and advancement of a community of physically and psychically homogeneous creatures*'. Both philosophies, in their different ways, however, utterly deny the significance of the individual and the concept of freedom in favour of the collective and the priorities of duty, obedience and submission.

However, from some perspectives, collectivism and individualism may not be wholly incompatible. Theorists such as Rousseau, Marx and many anarchists believed that genuine individual freedom and fulfilment could only be achieved through collective endeavour and common purpose. Modern liberals, coming from the opposite direction, have adopted what is sometimes called developmental individualism with a stress on personal growth and self-realisation, which accepts some degree of collectivism – through representative, pluralist democracy; and state welfare – as a precondition of individual freedom for all.

There may also be internal paradoxes within some theories of collectivism. Advocates of direct democracy, such as Rousseau, argue that this is the only form of decision-making which preserves people's essential freedom and personal autonomy. At the same time, of course, it involves the surrender of the citizen's will to that of the community where his or her choice conflicts with theirs (for Rousseau, in the form of a social contract between the individual and the community in pursuit of the common good). Since the general will seeks the common good, any individual who deviates from it is in conflict with himself; if he is not made to conform to the general will, his own essential freedom and good are negated and therefore he must be 'forced to be free' – forced to conform to the general will.

At the least, this poses the clear danger of the 'tyranny of the majority' so feared by liberal individualists such as Alexis de Tocqueville (1805–59) and J.S. Mill (1806–73) – as Rousseau himself recognised. At worst, it unwittingly laid the ground for future dictators such as Hitler to hijack Rousseau's concept of the general will, and to embody it in themselves, as their personal claim to infallibility and to be the fount of true democracy. The paradoxes within Rousseau's theory of collectivism are such that he has sometimes been perceived as the father of both anarchism and totalitarianism.

Britain used to be regarded, until the 1980s, as a more collectivist than individualist society, whether dominated by organic Tory paternalism or by the post-war, Keynesian, social democratic values of the mixed economy and welfare state. With the rise of New Right conservatism, however, laissez-faire individualism increasingly predominated. This was celebrated by its supporters as the triumph of individual freedom and meritocracy over the dependency culture and dead hand of the state; but it was lampooned by trenchant comic satire as the 'loadsamoney' culture of selfish greed and shallow consumerism. Left-wing collectivists bemoaned the inequalities and iniquities fostered by the free market, while organic conservatives feared that the very fabric of social stability and order would be torn asunder.

The subsequent 'new' Labour governments have not returned to old-fashioned, left-wing collectivism. The ideological dominance of the New Right's free market individualism by the late 1990s was such that they could not – and, anyway, the pragmatic nature of the 'new' Labour leadership was such that they had no innate philosophical commitment to such collectivist ideas. Rather, they have pursued an eclectic mix of individualism and communitarianism, with reference to both the rights and the responsibilities of the individual in relation to the community, combined with a steady commitment to state provision of health, education and welfare.

Communism

The Idea

ORIGINALLY, A POLITICAL PHILOSOPHY OF COLLECTIVE ECONOMIC OWNERSHIP, EQUALITY of outcome, and directly self-governing communities in a stateless society; a pre-twentieth-century philosophy of communal ownership as distinct from state owner-ship. In the twentieth century the label was applied to centralised, state-owned and controlled, one-party dictatorships.

Development of the Idea

COMMUNISM IS BASED UPON THE VIEW THAT ALL HUMAN BEINGS ARE ESSENTIALLY social, altruistic and cooperative, and that the selfish and competitive traits of human behaviour are the products of pervasive socialisation in an intensely aggressive and selfish capitalist environment.

Communism, in the sense of the prohibition of private property, predates Marx – the most renowned theorist of communism – by more than two thousand years. Plato argued in his *Republic* for the prohibition of private ownership and even of the possessive relationship of marriage by the ruling Guardians, on the grounds that they could not take disinterested decisions if they had vested property interests. Early Christians preached and practised communal ownership of possessions – a lifestyle resurrected by the mediaeval monasteries. Thomas More again advanced the case for communal ownership in his *Utopia* (1516). The seventeenth-century Levellers and the even more radical Diggers were early English agrarian communards – 'primitive communists' – who quoted the biblical assertion that men should enjoy the world in common, and equated private property with original sin. They are widely seen as the first significant emergence of 'the people' as a political force in England. (Their labels were originally terms of abuse applied to radical left-wing collectivists whose ideas were seen by the ruling elites as unacceptably egalitarian, both economically and politically.)

The utopian socialists of the eighteenth and nineteenth centuries often sought to prove the merits of communal living by demonstrating it in action. French philosopher Claude Henri, Comte de Saint-Simon (1760–1825) constructed a new, 'ideal' system of government comprising three separate legislative chambers of invention, examination and deputies. In Britain, factory owner Robert Owen developed his humanitarian experiment at his New Lanark mill through a series of communes in which all wealth and material possessions were communally owned, people worked at what they enjoyed most and did best and received a comfortable lifestyle in return.

Revolutionary socialists regarded the utopians as fools and dreamers who expected the world to be changed by example without the ruling classes acting – probably brutally – to prevent the erosion of their dominance. Eighteenth-century revolutionary socialists such as François Babeuf (1796) believed that an egalitarian society could only be established with the forcible removal of the existing ruling class. He, and many of his followers, were guillotined in 1797, but his ideas strongly influenced nineteenth-century anarchists and communists.

The prime communist theorist of the nineteenth century was Karl Marx, who developed a 'scientific' theory of common economic ownership and the disappearance of state which was distinct from the 'utopian' communists and collectivist anarchists of his era such as Proudhon and Bakunin. Prior to Marx, the arguments for communism were ethical rather than political. They questioned the moral propriety of ownership rather than its social utility and they sought moral solutions to personal indulgence, egoism and greed. Marx added a new dimension to communist theory by asserting that communism was not so much a moral preference for social justice, fairness and equality as a scientific inevitability in the evolutionary development of human society.

Communism, according to Marx, was not just the generalisation of private property and realisation of universal envy as advocated by 'crude communists' such as the French utopians. Communism would be the positive abolition of the property principle, the final stage in human history, characterised by common ownership of the means of production and hence the abolition of classes and class conflict. This would necessarily be an international phenomenon which would produce true harmony between the peoples of all nations. Hence, there would be no further need for the defensive capabilities of the state acting as the political agent of the economic ruling class in each given territory, and the state would therefore 'wither away' – a vision of the future very similar, in the end, to that of anarchism.

These later theories of communism also had to adjust to the realities of industrialism as opposed to agrarianism. They were, therefore, also new in perceiving the establishment of communal societies on the scale of the nation state or at international level, not just within small, local or village confines.

However, communism in the twentieth century came to be associated with highly statist political regimes (rather than abstract theories) such as those in the Soviet Union and Eastern Europe, which professed to be based upon Marxism but differed profoundly from the original theory. They often largely achieved the communist economic goal of wholly collective rather than private economic ownership, but it was through a highly centralised and coercive state rather than through direct ownership and control by the people. The most notable features of these regimes were the paramount position of an official communist ideology and the monopolisation of political affairs by the official Communist party, which suppressed opposition, persecuted dissidents and excluded alternative political value-systems. These systems were, undeniably, politically elitist, but nevertheless established a genuine degree of economic equality and very thorough social welfare systems throughout the mass of the population. These regimes were, at the same time, politically dictatorial, oppressive and widely labelled as totalitarian by Western liberal critics.

Lenin was the first practitioner of Marxist communism, after the Russian revolution of 1917. He believed that an elite of professional revolutionaries – a 'vanguard party' – was necessary to create and lead a revolution in a society which had not even properly entered the capitalist stage. He was succeeded by Stalin, who established a highly centralised, statist, oppressive dictatorship which, with (often significant) modifications, was emulated by Mao Tse-Tung in China, Castro in Cuba, Tito in Yugoslavia, the Eastern European and North Korean regimes, Vietnam, Cambodia, Laos and many African states.

Communist China was much more empirically egalitarian than the Soviet Union. Cuba was more participatory and democratic. Yugoslavia was more pluralist and open and so on. From a Western liberal perspective, however, there was little to distinguish them. They all gave communism a very bad reputation and justified the Cold War period of intense ideological hostility between capitalism and communism which really only ended with the 'fall of the wall' – the collapse of the Soviet and most other communist regimes – from 1989. Soviet President Mikhail Gorbachev's policies of *perestroika* – economic reform – and *glasnost* – political reform – transformed the map of world politics irrevocably. The primary ideological conflict ceased to be that between communism and capitalism and, by the early twenty first century, was widely perceived to be a war of basic values between the Western liberal democratic regimes and their opponents – 'the axis of evil' depicted by US President George W. Bush in 2002 – most notably the Islamic or dictatorial regimes of Iraq, Libya, Syria and North Korea.

The first communist government which came to power through democratic election – in the liberal democratic, pluralist sense of that phrase – was that of Salvador Allende in Chile in 1970; he was overthrown and killed in a CIA-backed coup in 1973.

Evaluation of the Idea

COMMUNISM IS NOW FREQUENTLY DEFINED IN TEXTBOOKS AS BEING SIMPLY EITHER THE theoretical ideal founded by Marx, or the actual governing principles of the self-described communist states of the twentieth century. There are great differences between twentieth-century 'communist' practice and previous communist theory, which embodied an ideal of freedom – from want, oppression and exploitation – as the natural consequence of social and economic equality. The twentieth-century regimes sought to apply the theories of Marx as first practised by Lenin in Russia (hence commonly labelled Marxist-Leninist). However, they were all established in underdeveloped, almost pre-capitalist, economies, which was quite contrary to the original Marxist theory, and they were, therefore, profoundly different from the societies envisaged by Marx and almost bound to fail.

As with anarchism, therefore, the most frequent question asked of communism – despite Marx's claims of scientific prediction – is whether it is a utopian philosophy of human goodness and equality which can never, in reality, be achieved. This evaluation revolves, essentially, around irreconcilable views of human nature – either as selfish and egotistical or as altruistic and sociable. This question about the essence of human nature is not empirically resolvable in that there is, clearly, empirical evidence for both sides of the philosophical debate, and there is no clear or easy way of distinguishing nature from nurture. However, insofar as communal systems and societies have been constructed and have worked, communists continue to argue that human selfishness is a product of nurture rather than nature and that sociability is the basic human instinct.

Secondly, communism is often perceived – especially from a liberal standpoint – as a philosophy of anti-individualism which denies the fundamental rights of private ownership and economic freedom.

However, since these abstract 'natural rights' have only ever, in reality, applied to a minority of individuals even in the most affluent societies, the ethical virtues of communism continue to appeal. Communist theory embodies an ideal of freedom – from exploitation and want – as the natural consequence of economic equality. Communists would argue that capitalist 'freedom' is a fiction, that economic exploitation and oppression are wholly inimical to any genuine freedom and that any belief in freedom under capitalism is simply the product of false consciousness.

Even collectivist anarchists of Marx's era, however, feared the threats to individual freedom implied by Marx's theory of communism, largely because they rejected Marx's concept of a transitionary proletarian (workers') state to safeguard against bourgeois (capitalist) counter-revolution. Anarchists such as Proudhon believed that a workers' state would be as inherently evil and oppressive as the previous bourgeois state and, moreover, that it would entrench itself rather than 'wither away' as Marx predicted. Modern-day anarchists of both left and right point to the 'state communist' regimes of the twentieth century to support their arguments that freedom should not be sacrificed in the pursuit of equality. However, this perspective rejects the power of the state – any state – rather than the Marxist goal of stateless communism.

Finally, Marx's argument with some of the utopians continues to resonate: should private ownership be entirely abolished to end social inequality and conflict, or should the rights and advantages of ownership be extended equally to all, thereby universalising ownership and, perhaps, the attending traits of egoism and selfishness? Margaret Thatcher, apparently, agreed with the utopians on this point. However, since the basic goal of communism is the end of conflict, oppression and inequality, it seems inevitable that communists will continue to argue for the abolition of the very concept of ownership, and for the establishment of economic and social equality for the human species.

Consensus Politics

ORIGINALLY A LABEL APPLIED TO THE POST-WAR, 1960S AND 1970S, ECONOMIC BOOM ERA of moderate policy agreement between the main UK parties, centring upon Keynesian theories of a mixed economy, full employment and welfarism. Also described as *The End of Ideology* (Bell 1962), implying – as a good thing – the end of radical and polarised politics.

CONSENSUS POLITICS – THAT IS, SUBSTANTIAL IDEOLOGICAL AND POLICY CONVERGENCE between the main political parties in the UK in the post-war period – was generally seen as the consequence of economic stability, growth or boom, when the voters were relatively content and not seeking radical political or economic change, and therefore the political parties followed suit. It was also perceived as the product of a bipartisan (cross-party) desire to provide 'a land fit for heroes' after the tribulations of war – notably in the form of universal welfare provision – and of the Conservatives' acceptance of key Labour policies in the wake of Labour's landslide victory in 1945. Thus both main parties pursued centrist policies which largely reflected the inter-war ideas of the progressive liberal economist John Maynard Keynes (1883–1946), especially in his *General Theory of Employment, Interest and Money* (1936). He argued – contrary to earlier, classical liberal, free market theory – that governments could, and should, intervene in the capitalist economy to avoid the worst excesses of inflationary boom and especially of major slump, by pumping money into the economy (for example, by spending on public works) during a slump to increase demand, or by raising taxes during an inflationary phase to dampen demand. This approach was characterised by a commitment to full employment, a stable economy and active state intervention – at its core, a compromise between the advocacy of private property and that of welfarism.

Keynes' liberal ideas were, in fact, foreshadowed by those of some pragmatic conservatives such as Harold Macmillan who, with like-minded others in his party, had also contemplated ways of *'devising some coherent system between private enterprise and collectivism'* (1927). In 1938 he published *The Middle Way* in which he called for the nationalisation of the Bank of England and state subsidies for industry. These paternalist conservatives influenced and encouraged Keynes in developing his theories of demand management.

John Maynard Keynes

From the 1950s until the late 1970s, these ideas in favour of state intervention were more or less commonly accepted policy across the main political parties and among most professional economists. Among their main political architects in the late 1950s were the then Labour leader Hugh Gaitskell and the Conservative Chancellor Rab Butler, whose names were combined to create the term 'Butskellism' to describe this bipartisan consensus especially on economic policy. This had, in fact, been foreshadowed by widespread agreement within the wartime coalition government on post-war economic goals and strategies. After the war, of course, the competing parties rarely acknowledged any such ongoing consensus – they continued to harangue each other across the floor of the Commons – but (even then) there was more spin than substance to their disagreements. Actually, the word 'Butskellism' was originally a term of abuse employed by those on the more radical wings of both main parties. This was especially true of those on the left of the Labour party who regarded Gaitskell as having 'sold out' by abandoning the idea of extensive nationalisation (state ownership of significant industries).

The concept of consensus politics was first employed in the early 1960s by moderate liberal writers such as Daniel Bell who regarded this 'end of ideology' as the end of polarised, extremist and divisive politics and therefore, from their point of view, as a good thing and hopefully permanent. Liberal philosophy defines ideology in negative terms as 'extremist' ideas (such as radical left-wing socialism or radical right-wing fascism), in contrast with its own moderate, middle-of-the-road, open-minded and tolerant philosophy. Since Daniel Bell defined ideology purely as 'extremism', he argued that all ideology had ended in the post-war economic boom period of consensus politics, when all mainstream politics approached the centre ground of Keynesian social democracy. *'The ideological age has ended'* (Bell 1962).

However, this party policy consensus lasted only until the onset of economic recession and the Conservative party's adoption of monetarism and conversion to New Right laissez-faire economics in the late 1970s.

'Endism' was revived by a later theorist, the American social analyst Francis Fukuyama, who reassessed the theory of the 'end of ideology' to apply it to a different era and different set of circumstances. He applied it 30 years later to the world arena, with the establishment of capitalist market economies and variations of liberal, pluralist democracy in many African, Asian and Latin American states, and especially with the collapse of communism in 1989; and he redefined it as the 'end of history', arguing that all ideology had not ended. Rather, liberal democratic ideology had triumphed on the world scale. (The phrase 'end of history' was actually taken from Hegel, who had been referring, almost 200 years earlier, to Napoleon's victory at Jena in 1806 which marked the beginning of the end of the Prussian empire. Fukuyama's usage of the term – celebrating the collapse of twentieth-century 'communism' – was also a clear jibe at the Marxist thesis that classless communism would mark the end of history as class conflict.)

Many commentators have suggested that, with the rise of 'new' Labour in the 1990s, the UK party system has, once again, entered a renewed era of the 'end of ideology'.

Evaluation of the Idea

BELL AND FUKUYAMA WERE BOTH WRONG.

Keynes' advocacy of fiscal management, upon which the post-war policies of consensus politics were based, lent theoretical legitimacy to the idea that future crises of capitalism could be averted indefinitely. The 1960s and 1970s era of consensus politics between the main political parties was, indeed, a phase of mainstream political convergence and centrism but it was not, as Bell had believed, a permanent phenomenon. It ended with economic recession and a renewed phase of 'adversary politics' in the early 1980s when the two main parties in Britain polarised into the 'radical right' ideas of Thatcherite, New Right conservatism which, in turn, prompted a resurgence of radical left ideas within the Labour party. For example, the 1983 Labour manifesto proposed substantial nationalisation, the abolition of the Lords and withdrawal from the EU. It was described by right-wing Labour MP Gerald Kaufman as 'the longest suicide note in history' (and Labour did, indeed, suffer their worst ever post-war defeat in the 1983 general election). Thatcher explicitly rejected the 'soggy consensus' of the post-war Keynesian era and coined the derogatory term 'wets' to describe its supporters within the Conservative party (incidentally prompting one such moderate Tory, Lord Thorneycroft, to describe himself as 'not exactly wet and not exactly dry – more, rising damp'). Consensus politics, from the radical perspective, encourages half-baked compromises, entrenches stagnation, discourages dynamic innovation and undermines pluralism and effective policy diversity and choice.

Moreover, even during the height of the economic boom in the 1960s, the centrist consensus prevailed only among the leading elements of the main parties. Strong radical wings survived within both the Conservative and Labour parties; even for the party leaderships, consensus was more a pragmatic electoral necessity than an ideological conversion; and class divisions and antagonisms remained among the most marked features of wider British society. Outside of the political mainstream, meanwhile, the revolutionary New Left movement, combining – or at least containing under its umbrella label – Trotskyists, feminists, black civil rights activists, anarchists, Marxist intellectuals and budding ecologists – flowered in the UK and throughout Europe, and helped to generate profound ideological and cultural shifts especially among students and young people. Bell, therefore, was wrong. Nevertheless, he repeatedly defended his thesis (see, for example, Bell 1988).

Both Bell and Fukuyama approached the issue of consensus politics from a centrist, liberal standpoint, but in different ways. Bell described the post-war period of consensus party politics as the 'end of ideology' because he defined ideology purely in terms of extremism, and did not recognise his own centrist, moderate, middle-of-the-road politics as simply a different ideological stance.

Fukuyama (1989) perceived the wider collapse of communism on the world stage, not as the end of ideology, but as the *'end point of mankind's ideological evolution and the universalisation of western liberal democratic ideology as the final form of human government'*. Thus he did, at least, recognise centrist liberalism as an ideological stance in its own right. This is, therefore, in some ways a more sophisticated analysis than Bell's. Both theories, however, amount to blinkered philosophical self-justifying – and premature – variations on Western liberal triumphalism.

Liberal democratic regimes are, undoubtedly, increasing in number around the world, and they are, in relative terms, survivors, because they raise general – if not relative – living standards and they are flexible and quite responsive to public opinion.

However, if Fukuyama's 'end of history' thesis is correct – that is, if we are all liberals now because the doctrines of liberalism have become diffused throughout the growing number of liberal democracies around the world – then there is no diversity to tolerate, which is precisely the 'tyranny of the majority' which liberals fear.

But Fukuyama was also wrong – as he, himself, admitted by 2002. Orthodox communism has not yet entirely disappeared; the Cuban, Chinese, North Korean and some African regimes remain. Strong opposition to liberal democratic capitalism is also prevalent: the 11 September 2001 attacks upon America, the rise of Islamic fundamentalism, the electoral successes of the far right in Europe, the growing anti-capitalist movements and the uncertain impact of future economic recessions have led many to reject Fukuyama's basic assertion. Moreover, his sanguine vision of liberal democracy ignores – or accepts – profound economic inequalities and social tensions which undermine the ethical and practical claims of these regimes to be 'an unabashed victory', as he once put it.

Meanwhile, however, in the UK, many commentators have perceived a new, if different, era of consensus politics since the mid-1990s with the creation of the 'new' Labour party which has adopted many policies from – or very similar to – those of previous Conservative governments, notably on tax and spend, and law and order. This suggests that the long period of successive New Right Conservative governments from 1979 established an ideological dominance underpinned by a commitment to a market economy, ongoing privatisation and paternalist or even authoritarian social policies which 'new' Labour cannot, or will not, abandon. This is, therefore, a much more right-wing consensus than that of the 1960s' Keynesian era.

Examples include draconian law and order policies, Private Finance Initiatives (PFIs) and Public Private Partnerships (PPPs), where private capital is involved in the provision of public services. PFI was a creation of the Conservative government in the early 1990s, but it has been enthusiastically embraced by Labour in areas such as health, education, roads, prisons and the London Underground.

Since the early 1990s there has, therefore, been frequent reference – especially by radical right Conservatives such as those in the Conservative Way Forward faction – to a 'lack of clear blue water' between the Labour and Conservative parties, which is perceived as blighting the Conservatives' future electoral prospects. They seek to abandon any perception or reality of policy consensus and to pull the Conservative party further to the right, back to its Thatcherite zenith.

This view has been challenged, for example by moderate Conservatives such as Michael Heseltine who, at the 1999 Conservative conference, defended 'the centre ground, one nation, a country at ease with itself, call it what you will'. He warned the party not to abandon the centre stage, and not to give in to Blair's clever attempt to push them into the margins of extremism. 'I hear talk of a search for new policies with clear blue water between us. Take care, I say . . . We need the votes of the disengaged centre. Without them, without millions of them, there is no prospect of Conservative government.'

This new phase of consensus, however, is again only partial – 'clear blue water' still separates the two main parties especially on the euro and other key constitutional issues. It is also, doubtless, only short term, and will be shattered by a future economic recession, domestic or international crisis. It is also uncertain how widespread and strong it is across politics and public opinion in general, rather than simply among the mainstream political elites.

Conservatism

❖

The Idea

ORIGINALLY A PHILOSOPHY SEEKING THE PRESERVATION OF THE STATUS QUO BASED upon a theory of the organic state and mistrust of human reason and goodness. Recently conjoined by the 'New Right', derived primarily from classical laissez-faire liberalism, which favours a potentially paradoxical combination of economic libertarianism and political authoritarianism.

Development of the Idea

TRADITIONAL CONSERVATISM, OR TORYISM, IS ESSENTIALLY A FEUDAL PHILOSOPHY, BUT was first clearly expressed in writing by Edmund Burke, most notably in *Reflections on the Revolution in France* (1790). Burke began his political life as a Whig but, appalled by the violent excesses of the French Revolution, he abandoned his longstanding commitment to reform and espoused the values of traditional conservatism as we know it today. Its core doctrines are a basic mistrust of human goodness and rationality, and a belief in the organic model of state and society.

Traditional conservatism is '*a philosophy of human imperfection*' (O'Sullivan 1976). Toryism distrusts man's capacity to reason and act rationally. The political conservative has a deep sense of original sin, and a profound scepticism about the natural goodness of man. Burke did not advocate irrationality as such, but perceived limits to human reason and, therefore, preferred to rely on 'prejudice' which he saw as a positive concept of instinct, custom, habit, sentiment and emotional attachment.

The organic model likens state and society to a living organism (rather than to an artificial machine). Like any living organism, it has many different components, each with a different and specific place and role (brain versus hand, ruler versus ruled), and all must work together in a harmonious and coordinated – though necessarily unequal – way; therefore the whole entity is more than the sum of its parts, and the society as a whole – which is naturally hierarchical – is more important than the individual within it.

From these basic principles stem a belief in a static, harmonious, class hierarchy guided by the 'natural governors' who serve the common interest of the whole organic unit through a sense of *noblesse oblige* – literally meaning that privilege entails obligation. Thus the ruling elite has a duty to protect the interests of all, including the less well off, to protect the order, stability and harmony of society as a whole. Tories greatly value the preservation of tradition, in the form of long-standing institutions such as church, monarchy and Lords, partly because they have stood the test of time, partly because the organic society cannot be severed from its roots and expect to survive, and finally because – since human reason and the capacity to theorise cannot be trusted – real human history and '*the accumulated wisdom of the ages*' (Burke 1790) is a better test of practicality than is abstract theory. Tories claim that they are pragmatists, not theorists (which is why they have long been described affectionately as 'the stupid party'). They deny that their philosophy is an ideology in the sense of a package of abstract doctrines and theories. They also dislike change but, being pragmatic and flexible, they will accept a little change to prevent greater change: '*If we do not give them reform, they will give us social revolution*' (Hogg 1947).

The New Right strand of conservatism was adopted from classical liberalism in the nineteenth century but only came to prominence in the 1980s (e.g. Thatcherism in the UK and Reaganism in the USA). It centres on a desire to return to nineteenth-century liberal, free market economics. It is therefore radical and reactionary, seeking a return to the Victorian era of negative economic freedom with minimal state intervention in the economic sphere. It disliked the post-war rise of the 'nanny' welfare state and resulting 'dependency culture', and it favours the privatisation of economic and public services which had been nationalised in the post-war period of consensus politics.

What is 'new' about the New Right is that it combines economic libertarianism with a highly authoritarian brand of European conservatism whose origins predate paternalist Toryism. This disciplinarian school of conservatism prompted 1980s and 1990s Conservative party policies such as increasing police powers, a more punitive criminal justice system, curbs on trade unions, on local government, lone parents, gays, immigrants, travellers and squatters, as well as strict official secrecy and censorship.

There is, therefore, an apparent paradox within New Right philosophy between neo-liberal economic, laissez-faire libertarianism and neo-conservative political, social and moral authoritarianism.

Evaluation of the Idea

TRADITIONAL TORYISM DENIES BEING AN IDEOLOGY IN TWO MAJOR SENSES OF THE word. First, it mistrusts human reason. It therefore dislikes abstract theories and principles and is instead pragmatic – that is, it relies on practical responses to concrete circumstances. It therefore claims that it is not an 'ideology' in the neutral sense of a comprehensive and abstract theoretical package of principles and doctrines. *'To put conservatism into a bottle with a label is like trying to liquefy the atmosphere . . . for conservatism is less a political doctrine than a habit of mind, a mode of feeling, a way of living'* (White 1964).

By way of counter-argument, Toryism is certainly pragmatic, flexible and responsive but nevertheless it does have identifiable doctrines and principles – such as the organic theory, mistrust of human reason, belief in natural hierarchy, reverence for tradition and resistance to change. It is, after all, an '-ism' – and even pragmatism is a principle. As Heater (1975) points out, it can be a very stubborn or principled disposition or 'habit of mind'; it is quite predictable, and there are limits to its flexibility – for example, it was the traditional Tory MPs within the British Conservative party who collectively rebelled to defeat the introduction of Sunday shopping in 1986. Here, traditional conservative attachments to the Christian holy day and family home life clashed with the New Right pursuit of free trade and private enterprise – and the traditionalists won. It took a further seven years before the New Right succeeded in pushing through Sunday shopping – ironically, only with the help of the EU Court of Justice, an institution long mistrusted by the Thatcherites.

Secondly, Toryism also denies being an ideology in the sense that it is an organic theory: it likens society and state to a living organism where all the parts work together in interdependent – if unequal – harmony, and the whole unit is more than the sum of its parts and more important than any single part. It therefore does perceive class, but not class conflict – the whole organic unit has a common 'national interest' which the natural governors have a duty to serve and protect (*noblesse oblige*). It therefore also claims that it is not an ideology in the negative Marxist sense of a theory serving the interests of the ruling bourgeois capitalist class. Rather, it serves and protects the common interests of the whole organic society.

By way of counter-argument, however, Toryism also firmly believes in private property as a natural right. That does make it also an ideology in the Marxist sense of 'bourgeois ideology' – a set of ideas and beliefs which reflect and protect the interests of the ruling class in capitalism.

Tories and the New Right share a common belief in four main things: private property – although the New Right emphasis on the free market and unconstrained property rights is much stronger than the Tories'; hierarchy – although there is a clear difference between the Tory perception of an organic, static, class hierarchy and the New Right mechanistic, individualist ladder of meritocracy; law and order – although the paternalist, Tory 'Dixon of Dock Green' image of the friendly bobby on the beat contrasts sharply with the militaristic, New Right 'Robocop' version of policing; and, finally, Christian family values – again, paternalist versus authoritarian.

On the whole, there seem to be profound contradictions within modern conservative philosophy: both between traditional Toryism and the New Right, and within the New Right itself.

It is unsurprising that there are tensions between Toryism and the New Right. They derive from different philosophical roots and eras. They are conjoined within the same political party in the UK largely due to historical accident, because the first-past-the-post electoral system does not allow diverse political philosophies to split off into smaller parties with any realistic chance of electoral success. If the UK were ever to adopt a system of proportional representation for Westminster, the diverse philosophical schools within both the Conservative and Labour parties could – and probably would – break up into different parties of more theoretical coherence, with more chance of balanced representation.

The apparent paradox within the New Right itself is a matter of debate. The New Right advocates 'limited but strong' government, which sounds contradictory but may not be. Within its prescribed and limited role government should be strong: *Limitation of government doesn't make for a weak government. If you've got the role of government clearly set out, then it means very strong government in that role. Very strong indeed*' (Thatcher, quoted in Gamble 1988) The neo-liberal and neo-conservative strands may be seen as complementary – two sides of the same coin – that is, the economic free market tends to create growing inequality, resentment, social unrest and disorder and therefore needs a strong state in law and order, social and moral policy, to keep the lid on the instabilities generated by a laissez-faire economy. Thatcher expressed this positively: '*What this country wants is less tax and more law and order*'. A critical journalist, Neal Ascherson (quoted in Gamble 1988), expressed it more negatively: '*The trouble with a free market economy is it takes so many police to make it work*'.

However, there is a stronger case for saying that the two strands of New Right thought are paradoxical, especially given their diverse philosophical origins – laissez-faire liberal economics and conservative authoritarianism. One obvious focus of conflict is the question of human nature: the rationalist, neo-liberal view should not require the degree of authoritarian control and constraint to which the neo-conservative view subscribes. A second, less obvious, contradiction centres on the New Right's view of the proper role of women. Their meritocratic individualism should lead them to espouse liberal feminist values and a commitment to equal opportunities for women in the public sphere of economic and political life. However, their conservative dimension prompts them to defend traditional family values and anti-feminism in a conspicuously reactionary way.

After the Conservatives' second disastrous defeat in 2001, their natural constituency seemed to have shrunk to little more than the English countryside and south-east suburban heartlands with most of their active members in their dotage (average age 62). Moderate Conservatives such as Michael Heseltine said that the party had become '*a right-wing, xenophobic party talking to itself in an introspective way*' (*The Observer*, 10 June 2001).

Such moderate Conservatives have since been seeking to emulate the American Republican agenda of 'compassionate conservatism'. The rhetoric of some leading Conservatives such as Iain Duncan Smith, Oliver Letwin and David Willetts in 2002 implied a return to a more socially inclusive and paternalist Tory agenda; a new 'caring' Conservatism, enunciating a compassion for the vulnerable in society and a concern for those most in need. Iain Duncan Smith, for example, has spoken with sincerity of his shock on viewing scenes of decline and hardship in Glasgow's Easterhouse estate. However, this rhetoric has yet to be matched by concrete policy initiatives or backed by the wider party – a substantial number of whom still back the party as the champion of the populist paradox: free market economic libertarianism and moral authoritarianism. The imposition, late in 2002, of a three-line whip against a Bill in the Commons which allowed unmarried – straight and gay – partners to adopt children, seemed wholly to contradict the party's new language of tolerance, and prompted the resignation of Conservative frontbencher John Bercow.

The divided and diminished state of the British Conservative party since 1997 reflects its profound ideological schisms. It has yet to decide what kind of conservatism it wants to represent – and, even when it does, it must win back an electorate which has increasingly come to question both tradition and reaction.

Constitution

IN POLITICAL TERMS, A FRAMEWORK OF RULES AND PRINCIPLES WHICH ARE INTENDED TO regulate the relationships among the diverse branches of state and between the state and its citizens. The rules may be written or unwritten, legal or non-legal, laws or traditional conventions, framed by special processes for change or not. They need not be liberal democratic – a constitution may entrench a dictatorship – but the principle of 'constitutionalism' is a fundamental doctrine of liberal democracy.

A CONSTITUTION IS THE SET OF RULES AND PRINCIPLES BY WHICH A STATE IS GOVERNED and, in the formal sense, constitutionalism is simply the practice of establishing constitutions, whatever their content may be. A constitution – of any sort – is meant to establish the authority of the political decision-makers. Constitutionalism is perceived by liberal democratic theory as the advocacy or enforcement of a set of rules and principles which set genuine limits to the power of state and government. Thus, for example, liberal theory advocates doctrines such as the separation of powers, pluralism, the rule of law, decentralisation, tolerance, civil rights and liberties etc. – all intended to impose limits and constraints upon the powers of state and government institutions. However, one-party states often produce intricate constitutions which may nominally stress civil rights and liberties (e.g. the Soviet constitution of 1936) which are not upheld in practice. There is no inherent guarantee, therefore, that a constitution will limit the powers of government or protect against tyranny, or even seek to do so – it may simply entrench, and seek to legitimise, dictatorship. Nevertheless, liberal democratic thinking regards constitutionalism as a necessary, if not sufficient, external check upon the powers of government and state.

If a constitution is outlined in a single, legal document it is described as written or cod-ified – for example, the American constitution of 1787. Israel and Britain are rare examples of states with unwritten or uncodified constitutions, because there is no sin-gle, legal document to which they can point as their definitive constitution. Their political rules derive from many different sources – some written and some not, some with the force of law and some not. The diverse sources of the British constitution include Acts of Parliament (statute law), EU law, case law, common law, conventions – unwritten customs which are traditionally regarded as binding, but which have no legal force – historical documents and authoritative writings which are also not legal-ly binding but merely interpretive. However, the distinction between written and unwritten constitutions should not be overstated: all written constitutions are supple-mented, amended and developed in informal ways (witness the rise in the *de facto* power of successive American presidents without any formal constitutional amend-ments). Conversely, the British constitution is, in practice, becoming more written and more legally codified, mainly because of the growing quantity and impact of EU laws and regulations, which take legal precedence over all other sources of the constitution; and also because of the large number of constitutional reforms introduced by statute since 1997 – such as devolution, reform of the Lords and the Human Rights Act. This trend will continue.

The British constitution is also flexible; that is, it requires no special legal procedures for amendment, but can be changed by an ordinary Act of Parliament. Thus there is no distinct or easily identifiable body of constitutional law. This does not necessarily mean that the constitution is quick or easy to change; some critics (e.g. Ponton and Gill, 1982) have – at least in the past – argued that the British political system is too static and outdated in many respects. A rigid constitution, by contrast, has superior legal status to ordinary legislation, that is, it requires a special process for change which is different from the normal law-making process: for example, the USA requires two-thirds of Congressional votes, plus a majority in three-quarters of the state legislatures; and the Australian constitution requires a referendum for major change. A constitution may be written but also flexible – for example, New Zealand – so there is no necessary connection between these two traits.

Again, in practice rather than theory, the British constitution is gradually becoming more rigid as the principle becomes increasingly accepted and expected that referenda should be held on issues of major constitutional change such as electoral reform, devolution and joining the euro. Although such referenda in the UK are invariably merely 'advisory' to maintain the semblance of parliamentary sovereignty, no govern-ment could, in reality, ignore a referendum result. Instead it can, of course, choose not to hold a referendum, as Labour has done since 1997 on the question of electoral reform for Westminster (despite a manifesto promise to the contrary). Whereas in many rigid constitutions, a refrendum is a legal requisite for formal amendments, in the UK the whole question of referenda – whether and when to hold them, what questions to ask, how to word them and how to fund them – is entirely at the whim of the government of the day. No Conservative government has ever held a referendum because it would go against their philosophical belief in strong, responsible and centralised government. Sceptics may suspect that Labour governments only offer them when they are confident of winning a vote which will legitimise what they intend to do anyway.

The British (like the French) constitution is also unitary: that is, it has one sovereign legislature. Although there is local government and there are now also local Parliaments and assemblies throughout the UK, these bodies are still subordinate to the centre and their existence and powers are wholly determined by Westminster, which can limit their remit or, indeed, abolish them altogether at any time. (This does not mean that the law must be uniform throughout the whole country; but differences are only those permitted, if not decreed, by the centre.) This contrasts with a federal constitution such as that of the USA or Australia, where the local executive and/or legislative bodies have strong and autonomous powers within their own defined areas of responsibility. The centre has decision-making power over matters such as national security, defence and foreign affairs but it cannot impinge on the powers of the local bodies (nor vice versa) – they are, in theory, equal and autonomous and there are mutual checks and balances between them. Hence there is no single centre of sovereignty.

The unitary nature of the UK is also already challenged, however, by the supranational power of the EU over Parliament; and it is likely to come under more challenge from below as the Scottish, Welsh and Northern Irish assemblies consolidate their roles.

In theory – *de jure* – therefore, the British constitution is unwritten, flexible and unitary. In practice – *de facto* – however, all of these features are changing.

Evaluation of the Idea

L IBERAL THEORY STRONGLY BELIEVES THAT A WRITTEN, LEGAL CONSTITUTION WILL constrain the powers of state and government and thus protect the rights and freedoms of citizens living within the state.

Marxists and anarchists disagree. Marxists regard the constitutional state of liberal thinking as a false legitimisation of the political superstructure of a capitalist economy, whose purpose is to protect the interests of the minority ruling bourgeois class against the interests of the majority working class. The concept of the 'limited' power of the sovereign, bourgeois state is a product of the false consciousness of the bourgeois ruling class itself. They are self-deceived as much as deceiving.

Anarchists go further than Marxists to argue that the constitutional state of liberal democracy is a falsehood, a sham and a facade – a veritable conspiracy – which, in reality, has no effective limits to its power and simply embroils the public in accepting and colluding in their own oppression through the artifices of constitutions and ballot box democracy.

Specific criticisms of the British constitution concern its unwritten, flexible and unitary features, which render it exceptionally uncertain and even unknowable, and which allow its rules – insofar as they exist – to be bent and broken with relative ease, especially by the executive arm of the state.

However, there may be virtues to such a flexible constitution. It allows for easy amendment and updating in accordance with changing circumstances and the evolving desires and values of the people, without surrendering to small, obstinate minorities or to outdated, perhaps misinterpreted, statements of rights which are enshrined in stone;

the contemporary American assertion of the universal right to bear arms is frequently cited as an example of a wilful misrepresentation of an anachronistic frontier code that was never meant to apply to the mass of citizens in the modern day. Moreover, rigid constitutions may – from a liberal perspective – not allow for changing social norms such as the acceptance of the right to vote for women, blacks and young people, the legalisation of abortion or gay rights, alcohol or soft drugs.

Nevertheless, unwritten and flexible constitutions such as that of the UK are more frequently criticised than praised for their lack of clarity and enforceability. For these reasons, the liberal Alexis de Tocqueville, in the nineteenth century, went so far as to say that that there was no such thing as the British constitution.

This always overstated the case; there were always at least a few clear and enforceable rules, such as the legal requirement of the government to call an election within five years (precluding major war or crisis) and the conventional requirement that the monarch will choose as prime minister the leader of the majority party (if there is one) in the House of Commons. Moreover, since, as described above, the defining features of the British constitution are changing and gradually solidifying, de Tocqueville's thesis is becoming less true over time.

However, it remains the case that, although a more or less identifiable body of constitutional code exists at any given time within the UK, it can be amended, repealed or replaced at any time by a Commons majority, no matter how small that majority may be. Any number of authoritative – or perhaps complacent – textbooks make reference to specific documents (such as the Magna Carta) and statutes (such as the Habeus Corpus Act 1679) which have been repeatedly superseded, often with disturbing implications for the civil liberties of British citizens.

One example is the draconian anti-terrorist legislation passed in 2001 (in the wake of the 11 September attacks on America), which allows foreign suspects to be detained indefinitely without charge or trial. Another is retrospective – backdated – law which Parliament may pass, often to legalise government policy after it has been ruled illegal by a court. Retrospective law – for example, the backdated closure of an offshore tax loophole in Gordon Brown's 1998 Budget – breaches the principle of the 'rule of law', that the law should be 'knowable' at the time we are breaking it. In most written, liberal constitutions, such retrospective law is therefore prohibited, but there are no such constraints upon the type of law which may be passed by the sovereign UK Parliament. Conventions are even more flexible and difficult to enforce than are laws: for example, the circumstances in which ministers should resign over collective or individual responsibility, and the alleged 'politicisation' of civil servants who are constitutionally required to be neutral (most notably by Prime Ministers Thatcher and Blair). One final example: convention dictates that government ministers should be appointed from within Parliament, to ensure that they are democratically accountable; but in 1998 Prime Minister Tony Blair appointed Scottish media tycoon (and personal friend) Gus MacDonald, as a junior industry minister although he was neither an MP nor a peer. Unconstitutional action (rule-breaking) such as this is relatively easy with an unwritten, flexible constitution – indeed, given the uncertainty of the rules, it is often hard even to know what is unconstitutional action.

In sum, a majority government in control of a (domestically) sovereign Parliament, with a flexible constitution – which can be changed by a one-vote majority in the Commons – can effectively change the constitution at will; and even such legislative change is not always necessary, given the duration of conventional practice as the basis of constitutional decree. Hence Lord Hailsham's (1976) thesis of the permanent danger of 'elective dictatorship' by an overweening executive in the UK, which overturns the theory of parliamentary control of government and – given the lack of any Supreme Court or other overriding domestic check on executive power – does imply an inadequate degree of constitutional limitation on government, particularly in a state which claims to be a liberal democracy. The distinctly odd nature of the British constitution is a consequence of the historic – and arguable – fortune of the British state in not having undergone revolution, foreign invasion or other traumatic political upheaval over a long period, rather than of the innate superiority of Britain's constitutional arrangements.

Democracy

❖

The Idea

D ERIVING FROM THE GREEK, *DEMOS KRATOS* – PEOPLE POWER – LITERALLY, DIRECT SELF-government and decision making by the people. Now widely interpreted as indirect or representative democracy, where voters elect representatives to make decisions on their behalf. Specific types of indirect democracy include pluralist 'liberal democracies', the one-party 'people's democracies' of communism and the 'totalitarian democracies' of fascism.

Development of the Idea

A LMOST EVERY MODERN STATE CLAIMS TO BE A DEMOCRACY, FROM THE UK AND USA TO Cuba, Iraq and Zimbabwe. Democracy implies varying degrees of people power, participation, representation, responsible government and consent. Some pre-industrial political systems do operate direct democracy – for example, the Mursai tribe of Ethiopia, where the adult men make collective decisions around the campfire. Women, however, are excluded. Scarcely any modern industrial society can claim to practise direct democracy (Switzerland perhaps comes closest, with its very frequent referenda in a very decentralised political system; however, throughout much of the twentieth century, Switzerland kept having referenda on whether women should have the right to vote – and, since only men had the right to vote in those referenda, women did not get the vote until 1971).

Democratic participation may take many forms, from voting and standing for political office to meetings, marches, demonstrations, peaceful lawbreaking and violent political opposition. Even riots and terrorist attacks have democratic claims, since they are 'people power' in the literal sense – although all states and governments will deny those democratic claims when such activities are directed against them.

Representation is the most widely accepted variant of democratic government, but has diverse interpretations. The strongest interpretation of the concept of 'representative' is that of a delegate: elected power-holders who act as instructed by their voters, thus reflecting, representing and implementing the voters' wishes on every issue. The eighteenth-century political philosopher Jean-Jacques Rousseau argued that, if direct democracy was impossible, the next best thing – indeed, the only 'democratic' alternative – was a system of delegates: *'Thus deputies of the people are not, and cannot be, its representatives; they are merely its agents, and can make no final decisions. Any law which the people have not ratified in person is null, is not a law'* (Rousseau 1762). Alternatively, representation can mean the reflection of voters' interests (e.g. the traditional conservative concept of natural and responsible governors acting in the best interests of their constituents as those governors see fit); or it can mean the reflection of voters' social backgrounds and typicality by the political representatives (e.g. the percentage of female, ethnic minority, young or gay MPs in Parliament).

Responsible government means, primarily, government which is answerable and accountable – either directly to the voters or, as in the UK, to Parliament and thereby indirectly to the voters. A secondary interpretation is the traditional Tory (Burkean) idea of wise and sound government in the national interests of the voters.

Evaluation of the Idea

THE IDEA OF DEMOCRACY INVOLVES TWO (OFTEN CONFLICTING) QUESTIONS: BY WHOM are decisions made, and whose interests do they serve? Every modern state which calls itself a democracy in fact practises some form of indirect or representative democracy: the election of representatives to govern over, and on behalf of, the citizens. It may be a one-party, two-party or multi-party system, parliamentary or presidential, first-past-the-post electoral system or proportional representation; whatever form it takes, it is a limited variant of democracy, a retreat from 'people power' in the full sense. Representative democracy necessarily entails oligarchy – rule by the few – over, and (it is hoped) in the interests of, the majority.

Whether the resulting government is even elected by the majority depends on the voting system in operation. In Britain, no government has had over 50 per cent of the votes cast since the 1930s. The 2001 Labour government, for example, gained just 41 per cent of the votes cast, which (given a historically low turnout of 59 per cent) was only 24 per cent of the total eligible electorate. Clearly, this raises serious questions about the legitimacy of such indirectly elected representatives.

In Britain, representative democracy – the extension of the franchise – developed in the nineteenth and twentieth centuries under pressure from popular movements such as Chartism and the trade union movement, and was, in part, a conscious effort on the part of the political power-holders to forestall radical demands for more direct or extensive political democracy. In the words of conservative Quinton Hogg (Lord Hailsham), *'If you don't give them reform, they will give you social revolution'* (Hogg 1947).

This idea of democracy as universal suffrage is also a 'static' interpretation of the concept: that is, when (almost) every adult has the vote, the country is deemed a democracy, regardless of the goals or outcomes of the ballot box process. According to C.B. Macpherson (1966) other, non-liberal, systems – e.g. communist and third world one-party democracies – have a more 'dynamic' view of democracy as an ideal and goal of human equality, freedom, and fulfilment to be pursued. There, the emphasis is more on ends than on means, and democracy is seen as an ongoing search for progress. Many Third World countries (including one-party states) that do not follow the Western pluralist model of democracy are, according to Macpherson, actually closer to *the original notion of democracy as rule by and for the poor and oppressed*'. Equally opposed to the liberal concept of democracy is the fascist, and especially Nazi, concept which asserts that only the supreme, all-knowing and infallible leader truly understands and embodies the will of the people and hence that an absolute, fascist dictatorship is the only true form of democracy, that is, 'totalitarian democracy'.

The weakest criterion of democracy is the degree of consent underpinning a political system: that is, the agreement of the majority to accept and live by the decisions of the governors. Consent is more than mere compliance, which is the reluctant or apathetic acquiescence to a particular form of government – though it may be hard to distinguish between the two in practice. Political rulers cannot claim to be democratic if they merely possess power, that is, the ability to get things done and direct people's actions through threats, sanctions, force or coercion. They can claim to be democratic if they possess authority: the ability to get things done and shape people's actions through consent, respect and support. Authority thus generates rightful, legitimate power; it is a more stable basis of government than coercive power alone, and therefore most modern rulers seek at least some degree of legitimacy and consent.

The nineteenth-century sociologist Max Weber distinguished three types of authority: traditional authority, based on past custom and practice (e.g. the monarchy and House of Lords), legal-rational authority, based on rules and laws (e.g. the government), and charismatic authority, based on personality (e.g. Churchill). These may overlap: for example, judges may possess both traditional and legal-rational authority. Authority and consent, therefore, need not entail election: for example, opinion polls consistently indicate that the British monarchy, though not elected, is popular with the majority (around 70 per cent) of British people.

The problem with defining democracy in terms of consent is that, especially in the modern age of mass media, consent can be created by political power-holders – through manipulation of information and of public opinion – to legitimise their rule. In Nazi Germany, for example, there was undoubtedly a substantial degree of mass, active support for the regime; but there was also undoubtedly a well-developed and effective system of political indoctrination and propaganda in the schools, mass media etc., which made it difficult to distinguish real from manufactured political consent.

Most commentators would agree that the same point applies, to a greater or lesser degree, in every political system. We do not emerge from the womb as little flag-waving Nazis, or communists, or royalists, or parliamentarians; we learn to accept and support the system in which we live through a process of political socialisation. Through the various agencies of family, school, work, peer group (friends and colleagues), media and religion we acquire the necessary attitudes and values to enable us to accept and adapt to the system in which we live, and to enable that system itself to survive. All individuals, in all states, are subject to this process of socialisation

– sometimes by open indoctrination, often by more subtle, less honest and usually more effective methods.

Some political philosophies – such as political conservatism – broadly approve of the process of political socialisation because it promotes consensus, order and stability. Other philosophies – such as Marxism – disapprove of it because it masks a conflict of (e.g. class) interests and ideas which they see as the driving force of social change and progress. Either way, socialisation poses profound problems about consent as a criterion of democracy, because the most 'totalitarian' systems may be the most active in creating consent through intensive indoctrination, and therefore in this sense presumably the most 'democratic'.

There are, moreover, sound arguments against democracy. Individualist, liberal thinking has always been wary of democracy as an inherently collectivist concept which may promote the 'tyranny of the majority' and threaten the rights, interests and views of minorities and individuals – particularly if that majority is uneducated or propertyless, in which case 'mobocracy' triumphs. When liberals highlight the corrupting influence of power, they are referring to people power as much as to state power. Representative democracy also often implies a growing role for the state which may lead to an encroachment on property rights. Classical liberals were therefore downright hostile to the concept of democracy even as universal suffrage, never mind to more radical or direct concepts of genuine people power. There is also the argument that uninformed individuals may genuinely not know their own best interests. When modern liberals did come to accept the extension of the franchise, it was only on the basis that majority rule must be based upon informed reason and must not unduly reflect passions or selfish interests. Liberals remain fearful of emotional populism and demagoguery. Even J.S. Mill, while arguing that every adult should have the vote, believed that those with education should have more votes. The concept of 'liberal democracy' therefore embodies a whole range of doctrines and devices which actually seek to restrain popular rule and prevent government from reflecting the direct will of the majority.

Some post-war writers such as Jose Ortega y Gasset (1961) have adapted traditional liberal warnings about human nature to the modern age of consumerism; they argue that if people are self-centred and materialistic, democracy is dangerous and society itself is threatened, unless the voters are first trained to develop a sense of civic responsibility.

Those philosophies which believe human nature to be inherently irrational – such as traditional conservatism and fascism – are most wary of democracy in the true sense of 'people power'. Where they accept the concept of democracy at all, it is only by redefining it as some version of elite rule in the general interests of the people.

Further, there are purely practical arguments against democracy: it may be slow and inefficient in making changes or decisions, particularly in a crisis situation such as war. It may, arguably, even jeopardise national security; in 2002, the Labour government consistently refused to allow Parliament a substantive vote on the issue of a potential military attack against Iraq in case the process of debating and voting betrayed too much tactical information to the Iraqi regime itself. Democracy can also be expensive and bureaucratic in its implementation. The final problem – perhaps the main one in the modern age of mass democracy – is sheer apathy: people simply may not want to take an intelligent interest in the decision-making processes.

Devolution

❦

THE PASSING DOWN OF LIMITED LEGISLATIVE OR EXECUTIVE POWER FROM CENTRAL TO local bodies, where the centre remains sovereign, and the constitution of a state therefore remains unitary. This contrasts with 'federalism', where the central and local powers are, in theory, equal and autonomous in relation to each other.

Development of the Idea

DEVOLUTION INVOLVES THE PASSING DOWN OF POWERS TO SUBORDINATE ASSEMBLIES which can be overridden by the national legislature. It is therefore a limited form of decentralisation in comparison to federalism, where the regional bodies have autonomous powers in their own areas of responsibility which cannot be overridden by the centre.

The United Kingdom has long had elements of executive devolution in local government, and Scotland and Wales have long had their own Secretaries of State with Cabinet status. Scotland's legal and educational systems are also, historically, quite distinct. Until 1999 there was, however, no legislative devolution; Westminster was the sole UK legislature since the suspension in 1972 of the Northern Irish Parliament (Stormont) and the introduction of 'direct rule' from Westminster because of the growing political conflict in Northern Ireland at that time.

Encouraged by the rise of nationalist feeling in Scotland and Wales since the late 1960s, Labour and the Liberal Democrats have since the 1970s advocated legislative devolution for Scotland and Wales, and the Liberal Democrats also proposed elected local legislatures for the regions of England. A Labour government in 1977 introduced a Devolution Bill, and held referenda on the issue in Scotland and Wales in 1979. Wales voted against; Scotland voted in favour, but the 'yes' vote amounted to only 32.5 per cent of the total electorate, and the Bill required approval by at least 40 per cent of the electorate (due to a backbench amendment) so the issue was dropped.

Over the next two decades, support for the Scottish and Welsh Nationalist parties increased but the Conservative governments of that period were firmly opposed to devolution. In 1997, however, the Conservatives won no seats at all in Scotland or in Wales and Labour came to power with a mandate to hold new referenda on the question of devolution.

Scotland held a two-question referendum in September 1997: 74 per cent voted in favour of a Scottish Parliament and 60 per cent agreed that it should have tax-varying powers of up to 3p in the pound (turnout was 60 per cent). The Scottish Parliament came into being in May 1999 with 129 members elected by the Additional Member System (AMS): 73 elected by first-past-the-post and 56 'top-up' Members of the Scottish Parliament (MSPs) elected from regional party lists using the eight European parliamentary constituencies.

The Scottish executive is responsible for the following policy areas: health; education and training; local government, housing and social work; economic development; employment; transport; law and home affairs; police; environment; energy; agriculture, forestry and fishing; culture, sport and the arts; and the administration of certain EU laws in Scotland (e.g. civil nuclear emergency planning).

Westminster remains responsible for foreign affairs including relations with the EU, defence and national security, macroeconomic and fiscal matters, immigration, railways, shipping, airlines, pensions, employment law, broadcasting and telecommunications and much else. Overall, the Scotland Act lists 19 pages of powers that are reserved to Westminster.

In Wales, the government held the referendum one week after the Scottish vote, in the hope of giving the 'yes' side a boost. Despite this, the 'yes' vote scraped a 0.6 per cent majority on only a 50 per cent turnout. It quickly came to be known as *yr ie bychan* – 'the little yes'. The vote was geographically split with the eastern areas giving a decisive 'no' vote and the 'yes' vote increasing the further the areas were from the English border. Although there has long been a sense of national Welsh culture, centred especially on the Welsh language, there is far less support for political nationalism in Wales than in Scotland because of the perceived economic and political benefits of the union. The 60-member Welsh assembly is therefore much weaker than the Scottish Parliament, with control over the spending of the £8 billion Welsh Office budget but no taxation or primary law-making powers.

The Welsh assembly is also elected by the AMS system, with 40 first-past-the-post and 20 party list members. It operates on a local government style committee system with executive rather than legislative or fiscal powers – in effect, taking over the role of the Welsh Office in deciding how Westminster legislation is implemented in Wales, in the following policy areas: economic development; agriculture; industry and training; education; local government services; health and social services; housing; environment; planning and transport; sport and heritage.

At around the same time, but for different reasons – namely, the Northern Ireland peace process – an assembly for Northern Ireland was re-established at Stormont (for the first time since its abolition in 1972) following the peace deal on 10 April (Good Friday) 1998. In May 1998, a rapid referendum on the peace deal was held throughout Ireland and, unsurprisingly, won substantial support: Northern Ireland: 71 per cent 'yes' versus 29 per cent 'no' on 81 per cent turnout = 58 per cent in favour; Eire: 94 per cent 'yes' versus 6 per cent 'no' on 56 per cent turnout = 53 per cent in favour. The peace deal provided for a Northern Ireland assembly of 108 seats elected by proportional representation in the form of the Single Transferable Vote (STV); a 12-member executive chosen from within and by the assembly in proportion to the parties' strength in the assembly (thus, for example, Sinn Fein were guaranteed two seats on the executive); also a North-South executive council which was set up some months later, in return for which Eire gave up its constitutional claim to the North. There was also provision for a wider British-Irish Intergovernmental Council representing all five parliaments of the UK and Eire, and for decommissioning of weapons and prisoner releases within two years.

The limited nature of devolution – as opposed to federalism – has been illustrated by the repeated suspension of Stormont by Westminster since 2000, over issues such as the decommissioning of weapons by 'terrorist' and 'paramilitary' groups.

Evaluation of the Idea

DEVOLUTION IS A FORM OF DECENTRALISATION – ALBEIT A LIMITED ONE. THE UK HAS remained, for centuries, one of the most centralised political systems in the Western world because of the perceived disadvantages of decentralisation: the neglect or abandonment of the wider national interest; the risk of inconsistent, uncoordinated and potentially unjust provision of standards and services across different parts of the state; possible restrictions upon geographical mobility within the state; the danger that regional bodies may exceed their (weaker) local mandate to involve themselves in national issues, or that they may jeopardise overall control of public spending with populist and expensive local projects; the cost and potential inefficiency of added layers of local bureaucracy; and the possibility that devolution may entrench a regional 'elective dictatorship'.

However, the arguments in favour of decentralisation have become increasingly persuasive: that local people know local needs best; regional assemblies provide vital checks and balances against the potential 'elective dictatorship' of a minority-vote government in a sovereign, unitary, Westminster Parliament – especially one which may be neglectful of local wishes in areas where it is unpopular; regional assemblies also provide an added tier of democratic representation, participation and accountability; they have a mandate from local electors; they provide a training and recruitment ground for central government and Parliament; and they may even be cost-effective.

With specific reference to the UK, however, the devolution arrangements introduced by the 1997 Labour government were not entirely balanced or fair. For example, the arrangements for Scotland did not address the 'West Lothian question' (so-called because it was first raised by the MP for that area, Tam Dalyell): that Scottish MPs at

Westminster (already over-represented numerically) would continue to have law-making powers over areas of English policy such as health and education, while English MPs would have no such power over Scotland because the Scottish Parliament would be legislating on such matters.

Scotland also has a disproportionate share of Cabinet ministers and of central government finances. As English voters become increasingly aware of such imbalances, it may fuel calls for reduced voting rights for Scottish MPs at Westminster, fewer Scottish MPs at Westminster and/or the creation of elected assemblies for the regions of England to parallel the Scottish Parliament.

In April 1999, the government set up non-elected regional economic development agencies (RDAs) for the eight English regions outside London, presuming that this would be enough to redress the balance at least until the next election, but there were already growing calls for elected English regional assemblies. For example, in March 1999, even before the Scottish Parliament was established, a movement was set up calling for an elected regional assembly for Yorkshire. Some ministers of the time, such as John Prescott, wanted these to be part of the framework for an element of regional representation from all parts of the UK in a reformed second chamber at Westminster.

Frequent reference by the Labour government to the current devolution arrangements as the 'settled will of the people' seems, therefore, at best misguided and, at worst, misleading. Devolution seems very likely to be, not an event, but an ongoing process, with increasing impact upon English constitutional arrangements. English (as opposed to British) nationalist sentiment has been growing perceptibly since the turn of this century, and the flag of Saint George has replaced the Union flag as the symbol of choice for English nationalists of all sorts, whether liberal, conservative or chauvinist.

At the same time, if Scottish voters do not feel that their situation has significantly improved after some time, they may start to demand greater local autonomy, federalism or even independence. One 1998 poll indicated that 65 per cent of Scots believed that Scotland would be wholly independent by 2013. This was one reason why the Conservatives and others used to reject devolution, fearing that it might be the first step down the slippery slope towards the complete break-up of the UK.

In sum, for many, devolution is a step too far; for others – notably Scottish, Welsh and Irish nationalists – it does not go far enough.

Equality

❧

The Idea

MOST STRONGLY, THE IDEA THAT PEOPLE ARE DESERVING OF EQUAL OUTCOME IN terms of wealth, income, status and opportunities – a goal associated with left-wing socialist and anarchist philosophies; more narrowly, that people are deserving of equal opportunities or, at least, are of equal moral worth – a concept of 'foundational equality' associated with liberalism.

Development of the Idea

ON THE LEFT/RIGHT SPECTRUM, EQUALITY IS PERCEIVED AS A PRIMARY GOAL OF LEFT-wing theories of socialism and collectivist anarchism, against the right-wing, elitist and hierarchical theories of conservatism, fascism and racism. Liberalism – as always – stands somewhere midway.

There are different concepts and types of equality: for example, equality of opportunity as opposed to equality of outcome. The more limited concept of equality of opportunity is advocated – in two different senses – by New Right conservatives and by modern liberals. The New Right argue that everyone should have equal opportunity in the economic sphere in the sense of being equally left alone to succeed or fail on their own merits in the free market – that is, negative economic freedom: non-interference especially by the state, whether in the form of help or hindrance. Modern liberals, by contrast, argue that genuinely equal opportunity – foundational equality – may require positive state aid and intervention – for example, through state provision of education, health and welfare – for those who are disadvantaged by poverty or illness. Thus the state should provide a level playing field or safety net from which each individual can advance according to personal merit, talent and effort. This is equal opportunity through the concept of positive freedom, involving an active and interventionist role for the state where necessary. Essentially, liberals believe that inequalities should not be cumulative. Liberals also advocate formal equality in terms of political equality – one person, one vote, one value – and legal equality, that is, equal rights and entitlements for individuals in society through the rule of law. In the United States, for example, the guarantee of equal protection contained in the fourteenth amendment of the constitution – an amendment originally passed in 1868 to protect former slaves against the state – was later utilised by Justice Earl Warren (1953–69) and the Supreme Court to disbar wider racial discrimination and segregation. (However, a proposed amendment for equal rights for women to be enshrined in the US constitution failed in 1982.)

These two theories of equal opportunity – via negative versus positive freedom – differ significantly on the basic philosophical interpretation of social justice and on the proper role of the state, but they both clearly advocate inequality of outcome as desirable and meritocratic.

Socialists, broadly, argue that such assertions of equal opportunity are, at best, delusional and, at worst, deceptive. They assert that equality is only meaningful and just if it results in equality of outcome, that is, a significant reduction in the conclusive differences of wealth, income, economic security, personal achievement and social status throughout society. This is because they perceive inequality as a product of nurture rather than nature: a consequence of external, socially created and socially unjust barriers to personal achievement, such as birth, race, gender and religion, economic disadvantage, social deprivation, medical disability and disease, rather than innate, personal inadequacies. The essence of the socialist goal is a shared common humanity with no external disadvantages.

Equality may be categorised according to type as well as degree: for example, economic, social, legal or political equality. The dispute about equality of opportunity versus outcome focuses mainly on degrees of economic and social equality. Legal equality is the core principle of the rule of law: that everyone should have equal access to the law and equal treatment under the law. Clearly this cannot be divorced from economic and social equality, since the latter realities, in practice, largely dictate the former; but they are conceptually different. Similarly, political equality – meaning one person, one vote, one value, and equal access to political office – depends, in practice, upon economic and social standing but, in theory, need not.

Historically, modern liberals and socialists could philosophically agree upon policies such as the extension of the franchise, the abolition of slavery and the (genuine) rule of law. For example, in the UK, legislation has been passed in support of racial and sexual equality or, at least, non-discrimination (e.g. the Race Relations Act 1968 and Sex Discrimination Act 1976). These are liberal laws which parliamentary socialists would regard as necessary but not sufficient. Revolutionary socialists would regard such measures as merely bolstering inequality and false consciousness within an inherently exploitative and unjust capitalist economic system. For socialists of all sorts, economic equality is fundamental; traditionally, this implied collective ownership of the productive sector of society and radical – if not revolutionary – redistribution of wealth.

Evaluation of the Idea

TO WHAT EXTENT IS EQUALITY A DESIRABLE GOAL? A FUNDAMENTAL PHILOSOPHICAL divide between socialists and liberals is the potential conflict between equality and freedom: for example, a redistributive system of taxation to enhance equality may impinge upon the individual's freedom to keep and spend earned income. Similarly, the (socialist principle of) abolition of private education or health provision to promote genuine equality of access, opportunity and outcome may restrict the (liberal principle of) freedom of choice. As the liberal Lord Acton (1907) put it, *'The passion for equality makes vain the hope of freedom'*.

Libertarians reject all empirical claims of human equality, and strongly challenge how far moral claims about equal rights justify state or social action to enhance equality – artificially and unnaturally, as they see it. They argue that social, or state-imposed, equality undermines personal reward for personal merit, initiative and enterprise and is therefore unjust; it also generates economic stagnation and levelling down; it undermines personal freedom; and it creates social uniformity and mediocrity.

The organic view of society, embraced by traditional conservatives and fascists, is inherently in- and anti-egalitarian. *'Men are equal before God and the laws, but unequal in all else; hierarchy is the order of nature, and privilege is the reward of honourable service'* (White 1964). Thus inequality is both natural and desirable. *'Men are created different; and a government which ignores this law becomes an unjust government, for it sacrifices nobility to mediocrity'* (Kirk 1982). Toryism, like socialism, therefore perceives society in terms of a class hierarchy. Unlike socialism, however, Tories do not perceive class conflict – which would be unnatural in the organic unit – but, instead, a harmonious and integrative hierarchy of social classes, each accepting their proper place and function. This philosophy is reflected in the hymn 'All Things Bright and Beautiful': *'The rich man in his castle, the poor man at his gate, God made them, high and lowly, and ordered their estate'*.

Individualists such as liberals and New Right conservatives wholly reject any idea of sameness – and so would most egalitarians. At the heart of socialist and left-wing anarchist ideas of equality, however, is a concept of social justice which abhors unequal access, opportunity, treatment or social provision. The liberal concepts of foundational equality of worth and formal equality of rights are, say socialists, a meaningless fiction – at best, a moral exhortation – if economic and social structures erect barriers to equal attainment from the day of birth. Individualist challenges to the equality principle deriving from considerations of merit or incentive, under such conditions, are easily met. Equality enhances social cohesion and community, actualised freedom for all, genuine incentive for all and the realistic release and attainment of personal potential and merit.

Organic philosophies therefore perceive some sort of class or collective hierarchy as necessary, while mechanistic philosophies such as liberalism perceive individual inequalities as natural and just. Neither view regards equality as feasible, far less desirable.

However, socialists and left-wing anarchists argue that equality is a prerequisite of social justice, social cohesion, cooperation and community, that it underpins the common interest of society, promotes social harmony, is a precondition of genuine democracy and also of genuine freedom in the sense of personal autonomy and fulfilment. They also argue that material and social equality are the only meaningful forms, because all other forms of equality are dependent upon them and are a fiction without them.

The left/right divide is, fundamentally, an ideological battle between those who see equality as the bedrock of social justice and those who see some form of hierarchy as the most fair and natural social structure.

Positive attitudes to equality are relatively modern – i.e. post-French revolution. Classical and mediaeval philosophy would not have countenanced the concept. The debate now is waged over which type(s) of equality are desirable. Equality is often simplistically defined as 'uniformity' or 'sameness' – particularly by those who seek to decry it as an obstacle to freedom, individuality or meritocracy. However, advocates of equality – even utopian socialists – rarely employ the concept in such a basic way. They address economic, political, legal and social equality, equality of opportunity and of outcome, issues of nature versus nurture and potential conflicts within these diverse interpretations of the concept – most notably, the fairly limited concept of equal opportunity which assumes inequality of outcome. For example, the liberal inter-pretation of equal opportunity as positive discrimination – e.g. quotas for women, disabled and ethnic minorities in fields such as employment – is still largely illegal in the UK, but is legal (affirmative action) in the USA. It is the logical, but still controver-sial, consequence of desires merely to reduce decades or centuries of negative discrim-ination. In practical terms, within the UK, there remain clear inequalities of treatment, access, opportunity and attainment at every level – economically, socially, legally, sexually, racially and even for the young and the old. For example, according to the UK Land Registry (2002), 70 per cent of Britain is still owned by under 1 per cent of the population. The average child in Hackney will be one inch shorter than the

Hampstead child due simply to relative poverty and nutritional diff-erences. Each year since 1985, mortality rates among men and women between the ages of 16 and 45 have actually risen in the UK due to worsening income distribution and growing poverty at the bottom end of the socio-economic scale. One-quarter of old people and one-fifth of children are poor (by international UNDP calculations). Recently, politi-cians have taken to using the term 'social exclusion' to describe the situation and experience of those at the lower end of the economic ladder. Sceptics suspect that this may simply be a way of avoiding the word 'poverty', with its associated stigma and implications of political failure.

Homeless person

Globally, too, the gap between rich and poor is increasing. Currently, the three richest people in the world have assets that exceed the combined gross domestic product of the 48 least-developed countries (*Human Development Report 2001*, UNDP). South African President Thabo Mbeki opened the 2002 Johannesburg summit with the words, '*We do not accept that society should be constructed on the basis of a savage principle of the survival of the fittest*'. For good or bad, however, inequality not only remains a material reality, but – contrary to popular belief – is increasing.

European Union

The Idea

A N ECONOMIC AND POLITICAL FEDERATION, ESTABLISHED IN 1957, WHICH HAS EXPANDED
(by 2002) from 6 to 15 member states –
potentially in the future to almost 30 – and
whose agenda has been perceived as ranging
from an economic free market to a political
superstate. Originally known as the European
Economic Community, then as the European
Community (1967), and since 1993 as the
European Union (EU). The changing labels are
clearly illustrative of the broadening and
increasingly integrated embrace of the EU.

EU Flag

Development of the Idea

T HE THEN EUROPEAN ECONOMIC COMMUNITY WAS FORMED IN 1957. THE UK JOINED
IN 1973. The creation of the EEC was intended to establish a common market,
economic and monetary union and 'an ever closer union among the peoples of Europe'.
Thus the visions of a single market and a federal Europe date from the 1950s, not the
1980s as is sometimes suggested today. They were inspired by a desire for lasting
peace and security after two world wars; awareness of growing economic and social
interdependence and a desire for greater international cooperation between European
countries; the advantages of large-scale markets; greater world influence; and the wish
to challenge the blocs of the USA and the former USSR. The main economic principle
enshrined in the Treaty of Rome was free trade – the removal of barriers and the
establishment of common tariffs and policies (especially in agriculture, fishing, coal

and steel) across Europe. The 1960s also saw the creation of the controversial Common Agricultural Policy (CAP), a system of agricultural subsidies which by 2002 cost over 40 billion per year, almost half of the whole EU budget.

The EU is a supranational institution, that is, not just an international fraternity but a sovereign power over member states with a body of law that takes precedence over national law.

Britain initially refused to join for a number of reasons: a sense of superiority and national pride after victory in war; a hankering after lost imperial status; Britain's international status and links with the USA and Commonwealth; a sense of political and geographical separation from Europe – an island mentality; xenophobia (and mistrust especially of Germany and France); for the right-wing of the Conservative party especially, fear of loss of sovereignty and 'national' identity; and for the left-wing of the Labour party, dislike of the free market capitalist nature of the EEC. By the 1960s, however, it was clear that the EEC was an established success and Britain applied to join but was twice vetoed by France's President, Charles de Gaulle. Britain eventually joined in 1973, under Ted Heath's Conservative government. When the Labour party came to power in 1974 they were still very divided on the issue, so Prime Minister Harold Wilson held the first ever national UK referendum in 1975 on the question of staying in the EC. He lifted 'collective responsibility' and allowed his Cabinet ministers (including left-wingers such as Tony Benn) publicly to divide on the issue. Two-thirds of the country voted to stay in Europe, thus legitimising Wilson's own support for the EC. Elections to the European Parliament were first held in 1979.

Membership of the EU has profoundly divided the British political parties, Labour especially in the 1970s and the Conservatives especially in the 1980s and 1990s. Left-wing Labour MPs especially have always been hostile to the EU which they perceive as a 'capitalist club'. Blair's Labour government is now more Europhile – especially as the social dimension of EU policy making expands – and is currently pursuing the 'national changeover plan' making preparations to adapt to, and very likely eventually join, the euro (single currency). The Conservatives, under Margaret Thatcher, became increasingly suspicious of the EC in the 1980s as they saw it extending beyond a free trade community to a supranational political power (which, in fact, it always was). The perceived divisions and obsessions on the issue of Europe within the party contributed to its 1997 and 2001 election defeats. They apparently forgot Winston Churchill's comment in a speech in 1946, 'We must build a kind of United States of Europe'. Of the three main parties, only the Liberal Democrats are fully committed to the development of a federal Europe.

The UK's membership of, and future in, the EU has prompted the creation of two entirely new parties, both strongly anti-EU. One was multimillionaire James Goldsmith's Referendum party, which campaigned in the 1997 general election for a referendum on future entry into a single European currency and which, without winning any seats themselves, cost the Conservatives five or six seats by splitting the Eurosceptic vote. The party was dissolved upon the death of its founder. The second was the UK Independence party which is opposed to the whole concept of European union.

Three objectives currently dominate the EU agenda: the achievement of economic and monetary union; enlargement to include the new liberal democracies of central and eastern Europe; and the development of the political roles of the EU, notably the common foreign and security policies.

Evaluation of the Idea

THE MAIN ISSUE RAISED BY THE UK'S MEMBERSHIP OF THE EU SINCE 1973 HAS BEEN political sovereignty which, in turn, has two dimensions. The first is parliamentary sovereignty – said to be the linchpin of the British constitution since the English civil war in the mid-seventeenth century – which has been effectively negated by the primacy of EU laws and treaties. British courts are obliged by the European Communities Act 1972 to refuse to enforce Acts of Parliament which contravene European law (a principle established in the courts by the 1990 *Factortame* case about fishing rights in British waters). Even on entry in 1972, the British Parliament had to accept 43 volumes of existing EU legislation. Over 60 per cent of UK legislation now originates from the EU. Secondly, however, domestic governments and many voters are generally more concerned about the loss of national sovereignty, that is, their ability to pursue their own policies without external interference.

Economic sovereignty has become another important issue especially with the creation of the single European currency in 1999. The Labour government's granting to the Bank of England independent control of interest rates (immediately after the 1997 general election) was, in itself, a willing executive surrender of a key economic power which brought Britain into line with one of the conditions for joining the euro.

Critics also refer to the 'democratic deficit' within the EU because the Parliament is the only directly elected institution of the EU but is the least powerful. It is based in Strasbourg and now has 626 seats, of which Britain – like France and Italy – has 87. Only Germany has more, with 99. Other countries have fewer seats in rough proportion to their populations, ranging down to Luxembourg with 6. British Euro-constituencies are much larger than national constituencies with about 500,000 voters in each, and MEPs are elected every five years. The Labour government in 1999 changed the electoral system for Euro-elections from first-past-the-post to the closed party list system, a form of proportional representation where the party leaders rather than the voters choose the MEPs to fill the seats. The obvious criticism of this system is that the voter has no say in who are the actual MPs, who are likely to be loyal party placemen. The House of Lords rejected the closed list system for EU elections a record six times, but the government in the Commons pushed it through nevertheless. By 1999, some independent-minded and popular Labour MEPs – for example, Christine Oddy (Coventry and North Warwickshire) – were pushed so far down the party lists as to be effectively deselected by the leadership, with the voters having no say in the process.

The Parliament is a forum for debate, is consulted on major policy issues and can suggest amendments which the Commission often accepts, it can veto certain forms of legislation, can modify or reject the EU budget (as it did five times in the 1980s), can question the Council or Commission, can investigate public complaints of European maladministration (with an EU Ombudsman since Maastricht), can veto EU

Commissioners' appointments and can, in theory, dismiss the entire Commission by a two-thirds majority – never yet done, but it was pressure from MEPs which forced the Commission's collective resignation in 1999.

The European Parliament's profile is fairly low, many voters are apathetic or cynical about it and turnout at elections is relatively low (averaging under 60 per cent across Europe), with Britain's turnout usually lowest (e.g. 23 per cent in 1999). However, the Parliament's success against the Commission in 1999 may embolden it and stimulate voter interest in its activities.

The strongest expressions of hostility to the whole European project come from anti-EU parties such as the UK Independence party (UKIP): *'In 1975, the British people voted for the "Common Market" in good faith. They were told it was going to be a genuine common market – an association of independent, freely trading nation states. Instead, we have the European Union: centralised, bureaucratic, unaccountable and corrupt, eroding our independence and dictating policies that we would never vote for in an election. Not only is our currency under threat, but our entire legal system, our British nationality, our right to free speech and freedom of association, our police, our armed forces, our own agricultural policy, our right to trade freely and the parliamentary system that underpins British liberty'* (UKIP, 2001 General Election Manifesto).

(Ironically, the proportional representation system of election introduced by the Labour government for European elections allowed the UKIP to win three seats in the 1999 election.)

When Conservative Prime Minister John Major signed the Maastricht Treaty in 1991, he ensured the deletion of every reference to federalism ('the F-word') from the treaty and its replacement with the goal of 'an ever closer union', because 'federalism' has been used inaccurately by Eurosceptics to imply the complete absorption of member countries into a European monolith. In fact, of course, 'federalism' means the ordered division of sovereignty between central and local powers with constitutional guarantees of mutual spheres of autonomy. Thus the treaty also established the principle of 'subsidiarity' whereby decisions should be taken 'at the lowest possible level' compatible with efficiency and democracy. This was an attempt to return to member states some power previously lost to Brussels; and Scottish and Welsh nationalists argued that it also implied greater devolution of power within the UK itself (as was enacted in 1999).

Although the Maastricht Treaty gave the European Parliament more power, it also entrenched the system of 'intergovernmental' decision making in the Council of Ministers which, to critics, means a secretive and unaccountable club of national executives making most of the key decisions. Paradoxically, as it stands the EU strengthens national governments and bureaucracies at the expense of national parliaments and voters. If the European Parliament was to be given more genuine law-making power and ability to scrutinise and control the Commission and Council, that would further democratise the EU on the one hand, and reduce the potential for 'elective dictatorship' within Britain, on the other. Perhaps that is why the British government was foremost in resisting the granting of more power and influence to the European Parliament during the Maastricht negotiations.

A more positive view of Europe (Moravcsik 1993) argues that national governments benefit from EU membership, pooling sovereignty to achieve policy goals which would be unattainable alone; and that EU decision making helps to strengthen national governments by reducing the impact of domestic constraints.

Observers might, therefore, be forgiven for being sceptical about UK governments' expressed concerns about the loss of domestic parliamentary sovereignty, since post-war British governments have done more than Europe ever has to undermine Parliament's real power, from within.

Moreover, economic sovereignty has, actually, long been undermined by foreign ownership and investment from Europe and elsewhere, and by Britain's dependence especially on the health of the American economy – apparently with little hostility from the traditional right-wing Eurosceptics.

Most EU countries are more pro-Europe than the UK is, and many other countries such as Cyprus and Malta, including Eastern European countries such as Poland and Hungary since the end of the Cold War in 1990, are very keen to join the EU, taking the possible total up to at least 27. It seems likely that the Union will both deepen and widen within the next couple of decades, and Britain will have to decide whether it genuinely wishes to be 'at the heart of Europe' or to be sidelined and left behind.

Fascism

The Idea

A N INTER-WAR PHILOSOPHY AND POLITICAL SYSTEM STRIVING FOR MONISM – SINGLE leadership, party and ideology – combined with expansionist nationalism or racism and an economic philosophy of highly state regulated capitalism, based on a totalitarian political system which sought to control the private as well as the public spheres of life through a combination of mass consent and coercion.

Development of the Idea

T HE WORD 'FASCISM' DERIVES FROM THE LATIN *FASCES*, THE BUNDLE OF RODS WITH A projecting axehead, symbolising social unity and political leadership in the days of ancient Rome. The label was given by Benito Mussolini to the movement which he led in Italy from 1919 and which came to power in 1922. Thereafter, every European country had its fascist movement – for example, Oswald Mosley's Blackshirts in Britain and the Falange in Franco's Spain. Adolph Hitler's Nazi movement came to power in Germany in 1933 and is widely perceived as a unique and aberrant form of 'racial fascism'.

All of these movements developed in the inter-war years in response to economic depression and the political failures of the liberal democratic regimes in Europe. They were also a rejection of the German and Italian defeats of World War I and the humiliating reparations demanded by the victorious allies; and they were, finally, a product of the fear of rising communist sympathies in Europe. Many people – especially the

Benito Mussolini

lower middle classes – therefore flocked to fascism and Nazism, which had an undeniable claim to popularity. Writer Erich Fromm (1941) ascribes the psychological roots of fascism to 'the fear of freedom' – that is, the popular desire for strong leadership and security at a time of great economic and political instability and disorder.

Fascism is characterised by: an all-powerful state and leader; monism – a single party, ideology and centre of power; expansionist nationalism and/or racism; anti-communism; anti-egalitarianism; anti-liberalism; anti-individualism; anti-rationalism; anti-intellectualism; symbolism, myth and mysticism; a cult of war, violence and of youth; advocacy of private property but hostility to free market capitalism; and a combination of consent and coercion, propaganda and terror.

Clearly, fascist ideology is full of 'negations' – that is, it is a highly negative philosophy which opposes as much as it supports. This is unsurprising, given its origins as a fundamental rejection of inter-war liberal democracy and all of its attendant values.

All fascist movements were strongly nationalist, that is, they strove for unity around a sense of common culture which, in their case, also involved a powerful belief in the superiority of their own culture – ethnocentrism. This was usually coupled with an assertion of national decline or degeneration (blamed on some external contamination or conspiracy) from some mythical past age of glory to which fascist movements strove to return – that is, fascism was reactionary, and its goal was the restoration of national purity and dominance. The implication of the Italian fasces, for example, was that Mussolini was re-creating the greatness of ancient Rome. For Mussolini's brand of fascist nationalism, it was enough to be Italian (even if Jewish etc.). His movement was a very reactionary, ethnocentric and militarist form of nationalist expansionism based on a powerful sense of cultural superiority. It has been called 'integral nationalism': the individual was wholly subsumed in a sense of national identity, duty and dedication and had no personal identity or importance outside of the national interest.

Thus not all fascist movements were racist; this was mainly a feature of German Nazism. It divided human society into a hierarchy of perceived biological or genetic castes, headed by the culture-creating Aryan master race (herrenvolk). The intermediate, culture-carrying races were to be servants of the master race, and the most inferior, culture-destroying races – Jews, blacks, homosexuals, gypsies, communists, physically and mentally handicapped (even if they were German) – were to be eliminated. When Hitler spoke of the Jews as 'parasites' he meant it not simply as crude abuse but as a biological analogy. German expansionism had the goal of lebensraum – living space for the master race. This racial theory was not devised by Hitler but was adopted from nineteenth-century ideologists such as Gobineau, Wagner and Chamberlain. Hitler also applied – or, rather, perverted – the Darwinian idea of 'survival of the fittest' through a programme of eugenics, or selective breeding, in which the physically and mentally handicapped were sterilised and ultimately killed.

Evaluation of the Idea

THE TERM 'FASCISM' HAS OFTEN BEEN USED SINCE WORLD WAR II AS A PEJORATIVE or purely insulting term for any idea, philosophy or system perceived as right-wing, statist and anti-liberal, but it is best reserved for movements which adhere to the ideological package outlined above. That said, fascism is hard to pin down as a coherent ideology because of its very nature: it is intellectually crude and despises rationalism and logical theory, instead glorifying action, energy, instinct and emotion. '*Think with your blood*', said Mussolini.

The ideas of fascism embodied a rejection of the Enlightenment values of equality, freedom and reason which had dominated European politics since the French Revolution. As the Nazis put it, '*1789 is abolished*'.

Their claims to democracy were based on the charismatic and demagogic leadership of every fascist movement, which used populist appeals to the masses; their insistence on legitimising their regimes by elections and plebiscites and on involving the people in mass mobilisation and participation; and, in Italian fascism, by the support of the King and the Catholic Church which lent the movement added authority in the eyes of the people.

Above all, fascist leaders – especially Hitler – claimed to embody the 'general will' of the people (a perversion of Rousseau's directly democratic idea of the 'general will') and, as such, the leader had supreme authority to demand absolute obedience. '*His will is not the subjective, individual will of a single man, but the collective national will*' (Hitler 1969). This did not mean that he followed the will of the people, but that he was the only person capable of rightly interpreting the collective will. This meant that he was infallible. He could not err. This was also claimed by fascists to be the purest form of democracy. The idea of a 'Superman' or *Ubermensch* – a supremely powerful and omnipotent leader – was very loosely derived from the writings of the nineteenth-century German philosopher Friedrich Nietzsche.

This was not the kind of democracy which would be recognised by today's liberal regimes. All fascist movements used a combination of propaganda and terror to create and, indeed, coerce mass consent or compliance. The control and use of the mass media – newspapers and especially radio and film – were crucial to the rising popularity of fascism and confirmed it as a specifically twentieth-century phenomenon. However, once in power, fascist parties eliminated their rivals and manipulated the legal and judicial systems to legitimise their activities. They despised the division and diversity of liberal democracy and sought absolute unity under absolute leadership within the total power of the supremely organic state – 'strength through unity'. Nevertheless, in so far as fascism involved mass consent, participation and authority within a monist political system, it has often been labelled 'totalitarian democracy'.

For liberals and socialists, fascism posed disturbing questions about the essence of human nature, both in its theory of anti-rationalism and in the unquestioning enthusiasm with which so many accepted a fundamentally anti-egalitarian philosophy and pursued the tactics of terror and genocide, especially in Nazi Germany.

It also resurrected ancient questions about the essential role of the state – whether it is to provide security, liberty or equality – and especially about its proper limits – if any. For fascist totalitarianism, by definition, there were no limits to the rightful power of the state.

Finally, fascism had a peculiar relationship with socialism. On the one hand, Mussolini began his political life as a 'socialist' of sorts and Hitler called his movement National

Socialism: they were trying to appeal to all classes including the working class, and they did share some theoretical principles with communism such as collectivism, social Darwinism, the dialectic, opposition to liberalism and to the capitalist free market. Fascism rejected the individualism and self-interest of laissez-faire capitalism and the multinational or global variants of big business. Mussolini had been strongly influenced by the Italian revolutionary syndicalist Georges Sorel who rejected Marxist materialism and said instead, 'Man is moved by myth'. For fascism, mysticism replaced scientism and nation or race replaced class.

Post-war liberal and conservative Cold War writers tended to equate fascism – and especially Nazism – with Soviet Stalinism under the banner label 'totalitarianism'. They pointed out the many practical similarities between the regimes: a single, all-powerful leader, a one-party system, a single ideology with all opposing groups and ideas banned, monopoly control of the means of communication, strong state control of the economy, militarism, use of terror, lack of freedom and individualism, the subordination of law to politics, the goal of world domination, mass mobilisation of the people and control of private morality and civil society. Friedrich and Brzezinski, writing in the 1960s, devised a 'six point syndrome' of such characteristics; Schapiro, in the early 1970s, devised a model of 'three pillars and five contours'. The essence of all of these theories was the same: an academic rationalisation for defending the virtues of liberal democracy against the twin evils of fascism and communism.

This was liberal capitalist propaganda. Fascism was an extreme right-wing movement, stressing private property and hierarchy, which rejected and despised socialism and especially communism with their ideals of equality, internationalism and universal harmony. As the historian Hugh Trevor-Roper (1947) put it, 'Before all else, it was anti-communist. It lived and throve on anti-communism.' It was funded and politically supported by the business classes, who prospered by it. As the British fascist Oswald Mosley put it, 'Capitalism is a system by which capital uses the nation for its own purposes. Fascism is a system by which the nation uses capital for its own purposes' (quoted in Heywood 1992).

The Cold War School analysis is, incidentally, the opposite of the Marxist analysis of fascism and Nazism (developed by e.g. Trotsky, Miliband), which sees them as systems of right-wing, authoritarian, state capitalism that emerge when capitalism is in economic crisis and needs rescue by powerful state intervention, and whose defining feature is anti-communism. For Marxists, fascism is the extreme example of bourgeois hegemony, with the fascist state protecting bourgeois property interests through corporatism, suppression of workers' organisations and rights, aggressive nationalism and racism, imperialist war and the maximisation of private profit through state direction. Whereas Stalinism could never sensibly be seen as Marxist theory put into practice, fascism and Nazism provide perhaps the best examples of the congruence of political thought and action.

Some argue that fascism is history and that, given its legacy of oppression and genocide, humankind will never go down that road again. A current concern throughout Europe, however, is the apparent resurgence of the ultra-right, often in the form of neo-fascism: for example, Silvio Berlusconi's affiliations with the Northern League and National Alliance in Italy; the election of Joerg Haider's far right Freedom Party in Austria in 2000; the high vote for National Front leader Jean-Marie le Pen in the first round of France's presidential elections in 2002 (followed by the attempted assassination of President Chirac by a member of the far right Radical Unity group three months later); the rise of the far right in the Netherlands following the assassination of Pym Fortuyn; the election of British National Party (BNP) councillors in UK local elections in 2002; and even the vociferous presence of hard-right elements in the British Conservative party in factions such as the Monday Club. Deep economic recession, high unemployment and/or growing racial tensions in the future may help to provoke a significant revival of fascism throughout Europe.

Feminism

The Idea

A PHILOSOPHY WHICH ADVOCATES – AT LEAST – EQUALITY OF RIGHTS BETWEEN THE sexes. Originally an eighteenth- and nineteenth-century movement of middle-class women seeking the vote, it has developed into a wider and more far-reaching women's movement with diverse sub-strands including liberal feminism, socialist feminism and radical feminism.

Development of the Idea

WHEN SEVENTEENTH- AND EIGHTEENTH-CENTURY PHILOSOPHERS SUCH AS JOHN LOCKE and Thomas Paine asserted 'the rights of man', they meant exactly that; as did the American Declaration of Independence (1776) that *'We hold these truths to be self-evident; that all men are created equal'*. Hence the emergence of so-called 'first wave' feminism, of the liberal variety, with Mary Wollstonecraft's *Vindication of the Rights of Women* (1792) and J.S. Mill and Harriet Taylor's *On the Subjection of Women* (1869) which sought to reduce sexual discrimination primarily through a campaign for equal suffrage. Wollstonecraft (incidentally, wife of the anarchist William Godwin and mother of Mary Shelley, the creator of Frankenstein) argued that women were, like men, essentially rational beings and therefore as capable of self-determination and as deserving of liberty, rights and, above all, education. Mill's book encouraged the government of the day to pass the Married Women's Property Act 1870 which,

Mary Wollstonecraft

for the first time, gave married women the right to own property; previously, everything they possessed legally belonged to their husbands.

By 1928, women had won the vote on equal terms with men in the UK but, by the 1960s, it was widely perceived that this had done little to reduce ongoing economic, political, legal and social inequalities between men and women. Hence the emergence of 'second wave' feminism. Liberal feminists in the post-war era – such as Betty Friedan, whose book *The Feminine Mystique* (1963) marked the resurgence of feminist thinking in the 1960s – sought equal political and legal rights for women. They made considerable strides in the UK, with legislation such as the Abortion Act 1967, Equal Pay Act 1970, Sex Discrimination Act 1976, the liberalisation of divorce, taxation and property laws and the state provision of free and legal contraception. Women's whole lifestyles changed and even their health improved significantly as they bore fewer children, more safely. In the USA, liberal feminism went further and resulted in the legalisation of positive discrimination – that is, quotas – for women as well as for ethnic minorities in education and employment at around the same time.

However, the liberal feminist movement was predominantly white, Western and middle class and broadly excluded working class and black women who were much more socially disadvantaged. Moreover, manifest gender inequalities across all classes persisted, and so more radical forms of feminism emerged.

Socialist feminists have emphatically rejected the liberal feminist, reformist, approach, maintaining instead that sexual divisions in capitalism are due primarily to the operation of the economy, and therefore that a class revolution is the prerequisite of sexual equality. Socialist feminism began with nineteenth-century utopian socialists such as Charles Fourier, who argued for the abolition of oppressive, monogamous marriage in favour of short-term sexual liaisons in cooperative communes where housework and child-rearing would be done by specialists. The significance of economic factors in the sexual aspect of oppression was primarily asserted by Marx's collaborator Engels in his book *The Origins of the Family, Private Property and the State* (1884). He argued that the orthodox nuclear family is an economic unit bound up with the male ownership and inheritance of private property. Women themselves have long been the property of men within the legal framework of marriage which, in turn, has been a contract between the male breadwinner and the housewife of economic maintenance in return for sexual services. This is why, until the 1990s, there was no legal concept of rape within marriage. (One wonders whether Prince Philip knew to which philosophy he was subscribing when he said in 1988, 'I don't think a prostitute is more moral than a wife, but they are doing the same thing'.) Socialist feminists also stress the role of women as a 'reserve army of labour' in the event of an expansion of production such as in war. Women still provide a predominantly temporary and disposable source of labour, socially conditioned to accept low pay and status, thereby depressing wage levels without threatening men's jobs. Women's domestic work is also essential to the health and efficiency of the state in sustaining and servicing their male partners, nurturing and conditioning future male workers and releasing men for employment. The traditional nuclear family – male breadwinner, female housewife – provides capitalism with 'two for the price of one', also providing men with an incentive to remain in exploitative work to support their families. Marxist feminists emphasise the role of ideology and socialisation (e.g. women's magazines, Mills and Boon books etc.) in perpetuating gender inequalities and women's acceptance of them. Therefore, for Marxists, women's liberation will be a by-product of economic and social revolution, and women should devote their time and energy to the class struggle rather than to bourgeois women's organisations.

Radical feminists, who emerged only in the second half of the twentieth century, go further than liberals and socialists to argue the primacy of gender divisions over all other social cleavages, including class and race. Writers such as Kate Millett and Shulamith Firestone argue that patriarchy – where the male is head of the household – in the personal and private sphere of home and family, has always been the first and most important power relationship in the human social system – hence their famous slogan, *'The personal is political'*. Patriarchy in the private sphere confines most women to the home and therefore largely excludes them from the public sphere of work, economics and politics, and is therefore the root of sexual inequality throughout society and, indeed, human history. Social conditioning in the private sphere of home and family inculcates gender roles into future generations. Hence radical feminists draw a basic distinction between 'sex' – biological differences deriving from nature – and 'gender' – socially constructed roles which both men and women internalise through conditioning from birth, but which can be changed. Hence radical feminists reject the 'public-private split' – the divide between 'public man' and 'private woman'; for them, the priority is consciousness raising among women towards a sexual revolution which will transform gender roles and eliminate private patriarchy.

Evaluation of the Idea

Most Western Political Thought over the centuries has been rooted in the advocacy or assumption of patriarchy – rule by men. It has also largely been written by men, about men and for men. It is still, therefore, difficult even to get the concept of feminism taken seriously within the mainstream channels of political debate.

Arguably, too, feminists have damaged their own cause by their internal divisions and – for some – their extremism, which has allowed simplistic stereotyping by their critics. For example, radical feminists reject the 'public-private split' – the idea that there is, or should be, a division between the spheres of public, economic and political activity and the private arena of home and family – a split which liberals accept and even value. Whereas liberal feminists believe that encroaching upon the private sphere may amount to creeping totalitarianism, for radical feminists the priority is a sexual revolution which will eliminate private patriarchy. Marxist feminists are closer to radicals than to liberals on this point, that is, they reject the public-private split, but they argue that inequality is rooted in the public, rather than the private, sphere, and change must therefore begin in the wider economic system. For Marxists, gender explanations of women's inequality cut across class; socialist groups therefore face the particular, practical problem of whether women should maintain their own separate organisations distinct from the main (and mainly male) proletarian party. Modern Marxist feminists have increasingly recognised the complex interplay of economic, social and cultural factors in determining patterned, social inequalities, including those of both class and gender. This perception was the basis of Juliet Mitchell's revisionist work, *Women's Estate* (1971). She argued that social revolution was a necessary, but not sufficient, prerequisite of sexual equality and that the role of women as child-bearers, child-rearers and as sex objects would also have to be addressed.

Whereas liberals are inherently reformist, Marxist and radical feminists are both revolutionary – but they disagree on whether class or sexual revolution is the priority. They all agree that biological, economic and cultural factors all play a role in gender inequality but they disagree on the relative importance of those factors, and upon the solutions. For example, even liberals have long recognised that socialisation is a key factor in constructing gender roles: as J.S. Mill put it well over a century ago, *'I deny that anyone knows, or can know, the nature of the two sexes . . . What is now called the nature of women is an eminently artificial thing – the result of forced repression'* (1859). Nevertheless, liberals do not seek to challenge private family and marriage roles and relationships, whereas radicals see these as the root cause of sexual inequality.

Radical feminists, however, differ among themselves over whether women should – in a clear play on Marxist terminology – *'seize control of the means of reproduction'* (Firestone 1971) e.g. test-tube babies; or should pursue political separatism, e.g. women-only consciousness raising groups and activities; or – at the most radical – should pursue private as well as public separatism in the form of political lesbianism. As the graffiti has put it for over 30 years, *'A woman needs a man like a fish needs a bicycle'*. Radical feminism has also spawned anarcho-feminists and eco-feminists with their own particular concerns about the state and the environment. A few of the radicals insist upon the superiority of female traits and values – so-called 'supremacists' whose goal is matriarchy rather than equality. The most radical of the radicals have provided the focus or target for the crude political and tabloid stereotypes of hairy man-haters in dungarees, which have helped to ridicule and marginalise the very word 'feminism' since the 1980s.

Black and third world feminists, meanwhile, stress the great diversity of women in and across cultures, and often criticise first world feminists of all schools for racism. *'I despair. The debate surrounding the state of new British feminism makes me aware that one thing has not changed: new or not, British feminism is still self-confidently all-white'* (Mirza 1988). She describes contemporary British feminists as *'white media feminists with their self-indulgent, in-crowd, middle-class perspectives'* and says it is small wonder that they are rejected by the mass of both black and white young women. This is a useful reminder that it is dangerous and simplistic to over-generalise. The experiences of a successful, white, Western, professional woman would be utterly alien to a black, working class woman battling against racism and poverty as well as sexism.

There will, of course, always be anti-feminists, such as traditional conservatives and fascists who believe that gender hierarchy is natural, functional, inevitable and desirable. In the eighteenth century, for example, Prime Minister Horace Walpole described Mary Wollstonecraft's plea for women's rights as 'unnatural' and her as 'a hyena in petticoats'. New Right conservatism today contains a clear paradox in relation to the issue of women's equality. The neo-liberal strand of New Right thinking advocates individualism, equality of opportunity and meritocracy apparently regardless of sex, race, religion or creed; but the neo-conservative strand of New Right thinking strongly advocates traditional family values and hence patriarchy and gender inequality. It is no coincidence that Margaret Thatcher had no other women in her Cabinets. There are no conservative feminists.

Conservatism can even produce inverted chauvinism; for example, the glorification of the wife/mother stereotype. The irony is that some self-proclaimed contemporary 'feminists' come very close to this stance: Germaine Greer and Betty Friedan, for example, in their later writings have rejected the radical goal of androgyny where men's and women's roles would not be socially differentiated, and have celebrated the unique nature of womanhood and the superior roles of motherhood and domesticity – much to the disgust of many other feminists.

Finally, some commentators – usually conservative journalists, whether male or female – have argued that feminism has done its job so effectively that it is now obsolete. *'Feminism is no longer necessary because it has become a victim of its own success'* (Anne Applebaum, *New Statesman*, 16 January 1998). She argues that inequality before the law no longer exists (though she admits that reality does not always match the letter of the law); and she argues that further changes – in attitudes and prejudices, for example – cannot be achieved by legislation or activism but only by time. Katie Roiphe (*Sunday Times*, March 1998) similarly says that feminism has succeeded to the extent that women now have to search desperately for *'trivial definitions of victimhood'* like being complimented on their appearance or having doors opened for them by men. Some – such as Labour's former Education Minister Stephen Byers – have gone so far as to argue that men can no longer keep up with women's successes and that a new phenomenon of 'laddish anti-learning culture' has emerged, producing the 'redundant rogue male', unskilled, unwanted and unneeded by women and reduced to scavenging Britain's sink housing estates in a deformed celebration of defunct masculinity.

These portrayals are selective and they ignore the wider picture. The divide between 'public man' and 'private woman' has not disappeared, and official gender statistics on pay, career opportunities, pension rights, health issues, domestic violence and so on suggest – for better or worse – that post-feminist triumphalism is premature.

Freedom

The Idea

LIBERTY, LACK OF RESTRAINT; PERSONAL AUTONOMY. METAPHYSICAL FREEDOM IS THE concept of 'free will': the freedom of choice to do one thing rather than another. The issue of political freedom concerns the nature and justification of external restraints upon choice, action and achievement. The liberal philosopher T.H. Green (1836–82) distinguished between 'negative freedom' – non-interference; and 'positive freedom' – the actualised capacity to fulfil one's real potential.

Development of the Idea

THE CONCEPT OF FREEDOM IS EMPLOYED BY EVERY POLITICAL PHILOSOPHY FROM anarchism to fascism, but in very different ways. Freedom is the primary doctrine of both anarchism and liberalism but, whereas the anarchist belief in freedom is absolute, liberals are ambivalent about human nature and therefore are more restrained in their regard for freedom. Socialists, on the other hand, favour equality above freedom. Some other philosophies do not – to say the least – regard freedom as an undisputed blessing. Tories and fascists rank order, stability, security and duty far over freedom. They assert that humans are lacking in rationality and are therefore not deserving of either equality or freedom. Erich Fromm's (1941) analysis of fascism and Nazism as the 'fear of freedom' argued that human beings were not sufficiently mature to cope with the concept of freedom and longed to revert to a sense of collective psychological identity and security.

The first modern assertion of freedom emerged with classical economic, laissez-faire liberalism of the eighteenth and nineteenth centuries, which believed that *'Heaven helps those who help themselves'* (Smiles 1859). A form of economic meritocracy where people succeed or fail only on their own abilities and efforts is a guarantee of social justice, according to early liberals. This borrows from – and perverts – the ideas of the influential British scientist Charles Darwin (1809–82) about evolutionary progress based upon natural selection and the 'survival of the fittest' (not actually Darwin's phrase). As the American classical liberal William Sumner (1884) put it, *'The drunk in the gutter is just where he ought to be'*.

Laissez-faire economic theory lays strong stress upon individual freedom, but it means 'negative freedom', not positive: that is, it stresses freedom from any external intervention, especially from any state interference – whether help or hindrance – in the economic sphere, rather than actual freedom to achieve desired ends and genuine personal autonomy, with state help if necessary (which is the modern liberal concept of 'positive freedom'). It is therefore a freedom which stems from the economic rather than the political system; from capitalism rather than from political democracy; and from private property rather than from political organisation. The laissez-faire concept of negative freedom is commonly described as economic libertarianism. Contemporary New Right conservatism – such as 'Thatcherism' in the UK – inherited this economic doctrine from earlier, classical liberalism. Obvious New Right policy examples during the 1980s included privatisation, the shift from student grants to student loans and cuts in welfare provision. New Right conservatism is hostile to the idea of state provision of social rights, partly because they perceive 'big government' as expensive and inefficient, and partly because they perceive that the 'nanny state' promotes a 'dependency culture' which undermines individual freedom of choice, initiative, self-reliance and responsibility. Rather, individuals should make active provision for themselves and their families – for example, in the form of private insurance – to cover unemployment, illness and old age.

The core doctrine of modern liberalism, by contrast, is 'positive individual freedom': the actualised freedom to achieve one's own potential and personal development and attain fulfilment, with state help and intervention where necessary. The first advocate of this concept was the late nineteenth-century liberal T.H. Green. He perceived that free market capitalism sets up barriers to genuine freedom for the working classes, women and children who were disadvantaged by poverty, ignorance and sickness. Positive freedom means not simply the freedom to starve in the gutter without anyone either pushing you down or helping you out. Positive freedom, for modern liberals, implies a positive and empowering role for the state and government, whether in a mixed market economy providing health, welfare and education to help individuals to make the most of themselves, or in the state guaranteeing, by law – ideally in a Bill of Rights – freedom from discrimination, freedom of information, freedom of speech etc. For example, the UK Liberal party's Beveridge Report (1942), which laid the foundations for the post-war welfare state, advocated positive freedom from the 'five giants' of want, disease, ignorance, squalor and idleness.

Modern liberals therefore regard the state and the law as capable of enhancing individual freedom; indeed, they cannot envisage genuine freedom for individuals without some state intervention and legal protection. However, the liberal view that *'Liberty is the right to do everything which the laws allow'* (Montesquieu 1748) would be regarded by anarchists as a complete contradiction in terms and a wholesale denial of freedom itself. Anarchists take the view of Rousseau (1762) that *'Man was born free and everywhere he is in chains'* – that is, the essential liberty of humankind has been corrupted and oppressed by the state.

Evaluation of the Idea

THE CONCEPTS OF 'NEGATIVE FREEDOM' AND 'POSITIVE FREEDOM' HAVE BEEN DEFINED differently by different philosophies at different times. The basic definitions are often expressed basically as 'freedom from' and 'freedom to'; these interpretations, however, are much too simplistic. Every 'freedom from' is a 'freedom to' – for example, freedom from ignorance is the freedom to be educated. The liberal interpretations of 'freedom from state' and 'freedom through state' are more valid, but not full.

The more far-reaching definitions of negative and positive freedom are as follows: negative freedom means simply non-interference – whether by state, government, family or friends: but imagine, for example, a baby abandoned in a field. Non-interference for the disadvantaged, deprived and desolate means death. This is why modern liberals object to the classical liberal notion that the individual is truly free if the state simply leaves them alone. Positive freedom means the genuine, actualised freedom to fulfil your own wishes, potential, powers and possibilities to the full. If you are reasonably mature, intelligent, educated, healthy and prosperous, then there is no need for external intervention or help. However, modern liberalism assumes that many individuals are not in that luxurious situation and therefore that positive state intervention is frequently necessary. More optimistic theories, such as Marxism and anarchism, assume that we can reach such a level of economic, social and political development that state help is not necessary at all, because community help is entirely adequate. For them, therefore, positive freedom means the abolition of the state and its replacement by genuine 'people power'.

Marxism and especially anarchism further believe, contrary to modern liberalism, that the state constrains freedom much more than it enhances it. Freedom is often asserted as one of the values integral to a capitalist economy, but Marxist thinking avers that the exploitation inherent in capitalist profiteering is a fundamental denial of freedom, not only for the workers but also for the alienated and estranged owners of productive enterprises – that is, the ruling class; and, moreover, that the bourgeois state protects this exploitative economy and therefore suppresses freedom for all involved. Anarchism goes furthest in its hostility to the state: it argues that the state – any state – is, by definition, a sovereign, coercive and oppressive power which can never do anything but suppress freedom.

Three key questions are: is freedom the primary political or philosophical priority – as against, for example, security, happiness, equality or democracy (all of which may conflict with freedom); secondly, what separates freedom from mere licence; and thirdly, are humans deserving or capable of exercising freedom?

Hobbes (given his very negative view of human nature) famously believed that the human priorities were order and security over freedom. Plato, centuries earlier, was one of the first to argue that freedom in the context of democracy led to the rule of demagogues (unprincipled agitators) who would rapidly establish themselves as absolute tyrants, and hence would subvert freedom entirely. As Madame Roland said at the height of the French revolutionary terror, *'Liberty, what crimes have been committed in thy name!'* Contemporary Western liberal democracy widely asserts that freedom and democracy are synonymous; but liberals have, in fact, always defended individual freedom against the excesses of collective democracy such as the tyranny of the majority and the omnipotence of mass public opinion encroaching upon the private or personal sphere of individual thought and action.

Liberals such as John Locke have also always distinguished between freedom and licence (excessive liberty), arguing that freedom does not mean the removal of law, because that permits the invasion of one's freedom by one's neighbours at the expense of other priorities such as justice, morality and the harm principle.

Most fundamentally, the belief in freedom involves the belief in human rationality to use that freedom responsibly; therefore diverse views on freedom depend upon different views of human nature, free will and perceptions of the individual as rational or irrational, and as taking or giving in nature. Those philosophies which reject freedom, such as fascism, are those with the deepest mistrust of human nature.

The primary political question is how far the state should intervene either to enhance freedoms – e.g. through civil rights, welfare or law and order – or to constrain freedoms – e.g. by promoting alternative priorities such as equality, security or law and order. Those philosophies which perceive the state itself as the greatest threat to freedom put enormous faith either in the community or in the individual as self-sustaining entities, capable of genuine autonomy. The strength and durability of contemporary states challenge all such anti-statist philosophies, whether left wing or right wing.

In philosophical terms, to be truly free, we would have to be the product of nothing but ourselves – not of genetic factors, social factors, family, friends, work, media, church or any other extraneous influences. But, by definition, we cannot be *causa sui* – the cause of ourselves. Nor can we be untouched by any external influences or constraints. Therefore we can never be truly free. This raises the concomitant question of responsibility: if we are genuinely free in our actions, we are also wholly responsible for them – and, if not, presumably not.

In the UK, it has long been said (in the absence of an entrenched Bill of Rights guaranteeing positive freedoms) that we are simply free to do whatever the law does not prohibit – *'the silence of the laws'*, as Hobbes (1651) put it – that is, a concept of negative freedom which is widely presumed to be extensive. However, the legal restrictions upon basic civil liberties in the UK are often substantial, and are increasing. Take, as just one example, freedom of speech (defended on the grounds that it is essential for the pursuit of truth, a requisite of liberal democracy and vital to human autonomy and dignity). Discounting debates about what should count as 'speech', the legal constraints in the UK include the laws on libel, slander, official secrecy, obscenity and pornography, race relations, sexual discrimination and harassment, blasphemy, contempt of court, incitement to disaffection, sedition, treason and terrorism – to name but a few. Politically, philosophically and legally, we may be less free than we think.

Globalisation

❖

The Idea

'GLOBALISATION' DESCRIBES THE POST-WAR GROWTH OF ECONOMIC, TECHNOLOGICAL and cultural connections across state borders, such that states and peoples are increasingly internationally interconnected – particularly since the collapse of communism. Globalisation embraces the growing economic power of large, multinational private corporations, the international reach and relevance of the Internet, drugs, terrorism, weapons of mass destruction, HIV and AIDS (40 million victims worldwide by 2003), BSE, climate change, ideology and even the growing ubiquity of a few key languages – notably English.

Development of the Idea

GLOBALISATION IS USUALLY SAID TO HAVE STARTED IN THE SECOND HALF OF THE twentieth century because of the spreading power and influence of the post-war superpowers and the rise of huge multinational corporations whose annual turnover could dwarf the gross domestic products of several small countries.

UK Foreign Office minister Peter Hain once neatly summed up the impact of globalisation as '*a world in which there is no longer any such place as abroad*' (4 March 2002). Today's world, he said, is a small place, and whatever happens across the globe can directly affect every one us, wherever we are.

'*Foreign policy used to be about what went on abroad: diplomatic handshakes in distant capitals, nation speaking solely unto nation, far removed from ordinary life. No longer. Today, events in far flung places have a direct impact upon our lives. We find ourselves in the midst of a vast network of relationships and interests that disregard national divisions*' (Mark Leonard, Director, Foreign Policy Centre, February 2002).

The main dimension of globalisation is economic – particularly the growing control of giant companies and conglomerates such as Shell or Microsoft. It has been estimated that by the mid-1990s, a mere 40,000 multinational private companies (out of many millions) accounted for one-fifth of the total global economy.

Since the 1960s, most governments have relaxed exchange controls on international capital flows (since 1979 in the UK). Thereafter, investment could cross national boundaries with ease. Technological advances and more efficient financial clearing systems also made it easier to move capital between financial centres in the search for marginally higher returns elsewhere in the world.

New international organisations have been created to manage some aspects of economic globalisation. For example, the World Trade Organisation (WTO) was established in 1995 (as a successor to GATT – the General Agreement on Tariffs and Trade) as the only international organisation which now deals with the global rules of trading between states. It currently has 143 member states and its role is to resolve trading disputes peacefully by agreement or arbitration – for example, issues such as tuna and dolphin fishing in the Pacific, and Venezuelan oil exports to the USA.

Technological development has added other dimensions to globalisation, from the Internet to global climate change centring on the 'greenhouse effect'; that is, pollution produced by cars, industry and power plants which is causing the average world temperature to rise. Experts fear that, if nothing is done, the polar ice caps will soon begin to melt, causing sea levels to rise and changing the world's environment irrevocably.

The ultimate ideological pronouncement of both economic and political globalisation was Francis Fukuyama's (1989) thesis of 'the end of history' which asserted the 'universalisation' of capitalist liberal democracy since the collapse of communism and the fall of the Berlin Wall in 1989. The manifest strength of political and strategic connections between America's President Bush and Russia's President Putin by 2003 did, indeed, seem to signal a new, post-communist, consensual world order.

Finally, there is the growing ubiquity of a few key languages: *'Every fortnight, somewhere in the world, a language dies. The catalogue of loss is astounding. Hundreds of native Australian and North American languages were crushed in the mid-20th century by well-meant educational and "assimilist" programmes . . . . Dozens of minority European languages are disappearing . . . And even comparatively enlightened African governments are corralling their multilingual populations into speaking just two or three officially approved languages – simply for administrative convenience . . . A comparatively optimistic prediction is that just half of the 6,000 languages now spoken will survive the present century'* (Morrison 2002).

Evaluation of the Idea

TWO KEY QUESTIONS ARE WHETHER GLOBALISATION IS A REALITY AND, IF SO, WHETHER it is, on balance, a positive or negative phenomenon.

Does globalisation imply that the state is no longer relevant and politics is dead? Against the argument that globalisation is overwhelming us is the ongoing strength and emotional pull of state, national, regional or narrower local loyalties. While power broadens globally, sentiment and attachment seem to deepen locally. If the economic and political power holders do not recognise and respond to strengthening local attachments – for example, of state, nation, region, race or class – conflict will likely ensue.

It has been suggested, moreover, that capitalist economists and politicians may have overstated the reality of globalisation in order to encourage the idea that the forces of market capitalism are irresistible. However, globalisation is creating its own challengers – perhaps, even, the seeds of its own destruction – in the form of the environmentalist, anti-capitalist and anarchist protest movements which have been proliferating in recent years. By 2002, anti-capitalist demonstrations throughout Europe were attracting over 250,000 supporters (e.g. Barcelona, March 2002); and peace protests even in London – as much anti-American as anti-terrorist – numbered hundreds of thousands.

Fukuyama was also wrong – as he, himself, admitted by 2002. His thesis of the triumph of liberal democratic ideology since the late twentieth century ignored the growing power of Islam as a pan-national religious and political creed; nor has orthodox communism entirely disappeared – the Cuban, Chinese, North Korean and some African regimes remain. The electoral successes of the far right in Europe and the uncertain impact of future economic recessions also challenge Fukuyama's basic assertion.

If globalisation is a reality, is it a virtue? The positive view of globalisation stresses the benefits of international communications (satellite, telephone and Internet links), the possibilities for growing international affluence and the benign influence of non-governmental organisations and international charities such as Oxfam and Amnesty International. From a free market perspective, freedom from economic regulation has increased the efficiency of the world distribution of capital and the returns on private investments. (Critically, however, floods of short-term capital outside of the control of the state can rapidly destabilise an economy in response to speculative rumours.)

Alternatively, globalisation of markets could be positively interpreted as a sentiment of socialist internationalism – for example, the Commonwealth Heads of Government Meeting (March 2002) calling for 'a generous spirit of globalisation across the third world' addressing poverty, development, democracy, trade and investment. Moreover, globalisation could be regarded as a positive counter to divisive and dangerous sentiments of exclusive nationalism and racism manifested by such groups as the UK British National Party and the French National Front.

From a critical left-wing perspective, however, globalisation means, quite simply, the (temporary) triumph of international, exploitative capitalism. There is a sense that giant corporations such as Microsoft or Shell are beyond the control of any individual state – hence the sense of a 'governance gap' where states are powerless to control global events. That feeling of impotence in the face of such huge multinational conglomerates has helped to fuel the antagonism and even violence of recent anti-globalisation demonstrations around the world, from Seattle to Genoa. The continuing targets of the demonstrators' anger are international organisations like the G8 group of industrialised countries and the WTO. Often, on the streets, well-known global retail brands are also hit. McDonald's is both a favourite target and symbol for anti-globalisation activists. The critical view of capitalist international '*imperialism as the highest form of capitalism*', however, is not new; Marx and especially Lenin gave it expression and empirical evaluation from the 1840s to the 1920s. By imperialism, they meant precisely the process of capital accumulation on a world scale in an era of monopoly capitalism, and their theory of imperialism was an investigation of accumulation in the context of a world market created by that accumulation (not, as 'vulgar' Marxists have presented it, merely the oppression or exploitation of weak countries by powerful ones).

The economic and political powers which dominate the global agenda tend to deny, decry or simply ignore the wider and negative implications of globalisation. For example, in Kyoto in 1997, the UN brokered the world's first treaty to tackle global warming. Signatories pledged to cut their greenhouse gas emissions in the next decade by just over 5 per cent from 1990 levels. But the USA dragged its feet on implementing the Kyoto protocol and in 2001, President George W. Bush abandoned the treaty altogether, saying that it was against his own country's economic interests. This was a valid viewpoint given that America contained 4 per cent of the world's population but consumed 25 per cent of the world's energy resources.

In May 2001, Bush further announced US abandonment of the anti-nuclear Anti-Ballistic Missile Treaty 1972 in order that America could pursue its 'son of Star Wars' interceptor nuclear missile system. In July 2002, he demanded – and won – total immunity for American forces from the newly established International War Crimes Court, by threatening to veto UN peacekeeping missions in Bosnia and elsewhere. Finally, Bush himself did not even attend the 2002 Johannesburg earth summit.

For some – for better or worse – globalisation implies the death of politics and the growing irrelevance of the state. However, alternative international and supranational powers are not yet an effective substitute. The United Nations, for example, seems to be relatively powerless in relation to the dominant states within it. It is still the domestic state – witness, above all, the USA as the only contemporary superpower – which seeks to harness the processes of globalisation to the transnational pursuit of its own prosperity and power.

Finally, on the globalisation of the English language, the positive perspective – unsurprisingly expressed most frequently by British and American commentators – is that the sooner everybody can speak English, the better for world peace, economic efficiency and global prosperity. Morrison's (2002) article notes, however, that when a language disappears, a whole culture and even the unique mental processes enshrined in its grammar may die with it. 'One world, one dictionary,' boasted Bill Gates when he launched Microsoft's *Encarta World Dictionary*. '*Let's hope*', says Morrison, '*that mankind never descends into that totalitarian abyss*'.

Human Nature

The Idea

A PHILOSOPHICAL PERCEPTION OF THE ESSENCE OF THE HUMAN CHARACTER, UNAFFECTED by the influences of society or state. Very broadly, political theories can be categorised according to whether they are pessimistic or optimistic about human nature and, consequently, according to what they regard as the proper role – if any – of state and government.

Development of the Idea

B ROADLY, OPTIMISTIC VIEWS OF HUMAN NATURE SUBDIVIDE INTO THE ANARCHIST/ socialist and the liberal/capitalist. The anarchist view is the most optimistic of all, viewing human nature as perfectible; as William Godwin (1793) said, *'Perfectibility is the most unequivocable characteristic of the human species'*. This view is undeniably utopian. The socialist view is collectivist: it perceives human nature as social, giving, altruistic and gregarious. This view suggests that an economic system based upon collective ownership, cooperation and profit sharing is the most appropriate, productive and efficient.

The Marxist view of human nature is debated. Insofar as he is widely argued to perceive human nature as a blank canvas, conditioned by economic and social circumstance, it is held that there is no definitive view of human nature in Marxism. On the other hand, Marx had a vision of human equality and emancipation which is only remotely feasible if it is based upon an assumption of the possibility of basic human goodness.

The liberal view is individualist: it perceives human nature as rational, but in a self-seeking, egotistical, essentially selfish, sense. This implies that a capitalist economic system is natural and fitting. The debate between liberals and socialists revolves around the question of whether human motivation is essentially self-referential or other-referential.

The most pessimistic views of human nature include those of traditional conservatives, who believe that humans are born essentially sinful and lacking in reason, and are therefore in need of guidance and control; and those of fascists, who believe that men (they discount women) are fundamentally irrational and are guided by instinct and emotion – as Mussolini said, *'Think with your blood!'* Fascism borrows from classical elite theory which argued that non-rational elements in human behaviour – 'crowd psychology' – will lead most people to sublimate their individuality into a mass willing to follow a strong leader, especially in times of crisis.

The most renowned pessimists in political philosophy were Machiavelli (sixteenth century) and Hobbes (seventeenth century). Hobbes (often wrongly depicted as either a conservative or a liberal) did not believe that humans were either essentially sinful or essentially rational. For him, humans were simply survivors – self-sustaining entities who would do anything rather than submit to extinction. He believed that humans are essentially both fearful and competitive, and that these impulses motivate us in cyclical turn to strike down and triumph over our fellow humans. Only an absolute government could control this *'war of all against all'* (Hobbes 1651).

Thomas Hobbes

Machiavelli, on the other hand, took it for granted that men are naturally evil and will do whatever seems good to them – or for them – without reference to equity, virtue or justice, as long as they are unconstrained. The job of politics is not simply to hold those evil impulses in check but to direct them towards the security and supremacy of the state.

Many such political philosophers have employed the concept of the 'state of nature' – a natural order that existed before societies and states were created – not as a historical assumption but as an analytical device to explain why and how states and societies came into being. Probably Hobbes' nightmare vision is the most famous of these: *'In such condition, there is no place for industry because the fruit thereof is uncertain: and consequently, no culture of the earth; no navigation, nor use of the commodities that may be imported by sea; no commodious building; no instruments of moving and removing such things as require much force; no knowledge of the face of the earth; no account of time; no arts; no letters; no society; and which is worst of all, continual fear, and danger of violent death; and the life of man, solitary, poor, nasty, brutish and short'* (Hobbes 1651). William Golding's twentieth-century novel *Lord of the Flies*, about the rapidly disintegrating morals and behaviour of a group of young boys shipwrecked on a desert island, was premised upon the Hobbesian view of human nature. Other writers, such as Rousseau, envisaged the state of nature as a lost paradise, a garden of Eden, the realm of the noble savage who was corrupted by the arrival of society and state. Daniel Defoe's novel *Robinson Crusoe*, for example, depicts a civilised, eighteenth-century man who is shipwrecked and survives on his natural rationality, self-reliance and industry.

Generally, optimistic views of human nature argue for limited state and government or for the wholesale abolition of the state, on the grounds that humans are rational and responsible enough to make their own decisions, while pessimistic theories argue for strong government, culminating in the totalitarianism of fascism.

Evaluation of the Idea

THE MOST OBVIOUS QUESTION IS WHETHER THERE IS SUCH A THING AS AN ESSENTIAL 'human nature' – whether 'nature' can be separated from 'nurture', that is, from external influences such as family, society and culture. Some philosophies – particularly conservatism and liberalism – take the view that human nature is an immutable given; others – notably socialism and anarchism – that it is shaped by circumstance (in varying degrees).

It is ethically and practically difficult to test this question – for example, by separating infants from birth from all external social influences. The nearest we can approximate this situation is in the study of so-called feral children (wild or wolf children), for some reason abandoned at an early age and allegedly raised by animals. One such was Memmie le Blanc, the savage girl of Champagne, first sighted in 1731 when she was nine or ten years old. While one of her self-appointed guardians, Madame Hecquet, was printing her biography of Memmie, Rousseau published his seminal work, *Discourse on the Origins of Inequality* (1762). Rousseau looked back with nostalgic regret to the primitive origins of humankind, seeing in our simple beginnings a dignity, grace and vitality lost in sophisticated society. Through the stories, factual and fictional, of feral children, there emerges, perhaps, another narrative: the fragmented and haunting story of our continuing relationship with the savage image of ourselves. Most academic studies, however, focus largely on the feral children's invariable incapacity to speak or learn to speak, or to walk upright without training, or to demonstrate memory or self-awareness. They conclude that there is little, if anything, about man's higher mental abilities which can be considered innate. Indeed, even sexual behaviour, facial expressions and walking on two legs seem to require the shaping mould of society. We are born into this world with minds as naked as our bodies and we have to rely on society to clothe us. In other words, socialisation is fundamental.

Biological comparisons and conclusions about human nature have been attempted since the days of Plato and Aristotle – with limited success, since they are so various and deeply ideological in application. 'Sociobiology', according to its critics, is crudely reductionist and self-justifying: it presents only models of animal behaviour which it deems virtuous in human behaviour, and then seeks to present them as universal. Anyway, it is disputed whether the natural world is to be understood normatively or as a guide to human conduct.

Most textbooks and dictionaries of philosophy and politics assert that every political philosophy assumes a view of human nature. This is not entirely true. Jean-Paul Sartre (1905–80) was one of a few philosophers who asserted that '*existence comes before essence*', that is, humans are genuinely free to define themselves by their own values, goals and behaviour without being tied to any oppressive concept of 'human nature'. Hence the philosophy of existentialism.

Even for those many political theorists who do assume a view of human nature, how large does it loom in their overall philosophy? Thinkers since Plato have been manifestly ambivalent about just how central or immutable the human essence may be. For Machiavelli, for example, the evil inherent in human nature was an empirical observation to be factored into his theory of the proper role of the state, rather than a fundamental premise of his political theory. For anarchists such as Godwin, on the other hand, his political theory is absolutely premised upon the assumption of human goodness.

The second question is, if there is such a thing as the essence of human nature, is it good or bad? Human behaviour certainly seems dualist. Empirical evidence for both sides of the debate is plentiful: the giving and self-sacrificing behaviour of mothers, soldiers, heroes and spontaneous actors of charity; and the selfish and irrational behaviour of robbers, war-mongers, bullies and racists.

Some philosophies, such as Marxism, believe that human behaviour and values are 'plastic' – shaped more by nurture than by nature, that is, more by upbringing than by inborn traits. However, this does not mean that such philosophies have abandoned the idea of a human 'essence'; Marxism remains basically optimistic, while also believing that an inherent trait of human nature is its ability to be shaped by external forces. Rousseau (1762) said, 'Man is born free, but everywhere he is in chains' – implying that the essential goodness of man has been corrupted by the evil forces of state and society. This view has strongly influenced anarchists and socialists since the mid-nineteenth century.

Almost all theories of human nature imply a gap between the way humans are and the way they behave. If it is human nature to be egotistical and selfish, why do humans ever commit altruistic acts? If it is human nature to be selfless and giving, why do humans murder and steal? Even Hobbes, that most confirmed pessimist, believed that if humans contracted to form an absolute state, they would act in a more enlightened and rational way, such that life would no longer be 'nasty, brutish and short' (1651). Some writers therefore suggest that our capacity to change our nature, in a constantly changing world, is our most enduring feature. 'In a world where the pace of change is remorseless and sometimes extremely threatening, a theory of human nature has to make a developmental dynamic central to our explorations of who we are' (Hoffman 1994). John Dupre (2002) similarly argues that the crucial aspect of human nature is its diversity: 'Human nature is inherently a product of interaction between biology and environment . . . and the present diversity of human nature is also indicative of an indefinite range of forms human nature may come to take in the future.'

Perhaps humans are made so malleable by circumstances that we cannot usefully address the concept of human nature at all. It can safely be said that none of the basic questions about human nature – whether it exists and, if so, what it is – has been settled definitively, hence the vibrancy of such philosophical debate throughout the centuries.

Ideology

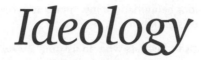

The Idea

THE MOST COMMON, AND NEUTRAL, USAGE OF THE CONCEPT OF IDEOLOGY IS ANY BODY of doctrines, beliefs and values held by any political philosophy or group, that is, any '-ism' such as Marxism, conservatism or liberalism. However, more narrow definitions – some positive, most negative – have developed since the nineteenth century to legitimise some political philosophies and condemn others.

Development of the Idea

THE WORD 'IDEOLOGY' WAS COINED BY THE FRENCH WRITER DESTUTT DE TRACY (*Elements d'Ideologie*, 1901) to mean 'the science of ideas': literally an idea-ology – a positive usage which emerged at a time when many academics were seeking to create or espouse a social 'science' – psychology, sociology, ecology and so on.

The most common usage today is a purely descriptive and neutral one (as suggested by Martin Seliger, *Politics and Ideology*, 1976): an 'ideology' as a set or system of related ideas, beliefs and values which may be used to understand and interpret events, and to guide and direct actions towards specified aims. According to this usage, the concept of ideology will have four elements: first, a concept of human nature; second, a theory about how human history has developed and why; third, an analysis of the role of the state as it is and should be; and, finally, some broad philosophical and policy prescriptions. By this usage, any '-ism' – communism, fascism, conservatism, liberalism, anarchism – is an ideology, and no value judgements are being made about whether it is good or bad.

In more narrow terms, ideology is defined as the values and principles which motivate political parties in pursuing the vision of society which they wish to create.

Ideology should therefore be a unifying force between party leaders, members and supporters.

Most usages of the concept of ideology have, however, been negative. Karl Marx, for example, argued that all ideas are a product of specific economic and social class systems. All thought is socially determined; individuals are not born with all of their ideas ready-made, but instead are socialised from birth into a certain pattern of values, beliefs and attitudes depending on their class position in society. '*Being is not determined by consciousness, but consciousness by being*' (Marx 1843).

This class-based picture of the world is limited, one-sided, partial and distorted; it is therefore not a true, complete and objective picture. Thus, for Marx, 'ideology' is a subjective and biased set of ideas and beliefs which reflect the interests of a particular class, and which constitute 'false consciousness' because they are believed to be a true and total picture of the world but they are not. This is clearly a negative view of 'ideology' as a distorted picture of reality.

In all class societies, moreover, the dominant class has the capacity to impose its own set of ideas and values upon the subordinate classes as a means of defending its own position. In contemporary capitalist society, according to Marx, the bourgeoisie – the ruling class – spreads its ideology through society by virtue of its ownership and control of the mass media, the political, judicial, military, industrial, educational and religious institutions etc. Hence '*The ruling ideas of every age are the ideas of the ruling class*'. Marxism itself claims to be scientific, objective and therefore not ideological. Marx effectively overturned de Tracy's definition of ideology as science, to portray it as the negation of science. Later Marxists such as Herbert Marcuse explicitly focused upon the role of science and technology in advanced industrial societies as examples of ideology in action. Marx himself, however, cited religion as one prime example. He argued that it was premised upon faith rather than reason; that it blamed workers' poverty upon workers' sin and idleness whereas the bourgeoisie were the truly sinful and idle; above all, that it purported to be a divine realm of God-given commandments but, in reality, was a social contrivance designed to protect and perpetuate the present economic system and the interests of the present ruling class. Religion was thus an ideological construct which induced working class passivity by persuading the proletariat that their reward was not in the here, but in the hereafter. Marx (1843), therefore, famously described religion as '*the opium of the people*'.

However, later Marxists, notably Lenin, redefined the concept of ideology to incorporate the notion of the value system of the working class – hence introducing the idea of competing class ideologies and the positive concept of a working class ideology.

Modern liberal thinking, on the other hand, associates ideology with radical or extreme and divisive, 'closed' systems of thought which claim to be absolute truth and which brook no opposition, posing the danger of totalitarianism. Thus liberalism would view Marxism itself – and fascism, Nazism etc. – as 'ideological', in contrast with liberal thinking which is moderate, open, tolerant and rational.

Yet another negative view of ideology is taken by traditional political conservatives, who – because they distrust human reason and man's ability to theorise rationally – dislike abstract or rigid theory of all sorts, preferring to adopt a pragmatic and flexible response to practical circumstances, based on experience and historical tradition. Traditional conservatism therefore also denies being ideological, in its own terms.

Evaluation of the Idea

IDEOLOGY IS OFTEN CITED AS THE MOST DIFFICULT, CONTESTED, CONTROVERSIAL AND yet the most frequently utilised concept in politics. The most basic definition may be a translation of the German *weltanschauung*, meaning 'world-view' – that is, an overall perception of the world and how it works, involving social values, moral views, empirical beliefs, and even rules of logic and science. The view of the world as perceived, for example, by a primitive tribesman, an Enlightenment philosopher and a modern-day teenager, may be crucially different and perhaps not capable of reconciliation.

Political theorists, however, have usually narrowed the concept of ideology down to interpretations which are much more value-laden and self-serving. Most recent usages have been negative and designed to denigrate others' ideas and to justify one's own. The Marxist interpretation of ideology as 'ruling class interests and values' is one obvious example. Twentieth-century Marxists such as Antonio Gramsci (1891–1937) placed growing emphasis upon the power and predominance of bourgeois ideology to explain the failure of Marx's prediction of revolution in Western Europe.

The liberal interpretation of ideology is another pejorative and self-serving example. In the early to mid-twentieth century there was a clear difference between the philosophies of 'left' and 'right' wing parties in the West such as the Labour and Conservative parties in Britain. In the post-war economic boom era, however, some political commentators perceived a growth in 'consensus politics', with the main parties shedding many of their ideological differences and advocating quite similar, centrist policies. Liberal writers perceived that middle-of-the-road, moderate, mixed economy, Keynesian ideas and policies were providing freedom and opportunity for all, eliminating the need for radical or extreme ideas. Thus, according to writers like Daniel Bell and Seymour Lipset, the post-war West was witnessing 'the end of ideology'. Being liberals, they regarded this as a good thing.

A similar theory, on the world scale, was advanced by Francis Fukuyama (1989) with the collapse of communism and the fall of the Berlin Wall: *'What we may be witnessing is not just the end of the Cold War, or the passing of a particular period of post-war history, but the end of history as such; that is, the end point of mankind's ideological evolution and the universalisation of western liberal democracy as the final form of human government'.*

These views all equated 'ideology' with extremism and fanaticism – again, a negative usage of 'ideology'. Critics have pointed out, however, that this thesis itself was clearly partisan – as shown by Lipset's (1969) remark that contemporary liberal democracy was *'the good society itself in operation'.* In other words, this perspective was as ideological and self-serving as any other.

Moreover, by the late 1960s, even as the 'endists' were advancing their theories, the West was witnessing the rise of the revolutionary New Left; the 1970s and 1980s saw economic recession and the polarisation of the main political parties in a new era of 'adversary politics'; and since the 1990s we have seen the world torn apart by nationalist and religious conflicts. Radicalism and diversity are clearly not dead.

Meanwhile, however, in the UK, many commentators have perceived a new, if different, 'end of ideology' since the mid-1990s with the creation of the 'new' Labour party which has adopted many policies from – or very similar to – those of previous Conservative governments, notably on tax and spend, and law and order. This suggests that the long period of successive New Right Conservative governments from 1979 established an ideological dominance underpinned by a commitment to a market economy, ongoing privatisation and paternalist or even authoritarian social policies which 'new' Labour cannot, or will not, abandon. This is, therefore, a much more right-wing consensus than that of the 1960s' Keynesian era. Since the early 1990s there has, therefore, been frequent reference – especially by radical right Conservatives such as those in the Conservative Way Forward faction – to a 'lack of clear blue water' between the Labour and Conservative parties, which is perceived as blighting the Conservatives' future electoral prospects.

Largely, however, the absence of ideology has been widely considered to be a virtue. Both radical right politicians such as Margaret Thatcher and radical left politicians such as Tony Benn have been labelled ideological, as though this, in itself, was sufficient condemnation. This usage of the concept of ideology combines the liberal fear of extremism and the traditional conservative fear of sheer theory. Presumably this view has persisted because of the strong influence of pragmatism and realpolitik within British politics. The present Prime Minister, Tony Blair, is a supreme example of the non-ideological politician, which may be one reason why he is the only Labour leader to have survived into a second full term of office.

Many contemporary social scientists, therefore, deny that ideologies are particularly relevant in modern politics, and argue that only a small minority of people have any logical and coherent views on social and political issues. Apparently, we are all pragmatists now. The danger of this view for contemporary politicians is that they are perceived as pursuing power for its own sake, with no ideology, principles or values at the heart of their political programmes. Even for the so-called pragmatists, however, it is hard to envisage how they can act at all without some underpinning core of values and goals.

In summary, many political theories view 'ideology' negatively; some because they see it as a cloak for partisan interests and false perspectives, some because they see it as fostering extremism and dogma, and some because they distrust abstract blueprints and grand designs of any kind. All of these negative usages of 'ideology', whether Marxist, liberal or conservative, deny that they are themselves ideological; but all can be argued to be manifestly self serving and ideological in one or more senses of the word – if only the neutral sense.

Imperialism

❖

THE ECONOMIC AND POLITICAL CONQUEST AND SOVEREIGNTY OF ONE STATE BY ANOTHER. Imperialism has widely been analysed – by liberals and socialists – as a form of international economic exploitation especially associated with modern capitalism; but critics of twentieth century communist regimes have also perceived many of them as imperialist. Also, imperialism may be seen as providing economic, political, military and other benefits to the colonies.

THE ORIGIN OF THE CONCEPT DATES BACK TO THE ANCIENT ROMAN IMPERIUM OR Empire. It may also mean the rule of an emperor, especially when despotic or arbitrary. The US presidency in the early 1970s was labelled an 'imperial presidency' by critics (such as Arthur Schlesinger Jr 1998) who perceived the powers of the office as excessive and too often abused by Presidents Johnson and Nixon. After the Watergate scandal of 1973–74, Nixon's resignation and some redress of the balance of power between President and Congress, the term fell into disuse.

In the UK, the term imperialism was adopted and the policy of imperial expansion pursued by Joseph Chamberlain from the 1880s (to strengthen the international power of the UK against Germany and France), against the wishes of those political opponents labelled 'little Englanders' who argued for isolationism. Imperialism often involves 'colonisation' by people who move from the 'mother country', taking with them the language, customs and loyalties of that country – and frequently seeking to impose them upon the local peoples. The nineteenth and early twentieth centuries were characterised by capitalist imperialism, where the northern, white European states rationalised their conquest of black African countries with reference to pseudo-

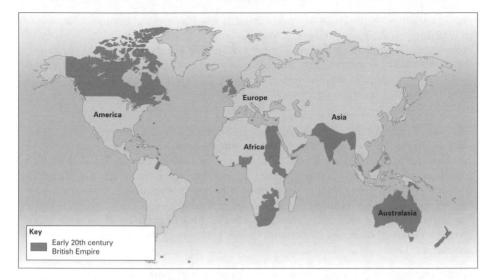

Key
Early 20th century
British Empire

scientific theories of social or racial Darwinism and to 'the white man's burden' – the assertion that superior whites had a missionary duty to civilise the blacks. The British poet, Rudyard Kipling (1899), put it most famously: *'Take up the White Man's burden – send forth the best ye breed – go bind your sons to exile to serve your captives' need; to wait in heavy harness, on fluttered folk and wild – your new-caught, sullen peoples, half-devil and half-child . . .'*. Or, as George Wyndham, a politician in the UK War Office in 1898, said to a German critic of imperialism, *'The day of talking about legality in Africa is over; all the international law there is there consists of interests and understandings. It is generally agreed by all the powers that the end of African operations is to civilise it in the interests of Europe, and that to gain that end, all means are good'* (in Blunt, 2002). By the turn of the twentieth century, a few states had come to dominate most of the world, either by direct conquest or by less formal economic and military pressures. This was the 'age of imperialism'. By 1900, over 90 per cent of Africa belonged to European and American colonial powers. By 1939, the UK alone owned and controlled over 13 million square miles of empire containing a population of 470 million people.

In the early twentieth century, radical liberals such as J.A. Hobson (1902) developed a critique of imperialism as a form of capitalist economic exploitation involving the search for captive markets, investment opportunities, cheap labour and raw materials and new products for cheap import.

This analysis was developed, in Marxist terms, by Lenin in his thesis of *Imperialism as the Highest Stage of Capitalism* (1915), where he argued that imperial expansion was a necessary and inevitable process for highly developed capitalism to offset the equally inevitable falling rate of profit which would otherwise spell its doom. Moreover, as well as allowing the working class to benefit economically from a small share of the super-profits derived from the empire, imperialism generated strong sentiments of nation-alism and patriotism among the working class which undermined their true class consciousness, dulled their revolutionary aspirations and promoted the economic and ideological dominance of the bourgeois ruling class. This analysis enabled Lenin to explain why capitalism had survived and prospered for so long. It also enabled him to justify Marxist revolution in underdeveloped economies such as Russia which were 'the weakest link' in the chain of world capitalist imperialism and therefore the easiest to overthrow – a virtual reversal of Marx's central argument about the necessity of progressing through all of the evolutionary economic stages to advanced capitalism before a workers' revolution was possible. Finally, Lenin argued, imperialism would inevitably lead to world war between the competing capitalist economies, and this, in turn, would lead to proletarian revolution which would bring down capitalism and usher in socialism.

'The war of 1914–18 was imperialistic (that is, an annexationist, predatory, plunderous war) on the part of both sides; it was a war for the division of the world, for the partition and repartition of colonies, "spheres of influence" of finance capital, etc. Out of such enormous superprofits (since they are obtained over and above the profits which capitalists squeeze out of the workers of their "own" country) it is possible to bribe the labour leaders and the upper stratum of the labour aristocracy. And the capitalists of the "advanced" countries are bribing them; they bribe them in a thousand different ways, direct and indirect, overt and covert. Imperialism is the eve of the social revolution of the proletariat' (Lenin 1973).

While imperialism fostered forms of nationalist and patriotic sentiment in the dominant state which were conservative or chauvinist in form, it also stimulated anti-colonial nationalism in the dominions – for example, Gandhi's mass movement of *satyagraha* or non-violent resistance in India – which underpinned the anti-imperialist movements in Africa and South-East Asia and which, by the late twentieth century, had led to the virtual collapse of the 'age of empire'. By the second half of the twentieth century, such popular resistance was making direct imperial rule prohibitively expensive. It was also increasingly unnecessary once capitalism was well established. More recently, states which eschew direct political conquest and sovereignty but pursue exploitative economic or cultural links with weaker states are described as 'neo-imperialist'. The UK's ultimate abandonment of formal empire in favour of the development of the Commonwealth, and the USA's dominant economic role – or 'dollar imperialism' – in the world in the late twentieth century, are perceived by critics to be examples of this new – and cheaper – form of neo-imperial exploitation and control. (See, for example, former President of Ghana, Nkrumah 1965.) The dominant states, of course, would call this 'overseas aid and international development'.

Evaluation of the Idea

ALTHOUGH IMPERIALISM IS WIDELY SEEN AS EXPLOITATIVE, IT MAY CONVERSELY INVOLVE preferential and protective economic links with the colonies and dominions, usually by imposing high tariffs on imports from countries beyond the empire – for example, Chamberlain's doctrine of 'imperial preference' (1897) for the British colonies, which contradicted the free trade ethos prevalent at the time. After World War II the policy was renamed 'Commonwealth preference'.

Even unwittingly, imperialism sometimes brought benefits to the dependent territories: economic investment, infrastructure, technology, formal education, improvements in medicine and health, a protective military umbrella etc. (Consider, for example,

Britain's Roman roads and baths.) The Monty Python film, *The Life of Brian*, put it well: '*But apart from the sanitation, the medicine, education, wine, public order, irrigation, roads, the fresh water system, and public health . . . What have the Romans ever done for us?*' asks a plaintive rebel.

However, few in the twentieth century defend the economic and cultural impact of imperialism upon its dominions – and fewer still uphold the racial Darwinism which often sought to legitimise it. Even at the turn of the twentieth century there were critics: for example, Edward Morel, a British journalist in the Belgian Congo, who wrote in 1903, '*It is the Africans who carry the "black man's burden" . . . What the partial occupation of his soil by the white man has failed to do . . . what the Maxim and the rifle, the slave gang, labour in the bowels of the earth and the lash, have failed to do; what imported measles, smallpox and syphilis have failed to do; whatever the overseas slave trade failed to do, the power of modern capitalistic exploitation, assisted by modern engines of destruction, may yet succeed in accomplishing . . . It kills not the body merely, but the soul . . . This is a crime which transcends physical murder*' (in Blunt 2002).

British imperial genocide also occurred much closer to home, in Ireland in 1845, in what English apologists call the 'great famine' – implying that unavoidable natural disaster was to blame for the ravages of the potato blight which killed up to two million Irish. This does not explain why the Irish population was so dependent on the potato when, during the time of starvation, eight ships left Ireland daily carrying wheat, oats, barley, butter, eggs, beef and pork for profitable export. As the British writer William Makepeace Thackeray (1982) wrote, '*It is a frightful document against ourselves . . . One of the most melancholy stories in the whole world of insolence, rapine, brutal, endless slaughter and persecution on the part of the English master . . . There is no crime ever invented by eastern or western barbarians, no torture or Roman persecution or Spanish Inquisition, no tyranny of Nero or Alva but can be matched in the history of England in Ireland.*'

A contemporary reinterpretation of the concept of economic imperialism has emerged with the argument that world capitalism and globalisation have virtually abolished the contemporary concept of the state – a poke in the eye for Marxist theory which anticipated the 'withering away' of the state only after the destruction of capitalism and the establishment of world communism. The 'vulgar Marxist' Kautsky, so derided by Lenin, perhaps anticipated this as early as 1915: '*From the purely economic point of view, it is not impossible that capitalism will yet go through a new phase, that of the extension of the policy of the cartels to foreign policy, the phase of ultra-imperialism, i.e. of a super-imperialism, of a union of the imperialisms of the whole world and not struggles among them, a phase when wars shall cease under capitalism, a phase of the joint exploitation of the world by internationally united finance capital.*'

Lenin (1973) scoffed in response: '*In the realities of the capitalist system, and not in the banal Philistine fantasies of English parsons, or of the German "Marxist", Kautsky, "inter-imperialist" or "ultra-imperialist" alliances, no matter what form they may assume, whether of one imperialist coalition against another, or of a general alliance embracing all the imperialist powers, are inevitably nothing more than a "truce" in periods between wars. Peaceful alliances prepare the ground for wars, and in their turn grow out of wars; the one conditions the other, giving rise to alternating forms of peaceful and non-peaceful struggle out of one and the same basis of imperialist connections and relations within world economics and world politics.*'

Until there is world peace, Lenin's analysis remains, perhaps, the more persuasive.

Individualism

❖

The Idea

T HE BELIEF THAT THE INDIVIDUAL PERSON IS THE MOST IMPORTANT HUMAN UNIT – NOT any collective, whether family, class, political group, society or state – and that the rights of the individual are more important than those of any other unit. It is usually associated with the idea of a limited state – for example, liberalism – or of a stateless society – such as individualist anarchism.

Development of the Idea

I NDIVIDUALISM IS WIDELY HELD TO BE A NINETEENTH-CENTURY CONCEPT, ALTHOUGH individualist theorists such as Thomas Hobbes and the classical liberals clearly predate this. Contemporary theories of individualism, however, originated mainly out of the Enlightenment and the American and French Revolutions. They stress the primacy of the individual and individual rights over the values of tradition and community, and include modern liberalism, New Right conservatism, anarcho-capitalism and egoism.

Unlike the term collectivism, with which individualism is frequently contrasted, there is not the same left/right diversity of usage; it is not possible to be a left-wing individualist. It is possible, however, to be either a centrist (i.e. liberal) or right-wing (e.g. New Right) individualist. Whereas collectivist theories (left- or right-wing) can advocate either equality or hierarchy, individualist theories invariably advocate inequality of outcome. At most, in its liberal form, individualism can advocate equality of opportunity. Alternatively, it can never (unlike uniquely right-wing theories) attach itself to organic theory which asserts necessary, desirable and inescapable group interest and hierarchy.

Whereas left-wing collectivism stresses equality and right-wing collectivism stresses duty, obedience and subservience (to nation, race or state), individualist theories generally stress freedom, whether negative or positive. They also have a more uniform view of human nature, which combines a faith in individual reason as the sole basis of belief and judgement, and a view that the overriding human motivation is a self-centred, self-interested pursuit of personal goals. Thus the individualist view of human nature is that it is rational, but in a self-seeking way, therefore always potentially corruptible, especially by power. This view is epitomised in the liberal Lord Acton's famous dictum, *'All power tends to corrupt, and absolute power corrupts absolutely'*.

Individualism was historically linked to liberalism, whose classical notion of laissez-faire economics and limited government – deriving from natural rights theories – upheld both the freedom and the responsibility of the individual to conduct his life as free as possible from state interference. This was modified by J.S. Mill's statement of modern liberalism in his essay *On Liberty* (1859) and by the development of the concept of positive, as opposed to negative, freedom, which allowed a more interventionist role for the state. However, classical liberal ideas continue to prevail in capitalist economies and value systems such as that of the United States, which stresses private enterprise, free trade, limited government and the celebration of 'rugged individualism' as former US President Herbert Hoover put it. These ideas were partially resurrected in the UK by the New Right Conservatives in the 1980s (only partially, because of the paradoxical nature of New Right philosophy, which also has an authoritarian dimension). They also generated individualist varieties of anarchism most notable for their strong hostility to the state, such as anarcho-capitalism and egoism.

Anarcho-capitalism is really a contemporary version of classical economic liberalism taken to its extreme and advocating a minimalist role for the state confined largely to national defence. Unsurprisingly, it was most enthusiastically embraced by American theorists of the 1970s such as Murray Rothbard (1978). Ethical egoism, on the other hand, was a philosophy developed in the nineteenth century, which asserted that the individual's own good should be his overriding goal and motivation and, moreover, that the individual is the centre of his own moral universe, with no obligation to accept the rules or restraints of others (see, for example, Stirner 1843). This does not preclude acts of generosity and altruism, as long as the motive is personal good; and personal conduct must be based on the – self-interested – constraining assumption that every other individual has the same moral autonomy as oneself.

Evaluation of the Idea

DOES INDIVIDUALISM DENY OR THREATEN HUMANS' SOCIAL ESSENCE? MARGARET Thatcher's famous dictum that *'There is no such thing as society, only individuals and their families'* amounted to a methodological individualism (derived from writers such as Hayek and Popper) which denied social causality for aggregate patterns of behaviour such as crime, on the grounds that societies – and even institutions such as the state and the law – are nothing more than the composites of the individuals who make them up. There is a certain simplistic logic to this view – society as an abstract entity cannot commit crime, only individuals can – but this ignores important socio-logical variables and factors underpinning changing trends in criminal behaviour (as detailed by writers such as Durkheim). More generally, it may be perceived that individual needs and wants are actually social constructs. Human behaviour changes from one society and social circumstance to another, suggesting that the individual is the product of society rather than the other way around. Moreover, even such ardent individualists as Hayek, Popper and Thatcher are happy to talk of – even to fetishise – the 'market' as a meaningful aggre-gate of individuals which itself develops the character of an autonomous actor. The motive behind Thatcher's assertion was probably more political than philosoph-ical: the New Right Conservative government of the day wished primarily to deny the relevance of rising unemployment or poverty as social explanations for rising crime figures.

Sir Karl Popper

Alexis de Tocqueville (1840), alternatively, was an early advocate of liberal democracy who, nevertheless, recognised the dangers of rampant individualism in burgeoning capitalist economies such as the United States. Although he admired many aspects of the American system of republican democracy, he also warned that American individ-ualism was '*a sentiment which disposes each citizen to isolate himself from his fellows and to draw apart with his family and friends*', abandoning '*the wider society to itself*', sapping '*the virtues of public life*' and eventually being '*absorbed into pure egoism*'. This would generate a narrow materialism, bitter economic competition and resentment at others' successes. Paradoxically, he argued, this could also generate a pervasive social conformism as every individual internalised the norms of prevailing public opinion, because the '*tyranny of the majority*' became the only valid intellectual authority when every individual was assumed to be the intellectual equal of every other. A further paradox, de Tocqueville argued, was that individualist attitudes could lead to the growing power and centralisation of the state, as alternative, social centres of power were destroyed and as obsessively private citizens were content to leave politics to the politicians. This threatened to produce '*a new kind of democratic despotism*' – not tyran-nical but suffocatingly benevolent – which could stifle both liberty and the very desire for liberty. To safeguard these, de Tocqueville – very much a liberal at heart – advocated vigorous decentralisation, free association, a free press and strong voluntary associations such as free political parties.

More contemporary writers such as C.B. Macpherson have also criticised the 'atomism' generated by individualist theories which perceive the desires and rights of the individual as taking precedence over – and, indeed, existing prior to – any form of social life. Macpherson (1962) indicts the 'possessive individualism' inherited from seventeenth-century social contract theorists such as Hobbes and Locke, with its '*conception of the individual as essentially the proprietor of his own person or capacities, owing nothing to society for them*'. Such rampant individualism could result in the ruthless pursuit of individual rights and the wholesale denial of social obligations, producing the kind of '*war of all against all*' so feared by Hobbes (1651). Hobbes' solution – unusually for an individualist theorist – was an absolute, sovereign state whose sole authority was to protect the individuals under it. If the state itself threatened any individual citizen's fundamental right of self-preservation – for example, by condemning a criminal to death – then that individual had the absolute right to resist the state. Clearly, however, the theoretical right of resistance is not the same as the actual capacity to resist, especially against such a strong state as Hobbes advocated.

Individualists, therefore, are faced with a central dilemma concerning the proper role – or, indeed, the very existence – of the state. Their faith in human reason usually leads them to conclude that little or no state is desirable; but their belief in human selfishness would suggest the need for some sovereign arbiter or controller to protect each individual from the selfish whims of each other. However, since the individuals who make up the state are equally corruptible by power, they, too, must be constantly checked and limited – not least by the individuals under the state.

Modern liberalism perhaps most clearly illustrates this dilemma: one person's freedom is another's constraint (e.g. welfare requires taxation) – how can the liberal state defend all individuals' freedoms equally or even optimally? How far does the proper role of the state extend before it stops enhancing individual freedom – if it can do so at all, which anarchists would entirely deny – and starts becoming coercive? How far is it possible for the liberal state to tolerate illiberal intolerance without destroying liberal tolerance itself?

Extreme individualism, in the form of anarcho-capitalism, rejects the state altogether, thereby creating new problems, such as how to curb the likelihood and negative consequences of deviant (erstwhile criminal) behaviour. Given their view of human nature as basically selfish, anarcho-capitalists cannot argue that such behaviour will altogether disappear; and they cannot espouse state laws, police and courts. Instead, they argue for private security and arbitration agencies – but those who cannot afford them will presumably be left without any such protection. Anarcho-capitalism also does not offer convincing answers to the problem of public goods: that is, facilities which can be withheld from one person only by being withheld from all and which must, by definition, be provided communally, such as street lighting, sewage, clean air and national defence. It is hard to see how these can be provided and paid for privately – what if one person in the street refuses to pay for the lighting? The last, obvious objection to unfettered free market capitalism is that it would generate mass exploitation, poverty, untrammelled survival of the fittest and precisely the 'war of all against all' which individualists such as Hobbes feared above all.

The appeal of individualism and its emphasis on personal freedom is obvious. However, it jeopardises traditional values, rootedness, social stability and order (from an organic perspective) and efficiency, equality, social justice, harmony and democracy (from a socialist perspective).

Justice

The Idea

JUSTICE MEANS FAIRNESS AND EQUITY. BROADLY, IT IS A CONCEPT OF WHAT CONSTITUTES a fair economic and social structure within society; narrowly, a concept of what is fair and rightful within a civil and criminal legal system. It is a highly subjective concept which different political philosophies interpret very differently.

Development of the Idea

PLATO'S *REPUBLIC* OPENS WITH THE QUESTION, '*WHAT IS JUSTICE?*', AND GOES ON TO refute the view that justice is simply the interests of those with power; that is, he separates the concepts of rights and powers to assert the principle of rights for non-power holders. Since then, Plato's question has often been viewed as the single most important issue in political philosophy – not least by Aristotle who, in his *Politics*, made a distinction between 'distributive' and 'commutative' justice fairly similar to what we might now distinguish as social versus legal justice. Distributive justice was concerned with the distribution of goods among a class – a matter of 'treating equals equally'. Commutative justice was concerned with giving to someone what he deserves, for example, when punishing him.

Today, the latter concept of legal or procedural justice is satisfied when the laws or rules in a given society are observed and upheld – whether or not those rules are 'fair'. This notion of justice parallels that of positive law and of the market economy: it has to do with efficiency rather than fairness (even where the concept of 'unfairness' is nominally built into the rules, for example, those concerning the laws of 'unfair dismissal' in the UK, where the tribunal is required to make a ruling purely upon the facts of the case as they pertain to the written rules, and not according to any subjective interpretation of the spirit of those rules). It seems, therefore, that there are at least two conflicting concepts of justice: one concerned simply with the consistent application of equitable and relevant rules and procedures, and one more concerned with fair outcomes. From the latter perspective, justice may sometimes involve 'bending the rules', for the noblest of purposes.

The question arises, however, on what basis were those rules originally formed? Presumably they were devised with some intention of a fair outcome as their consequence. Increasingly, social and legal justice have come to be seen as two applications of a single idea: the Roman Emperor Justinian's notion of the constant and perpetual will to render to everyone his due.

Evaluation of the Idea

THE FIRST QUESTION IS, ARE THERE FUNDAMENTALLY DIFFERENT CONCEPTS OF JUSTICE, or do they boil down to the same principle? Is there a valid concept of natural justice, independent of man-made law and human prescription? The story of the justice of King Solomon has been handed down over thousands of years: two women were claiming the same baby; eventually, Solomon decreed that the baby should be cut in two and half given to each woman. When one woman broke down and said that the other woman was welcome to the baby as long as it was not killed, the question of true motherhood was apparently resolved. The longevity of this story suggests that the essence of our concept of justice has not much changed.

Upon this concept of natural justice was built the idea of natural law conforming with 'universal moral standards' – which have, in turn, been the prescriptive base for many international codes of law, from the Nuremberg Tribunals after World War II, to the UN and European Conventions of Human Rights. Sometimes religious ideas of universal truths and divine laws of human behaviour have also been brought into play, from Aquinas to the Tao. The danger here, as always, is that humans are simply investing positive (man-made) constructs with divine will, either to legitimise them or to absolve their human agents from the responsibility of determining justice.

Harking back to Aristotle, the distributive concept of social justice may seem to conflict with the commutative concept of justice as right or desert in, for example, the Robin Hood principle (stealing from the rich – taking what one has no right to take – to give to the poor). Redistributive theorists such as the modern liberal, John Rawls, would conclude that Robin Hood acts justly, but not lawfully, unless he takes the title of sovereign and redistributes in the name of the state. Aquinas went further still when he argued that a person in extreme need was entitled to take another person's property to sustain himself.

By views such as these, positive or man-made law, is only just and fair if it accords with natural law, discoverable by reason, and premised upon moral law dictated by justice.

Something is 'legal' if it is in accordance with the law of the land; whereas something is 'just' if it is deemed fair and equitable. The idea of the rule of law seeks to equate law and justice, but sometimes – according to the concept of natural justice – the law may be regarded as unjust: for example, in the UK, the poll tax, legal immunities of diplomats, legal tax avoidance, retrospective (backdated) law, imprisonment before trial (remand), the high costs of litigation, etc. Conversely, an action may be seen as 'just', though illegal: for example, personal retribution – 'an eye for an eye'; breaking the law to prevent a greater crime; illegal political protest, such as airport and by-pass protesters; 'just' violence against an 'unjust' state (one man's 'terrorist' is another man's 'freedom fighter') – and the Robin Hood principle itself.

Both the concepts of law and justice are subjective; even whether an action is legal or illegal is often a matter of debate between senior judges, as, for example, the divisions among the UK Law Lords over the extradition of Chile's former President General Pinochet (1998) demonstrated. However, perceived conflicts between law and justice are sometimes used to justify 'civil disobedience': deliberate, peaceful law-breaking as an act of public, political protest. Some UK examples are: cannabis 'smoke-ins' in Hyde Park; the obstruction by the pressure group Greenpeace of nuclear waste discharges into the North Sea and its occupation of the Brent Spar oil platform; the refusal by some local councils – for example, Liverpool and Lambeth – to obey central government's 'rate-capping' laws; public refusals to pay the poll tax; secondary picketing by trade unions such as the National Union of Seamen; and the freeing of animals from research laboratories by the Animal Liberation Front.

Marxism and anarchism argue that laws – man-made rules, superimposed from above – are simply not compatible with justice as natural equity. Plato similarly argued that law was unnecessary, but only because just leaders with an inbuilt sense of rightness could govern the lives of their people – an elitist theory rejected by the contemporary left-wing philosophies.

Political theories further disagree on whether justice is primarily the characteristic of an act, a person or a state of affairs. Liberals lean to the first view, that situations are just or unjust only to the extent that they are the outcome of just or unjust acts. Aristotle seemed to lean to the middle view, that a man of virtue and justice, such as an impartial judge, must decide the rules of just action. Socialists lean to the latter view: that injustice arises from the distribution of goods and resources which are not necessarily the product of an act or a person but of an economic and social system – a state of affairs.

This debate, in turn, raises the question of whether justice is judged by its causes or its consequences. Modern ideas of legal and criminal justice generally look to causes – such as human intent and motivation – whereas left-wing notions of social justice look much more to consequences in terms of economic inequality, disadvantage and deprivation. The term 'social justice' first appeared in political debate in the early nineteenth century (e.g. J.S. Mill). The two most basic concepts of social justice embody the notions of merit and desert (i.e. liberal) and need and equality (i.e. socialist).

The liberal concept of merit is one which perceives that each person's social position and reward depend upon their individual talents and skills. Socialist critics of this view argue that market receipts are largely due to factors such as social background, heredity and luck, which have nothing to do with personal merit. They equate justice with equality of outcome and not merely of opportunity.

Parliamentary socialists, for example, seek positive action by central government to enhance equal distribution of both opportunities and outcomes via taxation, redistribution and welfare. This concept of social justice requires a large and active state to give people what they are entitled to in terms of basic social rights such as food, clothing, housing, education and welfare.

Right-wing, libertarian philosophers such as Hayek, however, argue that this involves the state in making an unacceptable number of value decisions, resulting in increased state regulation, which tends, inevitably, towards totalitarianism. Robert Nozick (1974), similarly, rejects any focus on the end state of distribution in favour of a concept of 'just transfer' of property from one person to another, and to another – that is, as long as the processes of transfer are just (open, voluntary, knowing and responsible), then very large end inequalities are, themselves, just. These right-wing ultra-capitalists reject the general concept of social justice as a denial of freedom, and defend any concept of justice that protects the unlimited acquisition of private property.

Aristotle raised the issue of 'treating equals equally', but that merely begs the question, who are equals and upon what basis is that determined? Left-wing theories of egalitarianism would conclude that all humans are deserving of equal treatment; while some right-wing theories of elitism would conclude that whole races are deserving of genocide.

Whether one or many concepts of justice are perceived, the basic question remains, why be just? If there is no inherent belief in the objective value of justice, there is no real point in a theory of justice. This is where Marxism, for example, is said to encounter philosophical problems: since it very largely dismisses value judgements as mere features of ruling class ideology, it is useless as a theory of justice (says, e.g. Scruton 1982). However, this view – from an avowedly partisan (anti-Marxist) perspective – ascribes a *'sceptical or subjectivist theory about the value of justice'* to one which rejects the restricted and self-serving capitalist concept of justice as largely and manifestly iniquitous.

Justice, in political philosophy, is closely tied to the concept of virtue – excellence of character, or *'dispositions which we praise'* (Aristotle 1946). Both he and Plato asserted that true virtue meant to be truly courageous, which also meant to be honourable, wise, just, prudent and, ultimately, happy. Aristotle also believed that, without justice, there could be no friendship, since justice is an 'other-regarding' and not merely a 'self-regarding' disposition and, without it, man as a social being cannot be fulfilled. This is, perhaps, the prime reason why we should be just and should value justice: we need others and, therefore, for the sake of mutual respect and friendship, we should do as we would be done by. We all have reason to be just.

Law

The Idea

THE BODY OF RULES OF STATE INTERPRETED AND ENFORCED BY THE POLICE AND THE courts. Law is widely seen to be compulsory rather than purely voluntary, hence its enforcement involves sanctions and punishments – although many political philosophies perceive the general body of law to be part of a 'social contract' between citizens and state.

Development of the Idea

LAW CAN BE DISTINGUISHED FROM OTHER SOCIAL RULES, FIRST, IN THAT IT IS MADE and enforced by states (as distinct from, for example, social norms about such things as table manners). Secondly, it is compulsory and hence breaches are subject to various forms of punishment by agencies of the state such as the police and prisons. Thirdly, there is a widespread, though not universal, perception that it is morally binding and should be obeyed – although the basis of this obligation is a matter of ancient debate. Finally, it is produced in fairly formalised, standardised ways and types which should be publicly known and recognised in order to be effective.

Law can be subdivided into types: in the UK, for example, there is civil law which concerns disputes between individuals or groups in society (e.g. landlord versus tenant) where the aim is usually compensation; and criminal law which concerns offences against society or state, where the state decides whether to take action and where the aim of proceedings is punishment rather than compensation. Another distinction is between public or administrative law, which applies to governmental bodies – hence, for example, a minister or government department can be taken to court and ruled *ultra vires* (illegal) if one of their policies contravenes the law of the land – as opposed to private law which enforces rights and obligations between citizens, such as property and contract law.

In the UK there are also diverse sources of law: Parliament, which creates statute law; EU law; 'judge-made' case law; common law dating from ancient, pre-parliamentary times; and now also law emanating from the devolved assemblies such as the Scottish Parliament. These different sources of law have different authority and status, with Parliament nominally sovereign but with the EU, in fact, overriding the law of Parliament. Many states have a core body of rules which they title 'the basic law', usually implying a written constitution of some sort. The UK is an exception.

Internationally, there are major substantive differences between different bodies of law, for example, the legal framework of liberal democratic societies versus Islamic Sharia law.

The philosophy of law – enquiry as to what intrinsic features it does or should possess – has a long and complex history. Early philosophers such as Socrates, Plato and Aristotle believed law to be the product of reasoned discernment of fundamental – perhaps natural – principles of right and proper social conduct. Others perceive that higher law has been laid down by God's divine will and that this is the necessary basis of human law. Yet others, such as the Scottish philosopher David Hume (1711–76), ascribe the origins of law primarily to custom and convention.

'Law and order' may mean a situation of (or desire for) general conformity to the law, especially to criminal law in such areas as theft, violence and breach of the peace, and perhaps also rigorous punishment of illegal acts; this is a popular concern of politicians. Liberals and especially conservatives perceive law and order as an essential basis for effective freedom or social stability and harmony. As the liberal John Locke (1962) said, '*Without law there is no liberty*'. More broadly, it may mean respect for the rule of law. The rule of law is, itself, a concept with diverse interpretations. It is sometimes (dubiously) employed in the UK as a factual assertion of the basic principles and practices of the British constitution, but more commonly the rule of law is put forward as a statement of an ideal, embodying principles such as legal equality and certainty, just law and judicial impartiality which systems such as the UK may aspire to achieve, and often do achieve – but not always. For anarchists and Marxists, conversely, order can – and should – exist without law; that is, people should be able to decide their own rules and create their own social harmony without the state dictating and imposing laws from above. If law exists without order, that is 'anarchy' in the sloppy usage of chaos and confusion.

Law may be studied structurally or sociologically. Writers such as Hans Kelsen (1973) have attempted a value-free – hence 'pure' – analysis of the distinctive structures and logic of laws and legal systems. Kelsen asserted the 'basic norm' (not to be confused with a legal constitution, or law, as such) as '*a juristic presumption or postulate implicit in legal thinking*', prescribing that one ought to behave in accordance with the rules of the constitution and the laws authorised by such rules. Only with such a presupposition could the systematic unity and normative character of law itself be explained. Sociological studies of the law, on the other hand, seek to establish causal explanations or other empirical connections between law and other phenomena such as social class, economic and political power, poverty, drugs, religious norms, media-created panics about deviant behaviour and various theories of crime and punishment.

Evaluation of the Idea

IT IS SOMETIMES SAID THAT THERE IS – OR SHOULD BE – NO CONNECTION BETWEEN LAW and politics, in order to keep the enforcement of the law free from partisan or partial ends (justice should be an end in itself) – but that view is not tenable. On the one hand, law is widely employed in pursuit of the political goal of good order, therefore politics – and politicians – shape the law. On the other hand, politics as power should – certainly from a liberal perspective – be limited by law to curb its abuse. Which is servant and which is master, law or politics, is therefore problematic.

One fundamental question is whether the law is essentially made by man or by nature. 'Natural law' means rules of law made by nature – whether as a reflection of divine wisdom (as Aquinas said) or based on rational thought (as the Stoic philosophers believed). Natural law theories assert a higher than man-made law, based upon a fundamental moral code. Theorists of natural law such as Aristotle generally believe it is universally recognised and never fundamentally changed – for instance, the law of murder – and that human law is based upon it but subordinate to it. This allows some to challenge the validity of man-made law on the grounds that it contradicts natural law: for example, Christians have long challenged conscription by the state because it contradicts the biblical commandment 'Thou shalt not kill'. John Locke's theory of the natural rights of life, liberty and property strongly influenced the American Declaration of Independence (1776) and Bill of Rights (1791) and also the French Declaration of Rights (1789). International law especially has been influenced by theories of natural law and natural rights – for example, the Universal Declaration of Human Rights. Sceptics might argue that all such declarations of rights are statements of an ideal rather than a reality, but perhaps that suggests a critique of current political conditions rather than of the law itself. For the naturalist, law is validated by its content; for the positivist (e.g. Jeremy Bentham), law is validated by its form and process.

Natural law theories assert that positive law should be grounded in a code of natural morality; whereas liberals, for example, tend to believe that law should apply overwhelmingly to the 'public' sphere of economic and political life as distinct from the sphere of 'private' morality, which (subject to the 'harm principle' that the law should forbid only such behaviour as is likely to cause harm to others) is not for the state to dictate. For example, liberals would not seek to outlaw private and consensual, if 'deviant', sexual behaviour between adults such as homosexuality or sado-masochism. How far law and morality should correspond – and which should shape which – is, again, a matter of debate.

A related question is that of the relationship between law and justice. Laws are intended to achieve justice but, because laws are framed in terms of general standards and rules (Kelsen's point) which cannot allow for every variation of circumstance, the rigid application even of a just law may create injustice in a particular case. 'Equity' was developed (by the Court of Chancery in English law) to allow modification of the body of positive (man-made) law to safeguard natural justice. Clearly, such application of discretion in particular cases also threatens to create injustice, because it breaches the principle of legal equality and may benefit one party in a case where the strict application of the positive law may have benefited the other party. Alternatively, equity itself may become so routine and generalised that it may develop the same standardisation or rigidity that it was designed to remedy. Aristotle advanced the first, classic statement of the relationship between law, equity and justice, which has since been a central issue in philosophy – complicated, of course, by the fact that 'justice' and 'legality' are both, to some extent, subjective concepts.

The ultimate question is whether, or to what extent, humans actually need law in the form of 'rules of state'. Theories which perceive law primarily as a weapon of coercion believe that, at the very least, there must be limits to the scope and power of the law. Liberals, for example, perceive a need for law to control self-seeking individuals but, to safeguard liberty, there must be both moral and practical limits to law. Whereas conservatives tend to believe that anything regarded as 'sinful' should be criminalised, liberals adopt J.S. Mill's advocacy of the 'harm principle' (see above). However, this begs large questions about the definition and scope of 'harm' itself. Anti-state philosophies – notably anarchism – reject law altogether, believing that it can only be oppressive and corrupting of the essence of human goodness.

The neo-conservative school of New Right thinking, on the other hand, is distinctly authoritarian. It does not derive from the paternalism of Disraeli but from an earlier, reactionary and highly disciplinarian school of European conservatism. In the UK in the 1980s and 1990s it took the form of increased police powers, heavier criminal sentencing, political centralisation, more stringent secrecy and censorship and increased legal curbs on non-conforming or deviant groups in society. It was reflected in policy examples such as: militarisation of policing tactics and centralisation – some would say 'politicisation' – of police control under successive Home Secretaries; increased criminal punishments (e.g. a 'short, sharp shock' regime in the 1980s and boot camps in the 1990s for juvenile criminals); the legalisation of secret surveillance; a range of new legal constraints against trade unions, immigrants and asylum seekers, demonstrators and protesters, travellers and ravers; and new legal curbs against homosexuals, sado-masochists and lone parents.

New Labour also has a markedly authoritarian streak, whether deriving from an ethical concept of the responsibilities of the citizen toward the community, or from sheer populism, or both. Examples include the Crime and Disorder Act 1998, which introduced Britain's first child jail for 12–14 year-olds, curfews for under-10s, the extension of the US-style 'three strikes' policy to increase minimum sentences for burglary, and draconian new anti-terrorism laws in 2001.

Theories about the proper role and scope of law clearly relate fundamentally to diverse views of human nature. Whether most of us obey the law – most of the time – through intrinsic respect and consent for it, or through sheer fear of the consequences of disobedience, is perhaps the most fundamental question of all.

Left/Right

The Idea

A LINEAR CONTINUUM WHERE LEFT-WING IDEAS ADVOCATE VARIOUS FORMS OF COLLECtive economic ownership and equality, and right-wing ideas advocate various forms of private or personal economic ownership and inequality. Left and right are economic rather than political positions, because both can be associated with either 'strong' or 'weak/no' state and government.

Development of the Idea

THE TERMS LEFT AND RIGHT FIRST CAME INTO USE DURING THE FRENCH REVOLUTION: in the 1789 National Assembly, the revolutionary republicans sat on the left of the presidential chair while the monarchist supporters of the *ancien regime* sat on the right. Today the terms are commonly employed to describe a spectrum of political ideas from communism on the far left, through parliamentary socialism, to liberalism more or less in the centre, with conservatism on the right and fascism (including Nazism) on the far right. In terms of attitudes to social change, the left/right spectrum can be perceived as ranging on the left from revolutionary, through radical and reformist, to conservative and reactionary on the right.

Left-wing ideas are invariably collectivist, whether in the form of anti-statist philosophies such as Marxism and anarchism or in the highly statist form of Stalinism in the twentieth century. They are also invariably optimistic about human nature, but may pursue either a strong, even 'totalitarian' state or the complete abolition of state. Rightwing theories, however, range from the highly individualist philosophies which derive from classical liberalism – such as anarcho-capitalism and New Right laissez-faire economic theory – to the highly collectivist and statist forms of fascism which emerged in the 1920s.

Whereas left-wing collectivism stresses equality and right-wing collectivism stresses hierarchy, duty, obedience and subservience (to nation, race or state), right-wing individualist theories generally stress freedom, whether negative or positive – including, as Thatcher famously put it, the freedom to be unequal. Modern liberalism – as always – stands somewhere midway with its advocacy of equality of opportunity but not outcome.

In sum, the left/right divide is not between collectivism and individualism, nor between advocates of a strong state versus a weak state. It is, fundamentally, an ideological battle between those who see common ownership and equality as the bedrocks of social justice and those who see private ownership and some form of hierarchy as the most fair and natural social structure. The left/right divide is, thus, essentially an economic, rather than political, schism between the opponents and the defenders of capitalism – whether in its laissez-faire, liberal or fascist form.

Evaluation of the Idea

EVEN IN THE POST-1990S ERA, SINCE THE COLLAPSE OF 'COMMUNISM' OR, MORE accurately, of the statist economies of the Soviet Union and Eastern Europe, the concept of the left is still widely associated with the idea of centrally planned, collectivised economies – particularly by neo-liberal ideologues who seek to equate right and left simply with laissez-faire and command economies respectively.

Alternatively, it is sometimes argued, the terms left and right have been used in such diverse and disparate ways over the twentieth century – from Peron's authoritarian populism in Argentina, through the populist peasant movements in Eastern Europe between the wars, and Hitler's national socialism, to the communism of Stalin and Mao – that, arguably, no clear and analytically useful definitions are any longer possible.

However, it should be possible to identify valid usages of the concepts of left and right which avoid both the crude reductionism of the neo-liberal usage and the empty relativism of others. Any legitimate and useful definitions of the terms should hark back to their original usages during the French revolution and take account of the upheavals of this era and the resulting transition from pre-industrial, traditional, hierarchical societies to modern, industrial or even post-industrial systems where subjects have become citizens and genuine – if limited – elements of rights, social mobility and political democracy have developed.

The most rigid and reactionary right today – the ultra-conservatives – reject all of these modern developments and seek to turn back the clock entirely. The less rigid right – the neo-right – accept the economic modernisation and development of market economics but reject the accompanying organisation of the working class in the form of trade unions, the extension of rights to the working class and the idea of any positive state intervention and protection of such rights.

The left nowadays largely rejects the statist models of the orthodox, twentieth-century, 'communist' era in favour of more genuinely democratic and humanist arrangements which, while (for most, but not all, on the left) embracing economic modernisation, also radically reduce economic and political inequalities. The growing anti-capitalist movement is one example of an emerging left-wing philosophy which is both egalitarian and anti-statist.

While theorists and activists of both right and left may hold to these purist views in unadulterated form, most political systems, in practice, combine left and right characteristics. Obvious examples are the social democracies of Western Europe (such as Sweden, Belgium and Germany). There is no current example – even America – of a wholly free market economy with a truly minimal state; the New Right Conservative governments of the 1980s and 1990s in the UK and USA significantly strengthened the state and restricted basic civil rights, both through widening economic inequalities and strengthening the authoritarian aspects of the central state apparatus (for example, through increasing police powers, state surveillance of citizens and growing secrecy and censorship). Nor is there any genuinely left-wing regime today which combines economic collectivisation with widespread political and civil rights.

'New' Labour in Britain cannot be characterised as left-wing insofar as it maintains a distinctively authoritarian dimension – in its criminal justice and anti-terrorism laws, for example – and is *about wealth creation, not wealth distribution*' (to quote former minister Stephen Byers, speech to the London Business School, October 1999); but, insofar as it is addressing issues such as child poverty and the 'socially excluded' – the government's evasive term for the social underclass – it is clearly a shift away from the classic Thatcherite agenda. 'New' Labour has, for example, adopted the EU Social Chapter giving workers greater rights, it has introduced the minimum wage, the 48-hour week, minimum income guarantees for pensioners, the working families' tax credit and the largest post-war increase in NHS spending, funded by a 1 per cent rise in national insurance contributions.

It is currently fashionable – particularly among 'new' Labour commentators, including Prime Minister Tony Blair – to argue that the left/right schism – indeed, any analysis in terms of left and right – is anachronistic and redundant in the modern, consensus politics era. The combined effects of the fragmentation of social stratification and the dealignment of classes and class politics has led to a critique or even denial of a left/right model of politics.

Most notable has been Anthony Giddens' assertion of a 'third way' between the two political ideologies of statist socialism and free market capitalism which have dominated the post-war period. Giddens argues that socialism – which he defines narrowly as a form of economic management – is an 'exhausted' project. Since the collapse of the Soviet Union and its satellites in 1989, socialism as a reality is dead. Equally, socialism as a theoretical project has become ossified. Third way politics, says Giddens, recognises that the range of questions which escape the old left/right divide is greater than ever before. It operates in a world where the views of the old left have become obsolete, and those of the new right are inadequate and contradictory. If left and right are considered less encompassing than they once were, the centre ground is no longer one of compromise between them, but is the space for a new political force – what has been labelled the active middle, or the radical centre.

Tony Blair has similarly said, 'We must take on the forces of conservatism, left and right, who resist change – whether it is the right who believe the knowledge economy is just a passing fad, or those parts of the left happy defending the status quo, promoting tax and spend or yielding up the territory of law and order to the right. For the twenty-first century will not be about the battle between capitalism and socialism but between the forces of progress and the forces of conservatism. The "third way" is not a new way between progressive and conservative politics. It is progressive politics distinguishing itself from conservatism of left or right' (speech at the 1999 Labour party conference).

It may be significant that neo-liberals have often also sought to deny the validity of the basic left/right model, because it positions them uncomfortably close to the collectivist and statist philosophies of traditional conservatism and fascism on the right of the spectrum as common defenders and allies of private enterprise capitalism. They often, therefore, 'wrap up' the left/right continuum into a horseshoe, such that communism and fascism are closely equated as the two ends of the horseshoe under the common banner of 'totalitarianism', while market liberalism is at the opposite side (i.e. the middle) of the horseshoe as the model of the good society and the enemy of statism in all its forms. From such a perspective, the defeat of fascism in World War II and especially the collapse of the Eastern European economies from 1989 has been portrayed as the final 'death of socialism' – including national socialism – and the ultimate triumph of liberal capitalism (namely, Fukuyama's thesis of the 'end of history').

However, this horseshoe typology is an ideological model of political systems which downplays the inconvenient features and similarities of some, while highlighting the distinctive traits which support the self-justifying thesis of liberal capitalism.

From most other perspectives, the left/right model of politics is not redundant. A current concern throughout Europe is the apparent resurgence of the ultra-right, often in the form of neo-fascism: for example, Silvio Berlusconi's affiliations with the Northern League and National Alliance in Italy; the election of Joerg Haider's far-right Freedom Party in Austria in 2000; the high vote for National Front leader Jean-Marie le Pen in the first round of France's presidential elections in 2002 (followed by the attempted assassination of President Chirac by a member of the far-right Radical Unity group three months later); the rise of the far-right in the Netherlands following the assassination of Pym Fortuyn; the election of BNP councillors in UK local elections in 2002; and even the vociferous presence of hard-right and racist elements in the British Conservative party in factions such as the Monday Club.

While it is undeniable that the left/right model was always two-dimensional and quite simplistic, incapable of addressing the complexities of modern philosophies such as ecologism and feminism, it clearly still has relevance in differentiating essential political values and principles – most notably, a belief in equality or hierarchy, and a critique or advocacy of capitalism. It is more likely that it will revive than disappear as a relevant tool of analysis in the forthcoming century, especially in any future periods of economic downturn.

Liberalism

❧

The Idea

A PHILOSOPHY DATING FROM THE EIGHTEENTH-CENTURY ENLIGHTENMENT PERIOD IN European history, advocating individual rationalism, freedom and rights, and therefore limited government and state. A distinction is commonly made between early 'classical liberalism', which advocated economic laissez-faire and a very limited state, and 'modern liberalism' which advocates more state intervention, a mixed economy, welfare and political rights.

Development of the Idea

LIBERALISM EMERGED FROM THE STRUGGLES FOR RELIGIOUS FREEDOM WAGED IN LATE sixteenth- and seventeenth-century Western Europe. The close link that existed between church and state ensured that the objective of religious freedom was associated with political dissent. Liberal theorists argued that the social order was a contract voluntarily entered into by those who were party to it rather than being an immutable structure handed down by God. Social contract theory was developed by liberal theorists such as John Locke. The belief that government emerged as the result of rational choice made by those who subsequently accorded their consent to its operations – that is, the people – ensured that the rights of the individual were prominent concerns of liberal philosophers. The people were viewed as the ultimate source of political authority and government was legitimate only while it operated with their consent.

At the heart of classical liberalism was a belief in the rationality – including the essential selfishness – of human nature, described by early liberals as 'possessive individualism'. Classical liberals therefore believed in 'negative freedom', that is, freedom from external interference of any sort, especially by government and state. The state was seen as inherently oppressive and hence as 'a realm of coercion', whereas private or civil society was 'a realm of freedom'. The state was a necessary evil to safeguard law, order and security, but its role should be minimal – a 'nightwatchman state' as John Locke put it or, as former US president (1801–1809) Thomas Jefferson said, *'That government is best which governs least'*. The state should exist to protect the three basic, natural or inalienable rights of life, liberty and property. Above all, classical liberalism believed in laissez-faire economics (literally meaning 'leave alone'): free market, private enterprise capitalism and the absolute right of the individual to enter and succeed or fail in the market on his own merits, without state help or hindrance. Thus it advocated a free market economy controlled only by the forces of supply and demand ('the invisible hand' as Adam Smith put it) and not by the 'dead hand' of state regulation or direction.

Classical liberalism believed that *'Heaven helps those who help themselves'* (Smiles 1859). A form of meritocracy where people succeed or fail only on their own abilities and efforts is a guarantee of social justice. This borrows from – and perverts – the ideas of British scientist Charles Darwin about evolutionary progress based upon natural selection and the 'survival of the fittest' (not, actually, Darwin's phrase). Economic inequality should be an incentive to enterprise. As the American liberal William Sumner (1884) put it, *'The drunk in the gutter is just where he ought to be'*. The repeal of the Corn Laws in 1846 marked the triumph of laissez-faire liberalism in England.

Modern liberalism, alternatively, was founded in the UK by John Stuart Mill, who wrote *On Liberty* (1859). Mill asserted *'one very simple principle'*: that the sole justification for (individual or collective) constraint on the liberty of any individual was to protect oneself or to prevent harm being done to others (not, in fact, as simple a principle as it sounds). Mill's essay was therefore the first comprehensive and systematic expression of the doctrine of individual liberty which has since been the central tenet of modern liberalism. *'Over himself, over his own body and mind, the individual is sovereign.'*

John Stuart Mill

Modern liberalism kept some of the main features of its classical liberal roots, notably the mechanistic theory of the state; thus it is individualist and rationalist and still believes fundamentally in individual freedom and in private property as a natural right.

However, modern liberalism agrees with classical liberalism that rational individuals are also self-seeking and self-interested, and therefore always liable to abuse others for personal benefit if they have the power to do so – that is, human nature is both rational and potentially corruptible: *'All power tends to corrupt, and absolute power corrupts absolutely'* (Lord Acton 1907). This has led modern liberalism to reject the worst economic and social consequences of its old laissez-faire doctrine of negative freedom from state intervention.

Instead, the core doctrine of modern liberalism is positive individual freedom: the actualised freedom to achieve one's own potential and personal development and attain fulfilment, with state help and intervention where necessary. The main advocate of this concept was the late nineteenth-century liberal T.H. Green (1836–82). He perceived that free market capitalism sets up barriers to genuine freedom for the working class, women and children and others who are disadvantaged by poverty, ignorance and sickness. Positive freedom means not simply the freedom to starve in the gutter without anyone either pushing you down or helping you out (i.e. negative freedom). Positive freedom implies, where necessary, a positive and empowering role for state and government, whether in a mixed market economy providing health, welfare and education to help individuals to make the most of themselves, or in the state guaranteeing, by law – ideally in a Bill of Rights – freedom from discrimination, freedom of information, freedom of speech and so on. For example, it was the Liberal party's Beveridge Report (1942) which laid the foundations for the post-war welfare state, advocating positive freedom from the 'five giants' of want, disease, ignorance, squalor and idleness. Modern liberalism is therefore also sometimes called 'social liberalism'. Its core doctrines are limited government, constitutionalism, the rule of law, separation of powers, pluralism, tolerance, civil rights and liberties, representative government, open government and society, decentralisation and internationalism.

Modern liberalism marks the accommodation of liberalism with the democratic state in the late nineteenth and early twentieth century. Liberal thinking has always been, at best, wary of democracy as an inherently collectivist concept which may promote the 'tyranny of the majority' and threaten the rights, interests and views of minorities and individuals – particularly if that majority is uneducated or propertyless, in which case 'mobocracy' may triumph. When liberals highlight the corrupting influence of power, they are referring to people power as much as to state power. Classical liberals were downright hostile to the concept of democracy even as universal suffrage, never mind to more radical or direct concepts of genuine people power.

Evaluation of the Idea

A T FIRST SIGHT MODERN LIBERALISM SEEMS STRAIGHTFORWARD, COHERENT AND rational – 'perfectly sensible', as Keynes said – but it poses some philosophical problems and dilemmas.

First, for all liberals, how far does the proper role of the state extend before it stops enhancing freedom – if it can do so at all – and starts becoming coercive? From a New Right or an anarchist perspective, the modern liberal view of the interventionist state as capable of promoting freedom is philosophically untenable. Even for modern liberals, the fine line between a liberating state and a coercive state is always difficult to draw. Consider the laws on the age of consent, anti-terrorism, car seatbelts, Internet access, underage drinking, soft drugs or compulsory schooling (to take a few random examples) – do they promote or constrain individual freedom?

Second, one person's freedom is usually another's constraint (e.g. for modern liberals, welfare requires taxation) – so how can liberals defend all freedoms equally? Does the core modern liberal doctrine of positive freedom move liberalism away from individualism and towards welfare collectivism? The undeniable answer is, yes. In the UK context, some voters even regard the modern Liberal Democrats as more 'left-wing' than 'new' Labour in this respect.

Does the doctrine of pluralism – diverse and competing power groups – which lies at the heart of liberal democracy, similarly lean liberalism towards collectivism? Again, yes, but this may be as close as modern liberalism can get to the notion of individual choice in modern party and pressure group politics.

The concept of 'liberal democracy' itself embodies a fundamental contradiction, because 'democracy' – people power – is inherently a collectivist concept and it implies full political equality, which seems to conflict with liberal individualism and its emphasis on freedom. Representative democracy also often implies a growing role for the state which may lead to an encroachment on property rights. This is why early liberals especially did not favour universal suffrage (far less any more radical or direct form of democracy); they feared 'mobocracy' and 'tyranny of the majority', especially of those without property. Even J.S. Mill, while arguing that every adult should have the vote, believed that those with education should have more votes than those without. The concept of 'liberal democracy' therefore embodies a whole range of doctrines and devices which actually seek to restrain popular rule and to prevent government from reflecting the direct will of the majority.

A further question is, can an insistence on private property accord with a denial of class and, moreover, allow for genuine equality of opportunity? Clearly, from a Marxist perspective, these apparently contradictory views would be perceived as false consciousness on the part of a capitalist elite (or their agents) determined merely to defend the ownership of private property. Moreover, in practice, it seems undeniable that modern liberal democracies have succeeded neither in eliminating social class inequalities nor in guaranteeing genuine equality of opportunity across the whole social spectrum.

Also, how far is it possible to tolerate illiberal intolerance without destroying liberal tolerance itself? Can tolerance extend too far? This central dilemma is raised by factors such as racism within liberal democracies; how far should it be curbed and controlled without unduly threatening basic freedoms of speech and expression? Conversely, how far can the rise of racist or fascist parties in a liberal democracy be tolerated without threatening the very existence of that liberal democracy? (As an unnamed judge once put it, *'Is racism an individual right or a social wrong?'*)

Some commentators have perceived, in the draconian legal responses to the terrorist attacks on America in 2001, the outline of a form of Western fundamentalism: *'In all systems of human thought, there are contradictions that advocates prefer to gloss over. One of the most acute in liberalism is between its claim to tolerance and its hubristic claim to universality'* (Bunting 2001).

Finally, if Fukuyama's (1989) thesis of the 'end of history' is correct – if liberalism has become *'part of the national character'* (Bullock and Shock 1967) and *'the gospel of our own time'* (Himmelfarb 1975) – that is, if we are all liberals now because the doctrines of liberalism have become diffused throughout the growing number of 'liberal democracies' around the world – then there is no diversity to tolerate, which is precisely and paradoxically the 'tyranny of the majority' which liberals fear.

Marxism

❖

The Idea

A NINETEENTH-CENTURY THEORY OF REVOLUTIONARY COMMUNISM WHICH CHARAC-terised itself as 'scientific socialism' and predicted the inevitable overthrow of the capitalist 'bourgeois' ruling class by the 'proletariat' working class due to the inevitable economic conflicts and contradictions within the capitalist system. These economic developments were part of a long chain of human history culminating in an egalitarian, classless, stateless society.

Development of the Idea

THE MARXIST ARGUMENT CAN BE SUMMARISED AS FOLLOWS. ALMOST ALL OF HUMAN history has been a progressive series of class societies, from ancient society (masters and slaves) through feudalism (lords and serfs) to modern capitalism (bourgeoisie and proletariat). In all class societies, there are two main classes (as well as many others): a ruling class and a subject class. The ruling class are those who own and control the means of production (i.e. the things used to produce other things, such as farming land, factories etc.) – in capitalism they are called the bourgeoisie. The subject class are those who own only their labour power (i.e. their ability to work) – in capitalism they are called the proletariat. The bourgeoisie exploit the proletariat (working class) – that is, they buy their labour power and use it to create and extract 'surplus value' in the process of production; this is the only possible source of

Karl Marx

profit in capitalism. There is therefore an inescapable conflict of interests between the two main classes.

Every class has its own 'ideology' – its own set of ideas which reflect and protect its own class interests. The ideology of the ruling class is by far the dominant ideology in society, because the ruling class owns and/or controls the means by which ideas are transmitted – the media, education systems, political and legal processes etc. – what Marx called '*the means of mental production*'. The personnel of these institutions – politicians, civil servants, television producers and presenters etc. – need not be the ruling class as such; but they always and inevitably act as agents of the ruling class, promoting its interests by defending and preserving the existing capitalist system and class hierarchy, by the partial nature and content of the ideas and values which they promote.

Thus '*the ruling ideas of any age are the ideas of the ruling class*' (Marx 1843). The dominant ideology in capitalism embodies and encourages support for, for example, private property, profit, competition, hierarchy, law and order, patriotism and the 'national interest', monarchy and parliamentary democracy (which Marx called 'bourgeois dictatorship', because no major party ever seriously threatens the capitalist system and the dominant position of the ruling class).

'Dialectical materialism' was the label which Engels applied to Marx's theory of progress through economic conflict. Marxism is a materialist theory, that is, it sees economic factors as primary. It examines the course of human history and argues that progress throughout human history is created by economic – especially class – conflict. '*The history of all hitherto existing society is the history of class struggle*' (Marx and Engels 1848). This, combined with economic crisis and recession, will eventually make the workers aware of the fact that the capitalist system is only serving the interests of the minority ruling class, and the workers will rise up in revolution to overthrow capitalism and create a transitional phase of proletarian (workers') dictatorship. When all industry is collectively owned, classes will have been abolished and communism will have been achieved. Only then will 'ideology' – class-based ideas and values – disappear, the state as political agent of the ruling class will 'wither away', true (direct) democracy will develop and the 'end of history' as conflict will be achieved. This analysis of human progress through economic conflict, says Marx, is not wishful thinking but scientific determinism – that is, it is inevitable.

Evaluation of the Idea

MARX CONTRASTED HIS 'SCIENTISM' WITH 'UTOPIANISM'. UTOPIANISM IS A FORM OF political theorising which develops an ethical critique and hence fundamental rejection of the existing social order by constructing a model of an ideal or perfect alternative, a utopia, based upon highly optimistic assumptions about the perfectibility of human nature and society. Marx was highly critical of earlier socialists and left-wing anarchists such as Proudhon, whom he labelled 'utopian socialists' because they criticised capitalism in moralistic, emotive and irrational terms but – said Marx – they had no adequate analysis of the means of changing society. Marx did not moralise about the evils of capitalism; he argued instead that the system's inevitable, internal, economic contradictions would cause it to self-destruct, just as previous economic stages such as feudalism had done before.

However, Marxism itself has often been labelled 'utopian', both because it seems to foresee a perfect – or, at least, much improved – future world, and because most other philosophies (notably traditional conservatism and parliamentary socialism) regard many aspects of the theory as unattainable fantasy. Conservatism argues that the Marxist view of human nature is, itself, over-optimistic; further, organic conservatives regard the concept of the disappearance of the state as wholly untenable. Parliamentary socialists, on the other hand, argue that, given the growing affluence and contentment of the working classes in modern capitalism, *'We have missed the revolutionary bus'* (Berki 1975). Certainly, the main problem for Marxists today continues to be the evidently non-revolutionary nature of Western working classes.

Marxist theory (since Gramsci in the 1920s) has used the term 'hegemony' (from the Greek *hegemon*, ruler or leader) to denote the predominance of one social class over others, for example, 'bourgeois hegemony' in capitalism. This stresses not only the economic and political control exercised by the dominant class, but its success in projecting its own particular 'ideology' – its own set of self-serving ideas and values which deny, conceal and justify the material realities of exploitation and alienation – so that this is accepted as 'common sense' and part of the natural order by those who are, in fact, subordinated and oppressed by it. Thus Marxism uses the term 'ideology' in a critical and negative way, to mean a partial and distorting class perspective. Marxism itself, therefore, is not 'ideology' in this sense, but a true and total scientific picture of reality.

However, critics such as Karl Mannheim have labelled Marxism a 'utopian ideology' because it does seem to take the side of the oppressed working class and to argue for a social transformation which would benefit them disproportionately.

Other critics, such as Karl Popper, reject Marxism's claim to scientism because it sets no time limit for revolution and therefore cannot be disproved, that is, it is not falsifiable as any good scientific hypothesis should be.

Assertions of scientism in politics generally are criticised, especially by liberals, for their claims to determinism: the idea that human development is predictable and inevitable. This fundamentally contradicts liberal ideas of free will and individual choice. As individualists, liberals also reject the idea that humans can be classified into groups like plants or rocks. Traditional Tory theory would criticise scientism on different grounds: that human nature is not inherently rational or logical and therefore that abstract scientific theory cannot be trusted. Other critics would argue that no analysis can ever be wholly objective and impartial and that self-proclaimed scientific theorists such as de Tracy, Marx and Hitler have all seemed to be rationalising, by reference to objective science, the goals which they subjectively desired. Finally, scientism can generate unjustifiable faith in an absolute truth or a single future human destiny, without regard to morals, ethics or value judgements; and this kind of blind faith can lead to the concentration camps and the gas chambers, that is, to dreadful errors which human intuition may have instinctively avoided.

Moreover, Marxism has been criticised for its overemphasis on economic causality – as distinct, for example, from political, military, cultural, environmental or even personal influences upon social change and social attitudes. The 'great man' theory of historical change, for example, stresses instead the decisive impact of individual leaders such as Hitler, Gandhi and Christ upon the course of human history. Alternatively, and at its most basic, as the German philosopher Herbert Marcuse put it, *'Not every problem someone has with his girlfriend is necessarily due to the capitalist mode of production'* (in *The Listener*, August 1970). It should be noted, however, that Marx's analysis is less reductionist than simplistic descriptions often portray it; for example, his account of the rise to power of Louis Bonaparte does take account of the 'great man' theory of historical change but still explains it in terms of wider economic factors.

Anarchism, in particular, rejects the cold, hard, unsentimental scientism of Marx, together with his insistence on the need for a transitionary workers' state after the revolution which, anarchists fear, would entrench itself as a self-serving, coercive power and never 'wither away'. (There were also personal antagonisms between the egotistical Marx and contemporary anarchists such as Bakunin (1990), who described him as a *'German authoritarian and an arrogant Jew who wanted to transform the general council of the First International into a personal dictatorship over the workers'*. The theory of Marxism has been irrevocably tainted by the practice of the twentieth-century 'communist' regimes, especially by the oppressive Stalinist system in the former Soviet Union and its copycat dominions throughout Eastern Europe. However, these regimes developed in circumstances so far removed from those demanded by Marxist theory – that is, in pre-capitalist economies – and with characteristics so antithetical to the theory – notably the overweening state as opposed to the 'withering away' of the state – that criticism of the original theory by reference to the later practice is hardly fair or valid. Marx's (1843) vision of communism was *'the positive abolition of private property, of human self-alienation, and thus the real appropriation of human nature through and for man. It is, therefore, the return of man to himself as a social, i.e. really human, being, a complete and conscious return which assimilates all the wealth of previous development. Communism as fully developed naturalism is humanism and as fully developed humanism is naturalism. It is the definitive resolution of the antagonism between man and nature, and between man and man.'*

To argue that the collapse of the Soviet model of 'communism' renders Marx's theory redundant is, clearly, wrong. The fact that the Russian Revolution of 1917 happened in the wrong time and place – where industrial capitalism had barely developed – may even be argued to vindicate Marx's theory. The twentieth-century 'communist' experiment was bound to fail there, and those economies must go through the necessary stages of early and developed capitalism before any genuine proletarian revolutions can occur.

Finally, it is increasingly argued that contemporary capitalist globalisation is rendering Marxist theory increasingly redundant. However, as with much else, Marx anticipated this and embraced it within his theory: *'The bourgeoisie has through its exploitation of the world market given a cosmopolitan character to production and consumption in every country. All old-established national industries have been destroyed or are daily being destroyed. They are dislodged by new industries that no longer work up indigenous raw material, but raw material drawn from the remotest zones. In place of old wants, satisfied by the productions of the country, we find new wants, requiring for their satisfaction the products of distant lands and climes. In place of old local and national seclusion and self-sufficiency, we have intercourse in every direction, universal inter-dependence of nations'* (Marx and Engels 1848).

Over the whole range of the social sciences, Marx undoubtedly remains one of the most influential and important analysts of the post-Enlightenment era.

Nationalism

The Idea

A SENSE OF COMMON CULTURAL IDENTITY BASED UPON FACTORS SUCH AS LANGUAGE, religion, history, territory and ethnicity, often seeking to create or defend a sovereign state in which to house the nation. Nationalism is often perceived as a single doctrine which can attach itself to almost any wider political ideology such as liberalism, conservatism, fascism and even socialism – hence as one of the most flexible of all modern political tenets.

Development of the Idea

NATIONALISM IS SAID TO BE A RELATIVELY MODERN – THAT IS, EIGHTEENTH-CENTURY – idea, arising from the collapse of traditional, small group loyalties (e.g. to village, region or tribe) under the strains of industrialisation and urbanisation. Previously, people gave their loyalty, not to a nation state, but to other forms of political authority – such as the feudal lord, the church or the monarch. The idea of the nation emerged with the French Revolution and with new theories of the sovereignty of the people and the rights of man.

The concepts of 'nation' and 'state' are sometimes confused but should not be. Whereas a state is a sovereign, political power over a given territory – which may be multinational – a nation (a much more recent concept than the idea of the state) is a cultural entity, a collection of people with a shared sense of common heritage, which may be based on any of a wide range of traits such as history, language, religion or ethnicity. Nationalism is, therefore, sometimes described as a psycho-political construct, because it is essentially subjective – a matter of sentiment and self-identity rather than objective character. Most states, such as the UK and USA, are multicultural and multinational (the UK, for example, comprises, at least, the English, Scottish, Welsh and Northern

Irish nations) – though politicians may choose to use phrases such as 'the British nation' for ideological reasons. To take another example, Nigeria has over 150 tribes and over 100 languages and dialects within it and, therefore, has little sense of cultural community. Equally, the United Nations is a prescriptive misnomer (dating from former American president (1913–21) Woodrow Wilson's League of Nations) which should properly be termed the United States. Alternatively, a nation may be landless or dispersed across many states – as were, for example, the Jews before the creation of Israel in 1948. Many nations today are still in search of a state: for example, the Palestinians, Kurds, Chechens, Basques and Quebecois. The aim of most nationalist movements is to create or maintain a nation state, where the common cultural group is geographically coterminous (equates) with a sovereign political unit. Their methods include unification and the creation of a new nation state, such as Germany; secession, i.e. break-away, such as Eire; irredentism (from the Latin *irredentista*, 'unredeemed'), i.e. movements seeking to redeem a lost territory, such as Argentina and the Malvinas, Spain and Gibraltar; or replacement of a foreign by an indigenous leadership, such as Palestine.

Nationalism is probably one of the most flexible of all political doctrines. Its earliest form was liberal, embracing the principles of self-determination and popular sovereignty as a challenge to the political authority and divine right of monarchy over its subjects. Its greatest prophet was the Italian Mazzini (1805–72). This form of nationalism was democratic (at least in the liberal sense), reformist and progressive. However, since liberalism espouses individualism and universalism, it ultimately looks beyond the nation to embrace a form of internationalism, and to support supranational bodies such as the EU. Liberal forms of nationalism are, therefore, inherently contradictory.

In the nineteenth century, conservatism – having once been wary of nationalism in its original, liberal, form – adopted it as an adjunct to its defence of traditional heritage, hierarchy and the status quo. This form of nationalism was organic, quite exclusive and suspicious of change. It was the basis of the 'age of empire' where northern states sought to impose both political sovereignty and cultural dominion over subject territories, especially in Africa and Asia.

This form of imperial nationalism, in turn, generated the anti-colonial nationalist movements of the twentieth century in, for example, India, Africa, Vietnam and Cuba. These were essentially about freedom and self-determination, but also about economic modernisation and industrialisation. They frequently attached themselves to socialist economic goals and were often positively revolutionary.

Finally, in the inter-war period, there developed intensely chauvinistic forms of nationalism in the form of fascism – aggressive, expansionist, militarist and ethnocentric – that is, embodying a sense, not only of cultural distinction, but of inherent cultural superiority, justifying their right to impose their control and culture upon other states through war and conquest. In the post-war era this form of nationalism has also been demonstrated by the Bosnian Serbs and Iraq's pan-Arab expansionism. (The concept of 'chauvinism' implies aggressive and prejudiced dedication to a cause based upon a belief in its superiority. The word is now commonly associated with feminist opposition to 'male chauvinism' but, in fact, the word derives from Nicolas Chauvin, a French soldier fanatically devoted to Napoleon. Chauvinism, therefore, properly refers to a concept of nationalism which believes in its own superiority or rightful dominance.)

Evaluation of the Idea

NATIONALISM HAS, ARGUABLY, BEEN THE MOST INFLUENTIAL POLITICAL CREED OF THE last two centuries, generating wars and revolutions, the collapse of empires, the birth of new states, the redrawing of boundaries and the rise of new regimes. Anthony D. Smith (1986) has described nationalism as a *'chameleon ideology'* because it is so flexible and adaptable that it can attach itself to almost any wider ideology. Probably the only philosophy which cannot absorb nationalism is anarchism, since the latter is so fundamentally hostile to any concept of statehood, which is usually the prime goal of nationalist movements.

Even Marxism which, in theory, is an internationalist philosophy – *'Workers of the world, unite! You have nothing to lose but your chains – you have a world to win!'* (Marx and Engels 1848) – accepts that the proletariat must first deal with their own, national bourgeoisie; and, in practice, Marxism and nationalism may go well together, especially in revolutionary, anti-colonial movements such as in Castro's Cuba, where the imperialist enemy and the capitalist enemy were one and the same (in this case, America). Marxism and nationalism are both collectivist and essentially democratic, and nationalism can be forward-looking and progressive – indeed, positively revolutionary. Hence the two may combine, uniting the quest for national liberation with the desire for social development.

Liberalism, for different reasons, is also ambivalent about nationalism. Liberal writers such as Kedourie (1974) reject the collectivist and emotional nature of nationalism, as well as its tendency to regression, exclusion, intolerance, violence and even racism and dictatorship. Nevertheless, the roots of nationalism lie in liberal notions of self-determinism and popular sovereignty – what Anthony Smith called the 'national ideal' – and some contemporary forms of nationalism are peaceful and constitutional (e.g. the Scottish and Welsh nationalist parties). Liberals do, therefore, recognise the paradoxical nature of nationalism, with its capacity for democracy or dictatorship, peace or violence and progression or regression. Even those liberals who dislike nationalism recognise it as *'the most vigorous and pervasive of all political creeds'* (Heater 1975).

Conservatives have embraced nationalism since the nineteenth century, but (in the UK) in a 'little Englander' way which is inward-looking and parochial, attaching itself to traditional and deferential symbols of cultural identity such as the flag or Crown, rather than to any democratic concept of citizenship. For them, nationalism is a means towards the ends of social cohesion, order and stability.

Fascist ideology in the 1920s adopted nationalism as its core doctrine, in an integral form which utterly denied the identity of any individual outwith the concept of nationhood. This form of nationalism is wholly at odds with the liberal form, given its aggressive, militarist and expansionist nature. Smith (1979) calls it *'a profound attack on the whole national ideal'*.

Even within the UK, there are currently many forms of nationalism. The Scots exhibit a political form of liberal nationalism in their desire for some measure of autonomy – whether devolution, federalism or outright independence. The Welsh, on the other hand, seek to defend and promote their nation's cultural heritage, particularly their distinctive language, without any strong desire for political autonomy. This is known as cultural nationalism, and has close associations with the concept of patriotism, a sentiment of loyalty and attachment to one's country. It is a 'bottom-up' form of nationalism that draws more on popular traditions, rituals, and legends than on elite or higher culture. In Northern Ireland, the republicans pursue an agenda of anti-colonial nationalism against the English conquerors and settlers. Their perception is that '*Catholics are blacks who happen to have white skins . . . The Northern Ireland problem is a colonial problem*' (de Paor 1977). The unionists are, essentially, conservative nationalists who remain deeply attached to the traditions of the UK Crown and flag. English nationalism, meanwhile, is in flux. For former Prime Minister John Major, it meant old maids on bicycles, warm beer and cricket on the village green. For liberal pessimists, it means skinhead football yobbos in Saint George T-shirts flaunting xenophobia – that is, irrational hatred of foreigners. Whereas Scottish and Welsh nationalism is assertive, English nationalism is defensive and often exclusive, wary of alien cultures and races. It leans to ethnocentrism – a sense of cultural superiority (in part, a heritage of empire) and, therefore, may even take the form of ethnic nationalism or racism.

In sum, therefore, nationalism can be left-wing or right-wing, democratic or dictatorial, reactionary or progressive. It looks both to the past and to the future. It is not a coherent political phenomenon. It may be one of the most cross-cutting of all modern political doctrines – and, in that sense, is both one of the most prominent and one of the most important, given its flexibility and impact upon the modern world.

Cultural or geographical identity is, ultimately, a subjective and emotive attachment – which is what makes nationalism such a potent political force, capable of manipulation and even manufacture by political leaders to their own ends. Anderson (1983) argued that nations are '*imagined communities*', one reason being that, no matter how small a nation (e.g. some Cornish people regard Cornwall as a viable nation), you can never know every member of it, no matter how strongly you may feel yourself to be a part of it. This implies that nationalism is not a natural phenomenon, but a political construct. Even many liberals regard it as something close to a surrogate religion. Many Western liberals would perceive the most obvious contemporary manifestation of 'artificial' cultural identity as that of the pan-nationalism of Islamic fundamentalism, a deeply reactionary form of religious nationalism which crosses state boundaries and profoundly threatens Western sensibilities. Marxists, of course, would regard all contemporary nationalism, whether liberal, conservative, fascist or Islamic, as a prime weapon of bourgeois ideological dominance in capitalist economies, dividing the international working class as a method of promoting false class consciousness and preserving the status quo.

Meanwhile, there are contemporary trends which threaten the profound power of nationalism in modern politics: on the one hand – on the grand scale – globalisation, supranationalism and internationalism; and, on the other hand – on the small scale – regionalism and localism – for example, recent decentralisation and devolution in the UK. Nationalism may not be a permanent political phenomenon.

Nazism

The Idea

A TWENTIETH-CENTURY PHILOSOPHY, ORIGINATING IN GERMANY IN THE INTER-WAR period, advocating a totalitarian one-party state, personal dictatorship, racism and genocide. Its full label, 'national socialism', was arguably misleading, since the movement was overwhelmingly racist and capitalist. It is sometimes perceived as a sub-type of fascism, and neo-Nazi movements continue to exist today throughout Europe and America.

Development of the Idea

W HEREAS ITALIAN FASCISM ASSERTED THE PRIMACY OF THE STATE, NAZI THEORY, BY contrast, asserted the primacy of the leader – the *führer-prinzip* – over everything else, including the state. The *Führer* – a quasi-sacred figure – was the embodiment of the spirit, virtue and 'will of the volk' (a perversion of Rousseau's idea of the 'general will') and, as such, the leader had supreme authority to demand absolute obedience. *'His will is not the subjective, individual will of a single man, but the collective national will'* (Hitler 1969).

This did not mean that he followed the will of the people, but that he was the only person capable of rightly interpreting the collective will. This meant that he was infallible; he could not err. The idea of a 'Superman' – a supremely powerful and omnipotent leader – was very loosely derived from the writings of the nineteenth-century German philosopher

Adolf Hitler

Friedrich Nietzsche. Nazi society was thus highly elitist: the leader dominated the heroic elite (the SS) who in turn controlled the unquestioning and obedient masses. Fascist and Nazi leaders were also usually very charismatic, attracting support by sheer force of personality, which is one reason why fascist movements rarely survived the death of the leader. This 'leader principle' was also claimed to be the purest form of democracy. Hitler happened to be elected into power in 1933, but consent through the ballot box was never the underpinning philosophical claim to democracy of fascist and Nazi movements.

This was not the kind of democracy that would be recognised by today's liberal regimes. All fascist movements used a combination of propaganda and terror to create and, indeed, coerce mass consent or compliance. The control and use of the mass media – newspapers and especially radio and film – were crucial to the rising popularity of fascism and confirmed it as a specifically twentieth-century phenomenon. (In previous centuries, neither the desire for mass democracy, nor the capacity to create it through mass indoctrination, existed in political leaders and elites.) Once in power, the fascist and Nazi parties eliminated their rivals and manipulated the legal and judicial systems to legitimise their activities. They despised the division and diversity of liberal democracy and sought absolute unity under absolute leadership within the total power of the supremely organic state – 'strength through unity'. Nevertheless, in so far as fascism and Nazism genuinely involved mass consent, participation and authority, they have valid claims to be labelled democratic, at least in the totalitarian sense.

Nazism – unlike Italian fascism – was not primarily nationalist but overwhelmingly racist: it divided human society into a hierarchy of perceived biological or genetic castes, headed by the culture-creating Aryan master race (*herrenvolk*). The intermediate, culture-carrying races were to be servants of the master race, and the most inferior, culture-destroying races – Jews, blacks, homosexuals, gypsies, communists, physically and mentally handicapped (even if they were German) – were to be eliminated. Hitler instigated the 'final solution' – the planned extermination of all European Jews – in 1941. When Hitler spoke of the Jews as 'parasites' he meant it not simply as crude abuse but as a precise biological analogy. German expansionism had the goal of *lebensraum* – living space for the master race. This racial theory was not devised by Hitler but was adopted from nineteenth-century European ideologues such as Gobineau (French diplomat), Wagner (German composer) and Houston Chamberlain (Wagner's English son-in-law). Hitler also applied a perverted form of the Darwinian idea of 'survival of the fittest' to his biological politics through a programme of eugenics, or selective breeding, in which the physically and mentally handicapped were sterilised and ultimately killed. Whereas in Italian fascism it was enough to be Italian, in Nazi Germany it was not enough to be German.

The way in which Nazism defined nationalism in terms of racism – the intermingling of 'blood and soil' – is illustrated by the following directive to all German schools: *'Teachers are directed to instruct their pupils in "the nature, causes and effects of all racial and hereditary problems", to bring home to them the importance of race and heredity for the life and destiny of the German people, and to awaken in them a sense of their responsibility toward "the community of the nation" (their ancestors, the present generation and posterity), pride in their membership of the German race as a foremost vehicle of hereditary Nordic values, and the will consciously to cooperate in the racial purification of the German stock. Racial instruction is to begin with the youngest pupils (six years of age) in accordance with the desire of the Führer "that no boy or girl should leave school without complete knowledge of the necessity and meaning of blood purity".'*

For Nazism, unlike Italian fascism, the race was prior to the state and blood purity was paramount. As Hitler put it in *Mein Kampf* (1969), *'The state is a means to an end. Its end lies in the preservation and advancement of a community of physically and psychically homogeneous creatures.'*

The German *volksstaat* rarely employed the concept or theory of totalitarianism, but was arguably more totalitarian in practice than was Italian fascism. In practice, with its Gestapo and SS, virulent racism and anti-Semitism, Nuremberg laws and 'final solution' – the Holocaust – Nazism was altogether the most organised and efficient, cruel and ruthless of all the fascist regimes (if it can rightly be called 'fascist', given its range of unique characteristics).

Evaluation of the Idea

NAZISM WAS OVERWHELMINGLY, BUT NOT ENTIRELY, RACIST. IT TARGETED AND SOUGHT to eliminate all possible sources of organised opposition to the Nazi movement. A well-known and moving quotation from German pastor Martin Niemoller (1892–1984) states, *'The Nazis came for the communists and I did not speak up because I was not a communist. Then they came for the Jews and I did not speak up because I was not a Jew. Then they came for the trade unionists and I did not speak up because I was not a trade unionist. Then they came for the Catholics and I was a Protestant so I did not speak up. Then they came for me . . . by which time there was no-one left to speak up for me'* (quoted in Bartlett 1992).

As in all fascist movements, the family was a central institution for Nazism and the role of woman was clearly delineated within it. As Nazi propaganda minister Goebbels put it, *'The mission of woman is to be beautiful and to bring children into the world'* (quoted in Roberts 2000). She was also supposed to be both athletic and womanly, and to refrain from such things as wearing make-up or smoking in public. But, above all, she was to have children and – together with the educational system – was to imbue in them the values of national socialism. Fascism and Nazism were the most patriarchal of twentieth-century political philosophies and, as such, they played a significant part in fuelling the emergence of post-war, 'second wave' feminism.

Nazism had a peculiar relationship with socialism. It styled itself as 'national socialism' ('Nazi' – NS – is an abbreviation for the National Socialist German Workers' Party) – that is, as a nationalist counter to the rising threat of international socialism – and its leaders often used the rhetoric of both nationalism and of socialism (fatherland, soil, comradeship, brotherhood and so on). Its origins lay partly in an anti-materialist form of socialist revisionism initiated by anti-Marxist, revolutionary trade unionists or syndicalists such as Georges Sorel at the turn of the twentieth century. Sorel (1950) said, *'Men are moved by myth'* – rationalism was replaced by mysticism, and the unresponsive proletariat was replaced, first by the nation as the focus of fascist attention, then by the race for Nazism. Like fascism, Nazism did share some theoretical roots and principles with communism such as collectivism, social Darwinism, the dialectic, opposition to liberalism and the free market etc. Fascism and Nazism rejected the individualism and self-interest of laissez-faire capitalism and the multinational or global variants of big business which the state could not control. However, they were staunch advocates of private enterprise – though it had to be heavily state-directed and regulated. They wholly denied the reality of classes and class conflict, Nazism instead asserting the primacy of the leader and race in an organic, exclusive and aggressive hierarchy. It was remotely 'socialist' only insofar as it was committed to a substantial welfare programme – as, however, are capitalist liberal democracies today – and its virulent anti-communism and anti-Semitism place it firmly on the far right of the political spectrum. Fascism and Nazism won support mainly from the middle and lower middle classes – who felt threatened by rising inflation and the power of big business on the one hand, and by growing unemployment and the creeping threat of communism on the other – and also from ex-soldiers who were resentful of the outcome of World War I and felt alienated by their return to civilian life with the loss of army discipline, security, pride and comradeship which this involved. Fascism and Nazism also appealed to young people attracted by the cult of action and alienated by 'the system'.

Many critics of Nazism have commented upon the irony that Hitler's Nazi philosophy celebrated all of the things which he, personally, was not. He was not German, but Austrian. He was the physical opposite of the tall, blond-haired, blue-eyed, Aryan ideal. He had Jewish ancestry. Psychoanalysts since Freud have made much of arguments that Hitler's inchoate theories glorified the antitheses of all that he despised in himself. This, of course, does not explain why so many millions of other people embraced Nazism with such fanatical enthusiasm. The mass support so readily given to the Nazi regime of totalitarian state control, racial genocide and international war begs quite fundamental questions about the basic nature of humanity.

As befits its anti-rational and anti-intellectual nature, Nazism was one of the most illogical and incoherent of modern political ideologies. It despised reason and rationality but claimed that its racial theories were scientific. It was wholly anti-individualist but elevated the leader as the supreme individual. It claimed to be revolutionary but was downright reactionary. It claimed to be the truest form of democracy but entirely despised anything approaching 'people power'. It claimed that Germany was threatened by a most unlikely world collaboration of Jews, international capitalist financiers and communists. Its very label – 'national socialism' – was, perhaps, its most contradictory feature, since it was essentially neither nationalist nor socialist. However, its very contradictions helped it to be all things to all people and lent it widespread popular support.

The ideas of fascism and Nazism embodied a fundamental rejection of the Enlightenment values of equality, freedom and reason which had dominated European politics since the French Revolution. As the Nazis put it, '1789 is abolished'. Nazism was born out of anti-communism, anti-egalitarianism, anti-liberalism, anti-individualism, anti-rationalism and anti-parliamentarianism. It is, perhaps, the most negative of all modern ideologies. It should also be remembered that it took the combined might of the British Empire and its European allies, together with the Soviet Union and the USA to defeat Nazism – perhaps only temporarily – in 1945. Its critics often seem to find it comforting to portray Nazism as an exclusively German aberration – a product of the combined influences of defeat in World War I and the humiliating

settlement terms imposed by the Treaty of Versailles, frustrated nationalism and incip-
ient racism, economic crisis and political instability. However, its potency, not only in
the 1930s but still today – witness the resurgence of neo-Nazi movements throughout
Europe and the USA – raises the most basic questions about the essence of human
nature and the very future of humanity.

'New' Labour

The Idea

THE LABEL ADOPTED BY THE LEADERSHIP OF THE BRITISH LABOUR PARTY FROM 1994 as it abandoned its traditional principles of common ownership and equality in pursuit of middle-class voters and a more pragmatic, right-wing, political agenda. It is perceived as blending diverse ideological elements from social democracy, conservatism (both traditional and New Right) and liberalism to produce what its advocates call the 'third way'.

Development of the Idea

THE TERM 'NEW' LABOUR WAS PUBLICLY INTRODUCED BY TONY BLAIR IN 1994, IN HIS first speech as leader to Labour's annual conference; though it has never, yet, been adopted as the official title of the British Labour party. Having lost four successive general elections, the British Labour party in the mid-1990s decided to 'modernise' in response to declining working-class numbers, economic globalisation, the collapse of communism and the discrediting of 'old fashioned' socialist ideas after almost 20 years of New Right Conservative government. Successive Labour leaders Neil Kinnock, then John Smith and now Tony Blair (who was elected party leader in July 1994) therefore pulled the party ever further to the right. Thus 'new' Labour was born, the most symbolic turning point being the abandonment in 1995 of the party's historic, constitutional commitment to Clause Four – which expressed their nominal

Tony Blair

pursuit of collective ownership (and which used to be printed on every party member-ship card): *'To secure for the workers by hand or by brain the full fruits of their industry and the most equitable distribution thereof that may be possible upon the basis of the common ownership of the means of production, distribution and exchange, and the best obtainable system of popular administration and control of each industry or service'.* Former Labour leader Hugh Gaitskell had attempted to revise Clause Four as far back as 1959, but had met a humiliating defeat at that year's party conference. Thirty-six years later, Labour's traditional, manual working-class constituency had shrunk and Labour had been in permanent opposition for 18 years. The motivation for change was far greater.

The term 'third way' was increasingly used in the late 1990s to describe this pragmatic repositioning – supposedly somewhere between free market capitalism and state socialism – which was adopted not only by the British Labour party but by others like the German Social Democrats. It involved concepts such as 'stakeholding' and 'social inclusion' – seeking to involve and provide wider opportunities for more people, including the disadvantaged, within a capitalist economy where every individual had both rights and responsibilities. The term 'third way' was, perhaps disturbingly for left-wingers, originally coined by Italian fascism in the 1920s, was later adopted by the post-war social democrats (especially in Sweden) and was then taken up by 'post-socialists' such as Blair in the UK and Clinton in the USA. As former DTI Secretary Stephen Byers said in 1999, 'new' Labour is about *'wealth creation, not wealth distribution'*. Some have described the 'new' Labour position as 'market socialism', arguing that markets could be made to serve socialist ends. Both traditional socialists and New Right conservatives have argued that this concept is a contradiction in terms. Blair has also employed the contradictory concept of 'one-nation socialism' – a clear rejection of class politics and implicit acceptance of a right-wing, paternalist concept of community. Blair's critics have, therefore, often criticised Labour for abandoning its socialist roots and merely being Thatcherism with a human face, in that the modern Labour party has abandoned its socialist beliefs of equality, cooperation, fraternity and collective ownership for free market individualism and social authoritarianism.

However, supporters of Blair assert that the modern Labour party is a qualitative break from Thatcherism, drawing upon older traditions of the Labour party and fusing them with left-wing liberalism through new political strategies.

Arguably, 'new' Labour is a combination of at least four distinct ideological strands: it still has elements of social democracy within it but in the modified form of communi-tarian ideas (rather than class politics) involving mutual rights and responsibilities; it has chosen largely to continue New Right economic, fiscal and law and order policies, combined with the pro-European and paternalist stance of the more traditional conser-vatives; and it has adopted a liberal programme of constitutional reforms.

Elements of social democracy in the 'new' Labour programme include the stress on community, social inclusion, and the concept of the 'stakeholder economy' enhancing social justice within a market economy. Policy examples include: the minimum wage, introduced when Labour opted into the Social Chapter of the EU Amsterdam Treaty; enhanced trade union rights, such as the Employment Relations Act 1999; substan-tially increased spending on health and education; the aim to abolish child poverty in two decades; targeted assistance for the poorest pensioners, etc.

The adoption of many New Right Conservative ideas and policies is manifest in Labour's ongoing privatisations and support for 'public/private partnerships' (e.g. air traffic control and the London underground); in their tax and spend policies – no increase in direct taxation, and 'prudent' public spending; in cuts in lone parents' and disabled peoples' benefits; and in authoritarian law and order policies, such as increased police powers, electronic surveillance, the introduction of child jails and the draconian anti-terrorist legislation of 2001.

The paternalist aspect of 'new' Labour is evident in its communitarian outlook that there are no 'unencumbered selves'. The government's moral responsibility to aid underprivileged individuals must be reciprocated by the individual's obligation to accept and make the most of such opportunities – exemplified by 'new' Labour's 'welfare to work' policies, which disallow unwarranted welfare dependency.

Finally, a fairly radical liberal programme of constitutional reform has included devolution, reform of the Lords, a Bill of Rights and freedom of information legislation.

This is a highly pragmatic policy mix, motivated by electoral opportunism rather than by ideological principle. Whether and how it may change to suit changing future circumstances and voters' opinions remains to be seen – in other words, 'new' Labour seems to be an ongoing process rather than a fixed ideological entity.

Evaluation of the Idea

'NEW' LABOUR IS FIRMLY OPPOSED TO THE OLD PARTY'S STANCE OF NATIONALISATION and the statist economy adopted in the late 1970s and early 1980s (culminating in the radical left 1983 Labour manifesto which proposed substantial state nationalisation, unilateral disarmament, abolition of the Lords and withdrawal from the EU – *'the longest suicide note in history'* as the right-wing Labour MP Gerald Kaufman described it). Supporters of the party today often argue that the goals of 'new' Labour – equality, community, cooperation and fraternity – remain the same as those of 'old' Labour – *'promoting a moral outlook that Keir Hardy and Clement Attlee would have shared'* (Mandelson 1996). However, 'new' Labour has transformed the means of achieving those aims, promoting an enterprise economy based on freedom and responsibility. 'New' Labour uses the language of freedom, responsibility, community and cooperation in a pragmatic update of social democracy for the twenty-first century. As Labour MP Tony Wright has said recently, *'We are dogmatists about ends but pragmatists about means'* (quoted in Morgan 1995). Or, as Blair said in 1994, there should be no confusion between *'means, such as wholesale nationalisation, and ends, such as a fairer society and more productive economy'* (quoted in Morgan 1995).

On the other hand, Blair clearly endorses the free market: in his first speech as Prime Minister to the Labour party conference, he proclaimed that *'a partnership between the public and private is the only language that this "new" Labour government will respect'*. In its early days, 'new' Labour did not resist the unions' growing distance from its enterprise – and, indeed, it established the 'Thousand Club' for wealthy business donors. Blair's transformation of the old Clause Four from *'the common ownership of the means of production, distribution and exchange'* into a vague statement emphasising a dynamic market economy and a just society, seemed to confirm the suspicions of the trade unions and the radical left of the labour movement that 'new' Labour was abandoning, or even betraying, its traditional supporters and its socialist roots.

It is often argued that one reason for the growing 'presidentialism' of the British political system and the increasing focus upon party leaders, their personal styles and images rather than upon the parties' policies is precisely because there is now so little ideological difference ('clear blue water', as many Conservatives have put it) between the two main parties. For example, senior Conservative Lord Onslow said of the 1997 Labour government in its early days, *'They're buggering up the constitution and ruining fox-hunting. Otherwise, it's a perfectly sound Tory government.'* He was only unduly pessimistic on the fox-hunting issue.

There is also a new, authoritarian dimension to 'new' Labour – in their criminal justice and anti-terrorism laws, for example – which is very reminiscent of Thatcherite neo-conservatism. Paradoxically, however, there is also a radical liberal aspect to many of 'new' Labour's constitutional reforms such as devolution, the Lords, Bill of Rights and freedom of information – even if these are enacted only on the government's limited, piecemeal and self-serving party political terms.

A further paradox of 'new' Labour has been this commitment to a more liberal and decentralising political agenda – for example, in terms of devolution – combined with its highly centralising processes of internal party control and decision-making. One conspicuous example occurred during the party's 2002 conference, when the leadership lost a vote on Private Finance Initiatives in the public sector and arrogantly proclaimed its intention to disregard the vote entirely. 'New' Labour has a top-down, leader-led, agenda, as much personal as political – which was one reason why Blair was so reluctant to lose close confidants like Peter Mandelson and Stephen Byers; and which is also why their enforced loss from the Cabinet was so politically significant.

In some respects, the Liberal Democrats are now to the left of 'new' Labour: for example, in advocating the renationalisation of Railtrack, and being prepared to consider increasing income tax to pay for state education. Also, in the face of the government's authoritarian stance on law and order, a leading Liberal Democrat said, *'To go back to the former shadow Home Secretary's [i.e. Tony Blair's] phrase, we've got to concentrate as much on the causes of crime as on dealing with the crime.'* (Simon Hughes, 24 June 2002) – a social approach usually associated more with left-wing collectivism than with liberal individualism.

The ideological essence of 'new' Labour is an ongoing, pragmatic response to the political successes of the New Right in the 1980s and the changing economic structures of the 1990s – in essence, a revised, more right-wing version of the post-war social democratic agenda. It is no longer radical, egalitarian or highly redistributive. It is safe to say that it is no longer socialist – if it ever was. As its name suggests, labourism, not socialism, was always the prevailing ethos of the British Labour party. It was born in 1900 out of a combination of the trade unions' desire for a parliamentary voice for the labour movement and a political representation of Christian or ethical principles of fraternity and compassion – not, ever, truly radical socialist goals of fundamental equality of outcome and economic collectivism.

Nevertheless, the latest ideological shifts, though not seismic, have disturbed and alienated many traditionalists – who, to date, have nowhere else to go in party political terms. The reawakenings of trade union activism – for example, in the firefighters' dispute in 2002 – signalled the end of 'new' Labour's extended honeymoon period. The pragmatic successes of 'new' Labour in 1997 and 2001 owed more to the acquiescence of the party itself and its thirst for power than to any widespread philosophical commitment to the new policies or campaign strategies. Mirroring the previous rise and fall of Thatcherism within the British Conservative party, these electoral calculations and tenuous ideological bonds will likely be the undoing of 'new' Labour when the country's economic stability and the party's electoral strength begin to fail.

New Right

❋

The Idea

A RADICAL, RIGHT-WING ALTERNATIVE TO TRADITIONAL, PATERNALIST CONSERVATISM which emerged in the nineteenth century and became predominant within the UK Conservative party and the US Republican party in the 1980s. It advocates an apparently paradoxical mix of free market economics, and authoritarian politics in non-economic spheres. Widely associated in the 1980s with Margaret Thatcher in the UK and Ronald Reagan in the USA.

Development of the Idea

THIS SECOND STRAND OF CONSERVATISM DEVELOPED IN THE NINETEENTH CENTURY with the decline of the old ruling class of paternalist landowners and the emergence of a new ruling class of free market traders, industrialists and financiers. The battle for dominance between these two dominant economic interest groups was epitomised by the struggle over the 1815 Corn Laws, which were good for the landowners and bad for the free-traders. Business and trading interests were originally represented by nineteenth-century laissez-faire liberalism, but the Conservatives recognised the changing balance of power in the country and set out to attract the growing class of traders and entrepreneurs. The 1846 repeal of the Corn Laws marked the triumph of free market interests over landed interests in Britain, and this new ruling class of entrepreneurs looked increasingly to the Conservatives rather than to

Margaret Thatcher

the Liberals to protect its interests. By the end of the nineteenth century the Conservative party had taken over the mantle of laissez-faire from the Liberals, and this has since been the second main strand of conservative philosophy after traditional Tory paternalism. The New Right has had most influence in the UK and USA (especially under President Reagan, 1981–89), but also in France, Germany and elsewhere in Europe. In Britain it is also commonly known as economic conservatism, Thatcherism or the Radical Right. It contrasts with traditional political conservatism (Toryism) in many important respects.

Given its liberal roots, the New Right is mechanistic rather than organic – it sees state and society as an artificial machine devised by man to serve man; and, like a machine, it can be altered and improved. It therefore sees the individual as the primary unit in society, with the state devised to serve the individual, and all individuals as being of equal basic worth – although, having unequal talents and abilities, they will end up unequal. All conservatives see inequality of some sort as inevitable and desirable. The New Right – again, given its liberal roots – has much more faith in human rationality than has Toryism, and is itself a more rational and doctrinaire theory. However, it also sees human nature as selfish and competitive; these instincts, it believes, must be given free reign in the market economy.

The New Right does not seek to conserve, and it has no reverence for tradition as such. Given its mechanistic theory and faith in human reason, it has a positive desire for change; it is radical and innovative, stressing individual initiative, enterprise, energy and drive. However, its attitude to change is both radical and reactionary: it seeks to turn back the clock to what it perceives as an earlier, better era, namely the Victorian age of the free market. Unlike traditional Toryism, it does not seek simply to conserve or to stand still. The New Right seeks to 'roll back the frontiers of state' in economic terms, and talks of 'a return to Victorian values'. Since the New Right has faith in human rationality and seeks radical change, it is much more 'theoretical' than is Toryism; indeed, it is principled to the point of being doctrinaire, and is much more overtly 'ideological' than Toryism in every sense. Hence the many famous slogans of Thatcherism: 'No U-turns', 'The lady's not for turning' and 'TINA – there is no alterna- tive'. This rigidity of attitude was most clearly illustrated by Thatcher's refusal to abandon the poll tax even in the face of its deep unpopularity and impracticality.

All conservatives are staunch advocates of private property, the New Right even more so than Toryism. The central doctrine of New Right economic conservatism is the unconstrained freedom to acquire private property, profit and wealth. It stresses free enterprise and the absolute right of the individual to enter and succeed or fail in the market on his own merits, without state help or hindrance. Thus it rests on a free market economy controlled only by the forces of supply and demand and not by state regulation or direction – i.e. negative economic freedom. However, there is an apparent paradox at the heart of New Right theory: although, in economic terms, it stresses freedom from state intervention, in all other spheres – political, social and moral – it advocates strong state intervention, not to promote freedom but to curb, constrain, control, censor and centralise. The economic dimension of the New Right is sometimes called 'neo-liberalism' and the authoritarian dimension 'neo-conservatism'. This authoritarian dimension of the New Right does not derive from the paternalism of the Disraeli era but from an earlier, reactionary and disciplinarian school of European conservatism. In the UK Conservative government policies of the 1980s and 1990s, it took the form of increased police powers, heavier criminal sentencing, political centralisation, more stringent secrecy and censorship and increased legal curbs on non-conforming or deviant groups in society. The New Right also opposes multiculturalism, internationalism and supranationalism, instead espousing an insular and often ethnic form of nationalism which is opposed to immigration and – at the least – sceptical of the EU.

Evaluation of the Idea

THE NEW RIGHT CAME TO THE FORE IN BRITAIN (AND AMERICA, GERMANY, FRANCE and elsewhere) in the 1970s for a variety of reasons. First, economic recession and 'stagflation' – unemployment combined with high inflation – seemed to prove that Keynesian interventionism had failed. Inflation, rather than unemployment, was seen as the main problem by the New Right, and they were quite prepared throughout the 1980s to allow increased unemployment for the sake of reducing inflation. This meant cutting public spending, abolishing inefficient state monopolies and curbing the 'over-powerful' trade unions. Many Conservatives also perceived a growing culture of welfare dependency upon the 'nanny state' which they rejected on grounds of both economic inefficiency and moral turpitude. The New Right sought to roll back the 'tax and spend' policies of the post-war era, to reduce the stranglehold of state bureaucracy and to foster self-reliance by individuals and their families.

They also rejected the 'permissive society' of the 1960s – the non-conformity and moral laxity of youth culture and of many previous Labour policies such as the legalisation of abortion and homosexuality.

Finally, UK membership of the EU since 1973 seemed to threaten national sovereignty and cultural integrity, and fostered an increasingly insular form of conservative nationalism and Euroscepticism.

Thus the New Right advocated 'limited but strong' government, which sounds contradictory but may not be. Within its prescribed and limited – that is, non-economic – role, government should be strong, said the New Right: *'Limitation of government doesn't make for a weak government. If you've got the role of government clearly set out, then it means very strong government in that role. Very strong indeed'* (Thatcher, quoted in Gamble 1988).

Margaret Thatcher once summed up her view of the proper role of government – and also the 'paradox' of the New Right – by saying *'What this country wants is less tax and more law and order'*. A critical journalist, Neal Ascherson, put it more sceptically: *'The trouble with a free market economy is that it takes so many police to make it work'* (quoted in Gamble 1988).

These last two quotes, in their different ways, imply that the economic libertarianism and political/social authoritarianism of New Right thinking are not so much paradoxical as complementary – two sides of the same coin. The laissez-faire 'survival of the fittest' approach of Conservative governments in the 1980s and 1990s resulted in growing economic and social divisions between rich and poor, and rising unemployment and poverty at the lower end of the scale, but also fewer state and welfare benefits for the losers. Stronger policing and political controls were required to keep the lid on real and potential crime, disorder and social unrest; but these more pervasive and often militaristic controls further alienated already deprived and disadvantaged groups. The 1980s was a decade of riots, and by 1997 the crime rate had soared to almost six million recorded offences per year.

However, there is a stronger case for saying that the two strands of New Right thought are, in fact, paradoxical, especially given their diverse philosophical origins. One obvious focus of conflict is the question of human nature: the rationalist, neo-liberal view should not require the degree of authoritarian control and constraint to which the neo-conservative view subscribes. A second, less obvious, contradiction centres on the New Right's view of the proper role of women. Their meritocratic individualism should lead them to espouse liberal feminist values and a commitment to equal opportunities for women in the public sphere of economic and political life. However, their conservative dimension prompts them to defend traditional family values in a conspicuously reactionary way.

It should also be said that not all Conservative politicians and writers fall neatly into the simplistic Tory/New Right categories described above. Some – especially in the youth wing of the British Conservative party – are libertarian, subscribing to the principle of extensive negative freedom from the state in every sphere: they advocate legalising heroin and even paedophilia. Others – such as neo-conservative writer Roger Scruton – subscribe to the authoritarian dimension of New Right thinking but not to laissez-faire economics. Yet others, such as the post-2001 Michael Portillo, apparently now subscribe to economic laissez-faire principles combined with social liberalism.

What they all share is a revulsion against socialism both in its theory and practice, '*as a form of mass domestication, destined to bring about the degeneracy of the species*' (Scruton 1982).

The contemporary British Conservative party is clearly still trying to decide what kind of conservatism it wishes to espouse. The New Right wing currently appears to be in some retreat, partly because of its philosophical incoherence and partly because of the manifest inadequacies of the free market itself. The rhetoric of leading Conservatives such as Duncan Smith, Oliver Letwin and David Willetts in 2002 implied a return to a more socially inclusive and paternalist Tory agenda; but it has yet to be matched by concrete policy initiatives or to be backed by the wider party. For example, less than a week after the party's 2002 conference about modernisation and social change, the 'nasty party' (as Conservative Chair Theresa May put it) returned with a three-line whip in Parliament against the adoption of children by unmarried couples. The divided and diminished state of the British Conservative party since 1997 reflects its profound ideological schisms.

The rise of the New Right – given its philosophical contrasts with traditional conservatism and its internal paradoxes – has given the modern British Conservative Party a schizophrenic character which it may have to resolve under new leadership; and, even if it does, it must win back an electorate which has increasingly come to question both tradition and reaction.

Parliamentary Government

A CONSTITUTIONAL ARRANGEMENT (E.G. THE UK) WHERE THE EXECUTIVE IS APPOINTED from within, and is subordinate and accountable to, the legislature – as distinct from a 'presidential system' (e.g. the USA) which advocates separation of the legislative and executive powers. Hence, in parliamentary government, the executive is not directly elected by, nor directly accountable to, the voters.

THE MAIN OVERLAP IN THE BRITISH POLITICAL SYSTEM IS BETWEEN THE LEGISLATURE – the law-making body, known as Parliament (comprising the Crown, Commons and Lords) – and the executive – the government, that is, the policy-making body (comprising the Crown, prime minister, senior Cabinet ministers and other junior ministers). The term 'parliamentary government' refers to this overlap, or fusion, between Parliament and government: the executive is chosen from within the legislature (from both MPs and peers), and is, in theory, subordinate and accountable to the legislature. *'The efficient secret of the English constitution may be described as the close union, the nearly complete fusion, of the executive and legislative powers'* (Bagehot 1867). The choice of government depends upon the strength of party representation and continued support in terms of seats and votes in the House of Commons. For example, an important convention of the constitution is that, if a government is defeated in a vote of no confidence by the House of Commons, it should resign (as last occurred in the UK in 1979). Government is also responsible – i.e. accountable – to Parliament through Question Time, debates, votes, committees, and financial scrutiny. Thus, through its link with Parliament – and especially with the elected House of Commons – Britain is said to have both representative and responsible government. The office of

The Houses of Parliament

head of government is separate from that of head of state (which, in the UK, is a monarch, but in other countries, such as Ireland, may be a president). The prime minister in the UK depends for his or her political survival, not directly upon the voters, but upon his or her majority in the Commons and, above all, upon his or her party; witness Thatcher's forced removal by her party in 1990 despite her comfortable majority in the Commons. The voters had no say in the process of her removal and replacement as both party leader and prime minister. Finally, according to UK constitutional theory, Britain operates a system of collective Cabinet government where the prime minister is *primus inter pares* – first among equals (although clearly, in reality, he or she is much more than that).

In this system of parliamentary government, the main functions of Parliament are to scrutinise and legitimise the detail and passage of (usually government) laws, to supervise and approve the government's raising and spending of money, to represent the voters through election and especially in any conflicts with the executive, and to provide a forum of debate on the issues of the day.

This 'Westminster model' provided by the 'mother of parliaments' in the UK has been widely copied by other liberal democracies such as India, New Zealand and Australia, largely as a consequence of Britain's imperial bequest.

The United States and many other countries, by contrast, have a presidential system. This (confusingly) does not refer to the fact that they have a president and Britain does not. It means that their system follows the principle of the separation of legislative and executive powers, as advocated by the liberal Montesquieu (1748). Thus, in the USA, the executive – the president – is separately elected from Congress (the US legislature), is outside of the legislature and is in theory equal to the legislature with mutual checks and balances. The president is elected for a fixed term and does not have the power to dissolve the legislature and call a general election. The head of government in the USA – the president – is also head of state, and is directly accountable to the voters rather than being indirectly accountable through the legislature. He is therefore much less dependent upon his party than is a British prime minister. Finally, his Cabinet, both in constitutional theory and in practice, are mere advisers, not collective policy makers.

These are fairly 'pure' examples of parliamentary and presidential systems. There may also be hybrids. For example, in France, while executive ministers may run for parliamentary office, if they become members of the government they do not sit in the legislature but appoint deputies to perform their legislative functions. Again, in Israel in 1992, the prime minister was directly elected by the voters, although the Knesset (legislature) retained the right to dismiss him. Such systems may be described as 'semi-presidential'.

Evaluation of the Idea

IN A PARLIAMENTARY SYSTEM, MEMBERSHIP OF PARLIAMENT IS WIDELY HELD TO BE A crucial factor in legitimising government ministers themselves – otherwise, since they are not directly elected, they have no democratic mandate whatsoever. However, in 1998, Prime Minister Blair appointed his friend, and Scottish media tycoon, Gus MacDonald as a junior industry minister although he was neither an MP nor a peer, breaching the key rule that government ministers should be chosen from within Parliament. (MacDonald was belatedly given a peerage by Blair.) This was one small but significant example of how easily the conventions of the British constitution can be bent and broken.

The original intention behind the parliamentary system of government in the UK – combined with the first-past-the-post system of election – was to ensure a stable and workable government which could pursue its mandate and enact the proposals promised in its manifesto. The government's dependence on Parliament, meanwhile, was intended to ensure that it remained representative and accountable.

However, since the nineteenth century, the party system has become entrenched and party discipline has become intense. This has led to a situation where Parliament tends to be dominated by a single-party 'majority' government in terms of seats but not votes which, with party discipline and strong backbench support, can usually ensure that its legislative proposals are passed by Parliament – even if they were not in the governing party's manifesto and even if they are clearly unpopular.

In his 1976 Dimbleby Lecture, the Conservative politician Lord Hailsham therefore coined the term 'elective dictatorship' to suggest that a majority government, in control of a sovereign Parliament, with a flexible constitution, could effectively change the constitution at will. He was, paradoxically, writing and speaking at a time when the British government was at its weakest for decades, with little or no majority (hence its defeat on a vote of no confidence in 1979). His thesis gained renewed strength during the Thatcher governments of the 1980s and especially after the general election of 1997, when Labour won a massive 179 majority of seats over all of the other parties combined in the House of Commons (on a minority of the votes cast) and seemed, to many critics, virtually unstoppable. Thus, for example, within its first year in office

Labour had pushed through many unpopular policies which were not in its manifesto, such as lone parents' benefit cuts, disabled people's benefit cuts, students' tuition fees, a five-year public sector pay squeeze, giving the Bank of England independence to set interest rates, increasing taxation of pension funds etc. The government forced through the introduction of the closed party list system for EU elections, by invoking the Parliament Act, despite a record six rejections by the Lords. They also killed off Michael Foster's private members' Bill against fox hunting – arguably a minor example of an 'unconstitutional' action, since private members' Bills should be no concern of the government. They guillotined the Amsterdam Treaty, Welfare Reform Bill, Employment Relations Bill, Asylum Bill, Criminal Justice Bill curbing jury trial, Football (Disorder) Bill which passed through Parliament in a fortnight, Police (Northern Ireland) Bill and the Greater London Authority Bill (to which they had added over 800 amendments!). They even guillotined a debate about hot-dog vendors in royal parks. As the Labour backbench MP Austin Mitchell once wrote, trying to control the executive was '*as useful as heckling a steamroller*' (contribution to a Durham University Union Society Debate, November 2001).

The (rare) exceptions to this balance of power within Parliament are: a backbench revolt – for example, the second VAT rise on domestic fuel, 1996; defeat by the House of Lords – for example, Section 28, 2001; or a minority government – for example, the Conservatives, April 1997. It is significant that the last successful backbench revolt on a policy issue in the Commons was in 1996 and that, despite many large revolts, Labour has never been defeated in the Commons since 1997. The Lords have often voted against the government since 1997, but they are weak and their defeats are generally easily reversed by the Commons. For example, the government invoked the rarely used Parliament Act 1949 to push through the lowering of the gay age of consent to 16. No majority government has been forced to resign by a vote of no confidence in the House of Commons since 1880. The last successful vote of no confidence was against James Callaghan's minority Labour government in 1979.

However, such minority-seat governments are very rare in the UK, given its non-proportional (first-past-the-post) system of election – despite the fact that no government since the 1930s has had a majority of votes cast; for example, Labour in 2001 gained 63 per cent of the seats in the Commons on just 41 per cent of the votes cast (on a record low turnout of 59 per cent). This, combined with Britain's flexible constitution – where major changes can be enacted by a one-vote majority in the Commons – together with the strength of party discipline in the nominally 'sovereign' Commons and the weakness of the second chamber – all compound the likelihood of elective dictatorship in the UK.

(The phrase has increasingly – and wrongly – been used to advance a critique of 'prime ministerial government' in the UK. Hailsham never referred specifically to the power of prime ministers in his lecture, only to the overweening power of the executive as a whole over Parliament. For Hailsham, as for Bagehot a century earlier, real power rested in the Cabinet as a whole, that collective body which has no formal constitutional recognition or role at all.) '*So the sovereignty of Parliament has increasingly become, in practice, the sovereignty of the Commons, and the sovereignty of the Commons has increasingly become the sovereignty of the government which, in addition to its influence in Parliament, controls the party whips, the party machine and the civil service.*' (Hailsham 1976).

There has thus been growing concern and criticism that Parliament is being increasingly sidelined and bypassed by an excessively powerful executive. Hence John Major – among many others – has accused Blair and the present Labour government of *'dumbing down British politics, putting style over substance and riding roughshod over Parliament'*, and veteran Labour backbencher Tony Benn announced (in July 1999) that he would stand down as an MP at the next election *'to spend more time in politics'*.

The American presidential system, by contrast, was designed to ensure checks and balances between the separate institutions of state so that no one body could become overweeningly powerful. The opposite problem arises here: the legislature is elected at a different time and in a different way from the executive, and it is quite possible that the opposition party may control either or both houses of the legislature, creating potential gridlock, or stalemate.

It is a matter of debate whether an unduly weak executive is preferable to an unduly strong one. Liberal democratic theory fears the latter most of all. Reforms which would reduce the likelihood of elective dictatorship in the UK include an electoral system of proportional representation (PR) for the Commons, a directly elected and strengthened second chamber, weaker party discipline or, indeed, a wholesale separation of powers. Of course, only the government of the day is in a position to enact such reforms – and it seems unlikely that any 'majority' government will tie its own hands in such a way. Labour's earlier enthusiasm for PR and a democratic second chamber, for example, has conspicuously cooled since it won such large majorities in the last two general elections.

Politics

NARROWLY, THE THEORY, STUDY OR PRACTICE OF THE ART OF GOVERNMENT AND STATE; broadly, the practice or reconciliation of factionalism, disputes and divisions, whether in family, work and other sub-state institutions or in government. Originally a term of abuse against those involved in factionalism, but now largely a neutral or positive term for various forms of governance and 'democratic' representation.

THE MOST BASIC DICTIONARY DEFINITION OF POLITICS DEFINES IT AS '*THE ART AND science of government*' or '*pertaining to the state and its affairs*'. This definition suggests that politics is simply the exercise of decision making in relation to public policy. Politicians are thus statesmen – power-holders employed by the state to make or legislate upon decisions of policy. Politics may also be slightly more widely defined as the exercise of activities concerned with the acquisition or exercise of power – which may range from electioneering to terrorism – or as the organisational principles and processes affecting such power. Politics is not only concerned with the nature of the rulers but also with the role of the state: how extensive its remit should be, what rights citizens may have against it and what relations may, and should, exist between states.

'*The study of politics is the study of influence and the influential*' (Laswell 1958). As so often, the root of the concept goes back to ancient Greece (*polis* meaning city state). The study of politics is sometimes labelled 'political science' – widely believed to be a modern concept but, in fact, Aristotle called it the 'queen' of sciences. Politics as governance has been studied since the days of Plato, who queried how rulers should be selected, what skills they should have and what obligations they should be able to impose upon their subjects. His pupil, Aristotle, examined different systems of rule and distinguished between 'tyranny' (rule by a single individual), 'oligarchy' (rule by the few) and 'democracy' (rule by the many). He was a vigorous critic of the latter.

However, politics may be further defined as the espousal of a particular set of ideas, principles or commitments in relation to public policy decisions (widely applied in the modern day as 'party politics'). This suggests that politics is about taking sides and advocating a partisan perspective. Politicians, undoubtedly, are widely perceived as partisan players in the public power, or party political, game. Voters, too, demonstrate political behaviour in this sense – widely studied by psephologists – whenever they cast their votes. The cynical view is that *'Politics, as a practice, whatever its professions, has always been the systematic organisation of hatreds'* (Henry Brooks Adams, quoted in Simpson 1996). The ultimate expression of politics as partisanship and conflict is that of politics as war – as stated by one of the most famous quotations in the history of political theory: *'War is nothing but the continuation of politics with the admixture of other means'* (Clausewitz 2000).

Below the level of state, however, phrases such as 'office politics' and 'family politics' make the same reference to conflict and partisanship. The golden rule that politics – like football and religion – should not be discussed at the dinner table, is assuming this concept of politics as argument and antagonism. In fiction, the perfectly rational Houyhnhnms of Swift's *Gulliver's Travels* demonstrated an ideal of the apolitical – that is, non-political – consensus. In sum, the diverse definitions boil down to politics as power and politics as conflict.

Evaluation of the Idea

THE FOCUS OF MOST POLITICAL PHILOSOPHY THROUGHOUT HISTORY HAS BEEN THE state, from the ancient city state to the modern nation state; and the origins, power, authority and functions of the state, together with its relations to the individuals within and under it in terms of mutual rights and obligations. *'We wish to understand by politics only the leadership of a political association, hence today, of a state'* (Weber 1948). Politics as power was, for centuries, held to be a purely public phenomenon, associated with the institutions of state and government. In the UK, for example, politics today is widely held to be enacted at Westminster and Whitehall, and perhaps more broadly by closely attached parties and pressure groups.

However, radical feminism, which emerged in the 1960s, fundamentally redefined the politics of power to apply it to the private sphere of home and family in the form of patriarchy – male dominance. They argued that 'the personal is political': personal, family and sexual relationships are, themselves, inherently political and power relationships, and they are also the underpinning causal factors of wider, patriarchal, political and economic power structures throughout society. This analysis has redefined and extended the concept of power politics for the last three generations. Orthodox, even male, liberal students of politics have followed suit and extended their definitions: for example, *'A political system is any persistent pattern of human relationships that involves, to a significant extent, control, influence, power or authority'* (Dahl 1984). Similarly, Leftwich (1983), argues that politics is a universal feature of human life, involving both cooperation and conflict over essential resources, not just within the state and its operations but also within and between all human groups, both formal and informal.

Philosophies such as Marxism and anarchism believe in the ultimate 'end of politics' as the end of both coercion and conflict, at both state and personal level, to be replaced by spontaneous harmony when economic exploitation is eradicated and the state is abolished. This is clearly a utopian vision – which is not necessarily to say that it is impossible, but that it is very idealistic.

To study politics, one does not have to be a 'political animal' (to use Aristotle's phrase) – that is, one does not have to be committed to any particular set of ideological beliefs, cause or party. This statement highlights the two fundamentally different usages of the concept of politics: first, politics as governance or power and, secondly, politics as partisan commitment or conflict. Thus 'political motivation' may suggest either the desire for power or the desire to pursue and promote a cause – or both. For 'non-ideological' politicians such as Tony Blair, it may suggest merely the former.

Some textbooks define the concept of politics in very narrow ideological terms: for example, Baker (1986) contrasts 'politics' with both 'totalitarianism' (as autocracy) and 'democracy' (as universal suffrage), defining politics as *'A belief in government by consent, the recognition and acceptance of diversity, the recognition that the field with which government may concern itself is limited, a belief in more open government and the rule of law'* (Baker 1986: 11–14). What he is describing is not politics, but liberal idealism. This is precisely an example of the application of politics in the sense of partisan ideology – which does not, of course, even recognise itself as such.

Baker is partially echoing Bernard Crick's earlier definition of politics as *'The activity by which differing interests within a given unit of rule are conciliated by giving them a share in power in proportion to their importance to the welfare and the survival of the whole community'* (Crick 1964). This is also what Bismarck (see Feuchtwanger 2002) and Rab Butler (see Howard 1987) meant when they defined politics as *'the art of the possible'*. They all accept the concept of politics as persuasion, bargaining and decision making but not as sheer force; holding a gun to someone's head is not, from these perspectives, engaging in a political relationship with that person. These views are all, essentially, defining politics as conflict resolution; again, a limited and partisan – liberal – definition, which resolutely refuses to recognise politics as conflict without resolution (is the Middle East situation not political?), or politics as the pursuit of purely sectional interest, or politics as pure power. It may be more valid to define politics as the search for conflict resolution, but even this is only one, partial and still partisan, definition. (When Hitler defined and pursued politics in racial terms as *'The art of carrying out the life struggle of a nation for its earthly existence'*, he was not seeking conflict resolution, but he was surely engaging in politics.)

Another 'positive', liberal – that is, ideological – definition of politics was advanced by Strauss (1959): that it sought either to change society for the better or to preserve it against change for the worse. Either way, by this definition, politics is purposive human action guided by an understanding of the good society and political action is moral action. *'Political philosophy is the attempt to truly know both the nature of political things and the right, or the good, political order'*, said Strauss. Bertrand Russell's scornful response was, *'The collection of prejudices which is called political philosophy is useful provided that it is not called philosophy'* (in *The Observer*, 1962).

Such positive definitions of politics are based upon a consensual view of society which assumes that there is a common good and the potential for a common understanding. Such views contrast with conflict theories such as Marxism, which – far from seeing politics as conflict resolution – argue that only the 'end of politics' will ensure genuine harmony.

Ask those who are not involved in politics as state governance what politics is about, and they will often reply that it is a dirty business – about sleaze, corruption, political or financial self-interest and the pursuit of other sectional interests which are perceived as simply dishonest. (Consider the second verse of the UK national anthem: *'Confound their politics, Frustrate their knavish tricks . . .'*.) They would agree with Isaac D'Israeli's cynical definition of politics as *'The art of governing mankind by deceiving them'* (quoted in Ogden 1969). The reputation of politics as state power is not high. When UK Education Secretary Estelle Morris voluntarily resigned in 2002 because, as she candidly admitted, she simply felt that she was not good enough at her job, the response of almost universal astonishment was most telling. Interestingly, voters often, also, express a dislike of 'unnecessary' political conflict and argument 'for the sake of it'; even the concept of modern 'party politics' is widely pejorative. Politics in every sense – as power, conflict and partisanship – is increasingly tarnished. Its sheer moral character is increasingly questioned. There is a growing feeling that politics should be left to non-politicians – that is, non-partisans and non-professionals. Hence the rise in unorthodox forms of political participation and direct action by non-governmental organisations, pressure groups and protesters in, for example, anti-capitalist and anti-globalisation demonstrations which are, themselves, often seen as 'anti-political'.

However, for good or bad, politics matters – whether as power or as conflict – because it is a daily reality which, in both senses, shapes all of our lives and determines all of our futures. It is not a purely theoretical concept, it is daily practice – either as power or as conflict, either at the state or at the personal level – and we are all both its subjects and its players.

Power

The Idea

THE ABILITY TO ACT, OR TO MAKE OTHERS ACT, BASED UPON THE CAPACITY TO COERCE and compel obedience. Power may take various forms – economic, political, military, social, personal etc. – and is a matter of degree. If it is based upon legitimate consent it is defined as authority, but power rests upon control and coercion, that is, the ability to reward and punish, regardless of consent. It is closely related to sovereignty: the principle of ultimate power and authority.

Development of the Idea

POWER IS THE ABILITY TO MAKE DECISIONS, TO ACT, OR TO GET OTHERS TO DO something through the threat or use of sanctions – rewards or punishments, even force or violence. It implies coercion rather than consent. The primary concept of power is understood as decision making: in terms of state, law making or policy making. However, if farmers or water workers can cut off the supply of food or water, that, too, is power; whereas a persuasive publicity campaign by Comic Relief or CND is simply influence. 'Influence' is persuasive effect upon others' ideas or actions; it may or may not be intended, organised or even consciously perceived, but it is based on respect or agreement (whether reasoned or unreasoned), and is therefore closer to authority than to power. Authority is the ability to act, or to make others act, because they believe that one has the right to do so – that is, it is legitimate power based upon consent and respect. Authority may derive, not only from election, but also from tradition, knowledge and experience, rules and principles, sheer personality or from simply giving people what they want and thereby winning their support. However, power-mongers despise such appeals to consent: *'Guns will make us powerful; butter will only make us fat'* (the German Nazi, Hermann Goering, radio broadcast, 1936).

The legalistic definition of *de jure* power – permission under law – should be distinguished from *de facto* power. Such 'naked' power is the ability to exact compliance without consent or legitimacy. Technically, it is different from 'force' or 'violence', which may (or may not) be wielded in support of authority – for example, the imprisonment of a criminal or the spanking of a child by a parent. 'Pure' power – that is, imposed will – may be entirely peaceful or even pacifist: for example, Gandhi's non-violent resistance to British rule in India. Power is based either upon autonomy – that is, the ability to act wholly independently and without regard for the actions of others – or it is based upon sanctions, that is, the ability to reward or punish. There are diverse types of power: economic, such as the ability to direct capital; legal, such as the ability to pass or enforce laws; military, such as the ability to direct an army or weapons of mass destruction; or purely personal, such as bullying. The epitome of power is the lawless gang which rampages through the streets generating fear and terror, or – at national level – the brutal military junta or rebel militia men who impose arbitrary violence and death, such as in Sierra Leone throughout the 1990s.

The most renowned theorist of power politics was Machiavelli, who argued that the primary goal of politics was the supreme control of the people within a given territory for the sake of the wider power and status of that territory – that is, *raison d'état* – the fundamental justification for sovereign statehood. Consent, law, justice and rights were irrelevant except insofar as subjects' belief in them formed the basis of further powers to be manipulated by the sovereign. Hobbes (1651), too, asserted that the primary human urge was *'power after power'*. 'Power politics' is now an emotive, and usually negative, phrase used to describe, primarily, an approach to international relations based purely upon the calculations of relative power and self-interest employed by the decision-makers responsible for international and foreign policy. This is closely related to the concept of realpolitik: a pragmatic, self-seeking approach to international state politics. However, the phrase 'power politics' may also be applied to domestic politics or, indeed, the office, school, family and other sub-state institutions.

Modern 'democratic' states claim legitimate authority rather than power over their members, but that claim is often disputed – most notably by anarchist theorists, who regard all states as inherently oppressive and coercive of freedom

The American sociologist C. Wright Mills (1956) coined the term 'power elite' to describe what he perceived as a unified body of privileged and self-interested power holders at the top of modern, industrialised, supposedly liberal democratic societies such as the USA. This elite comprised the top economic decision-makers, politicians, military personnel, bureaucrats, media owners and even church leaders. They might superficially seem divided and pluralistic but, in reality, said Mills, their common interests outweighed their conflicts and they formed *'an intricate set of overlapping cliques sharing decisions having at least national consequences'*. This power hierarchy, he said, negates the possibility of genuine representative democracy because the power elite serves only its own, minority, interests.

Evaluation of the Idea

T HE VERY DEFINITION OF POWER IS PROBLEMATIC. STEPHEN LUKES (1974) IDENTIFIED three dimensions to power. First, the one-dimensional view: at its simplest, power suggests the ability of one person to make another do something which he does not want to do, or to dictate whose decisions prevail in a situation of conflict (e.g. the teacher who puts a student in detention). The two-dimensional view focuses on both decision making and non-decision making: the latter implying either agenda-setting and preventing others from making decisions (e.g. parents censoring their children's Internet access), or the issue of potential power, which a person may have but choose not to use (e.g. the wife and mother who could – but does not – withdraw her family services at any time). The three-dimensional view concerns the ability to manipulate others' preferences: if one person can make another want something, or want to do something, that – presumably – is power. An advertising agency once defined its mission as 'revealing to consumers their latent wants' – for such unnecessaries as Pot Noodles or Odour Eaters – implying that we do not realise what we truly want until it is revealed to us by the powers of persuasion.

On a much more serious political level, this raises Hobbes' concept of the people giving their willing consent to surrender power to the absolute 'leviathan' – that is, all-powerful – state. The idea of humans consenting to coercion has always deeply troubled liberals. It implies either that the liberal concept of human rationality and autonomy is simply false – that is, that their basic assumptions about human nature are wrong – or that humans are so susceptible to the manipulations of authority and power that their essential nature is irrelevant.

What are the sources of power? Can it be purely personal and autonomous – e.g. the capacity to survive in a wilderness – with no relationship to other humans? Is a secret elite, which manages to avoid attack, powerful or powerless? There is also the problem of how to measure power – for example, competing types or conflicting sources of power, such as political versus economic or military. Finally, to use the concept of power at all is to assume a natural set of preferences which people would possess if no external impositions existed. Given some individuals' personal or sexual desire for pain and punishment, however, it is sometimes difficult to distinguish between genuine coercion, created wants and the innate psychological desire to be dominated.

These questions are real because modern theories of power, such as those discussed above, depend upon the answers. The most cynical theories of contemporary state-hood argue that modern day politics has simply been the – largely successful – attempt to convert the reality of naked and usurped power into the widespread perception of legitimate authority. Saddam Hussein's 100 per cent support in Iraq's 2002 presidential referendum was one example; George W. Bush's dubious presidential victory in the USA in 2000 was another; and the UK Labour government's 'landslide' victory in 2001 with just 24 per cent of the total electorate's votes was yet another.

'Pure' power, divorced from genuine authority, produces repressive regimes characterised by violence, disorder and instability. However, even if we think we have an intuitive appreciation of the concept of power, it is seldom value-free. It can take many forms, and it can be exercised for good or for evil. In the end, however, politics is so frequently defined as the exercise of power that this concept is one of the most important in the field. Students of politics are students of power: the who, how, why, where and when.

Liberals – and modern liberal democratic states – are deeply ambivalent about the concept of power. On the one hand, they are wary of it because it is a corrupting influence upon self-seeking humans, both at state and at personal level. They therefore advocate power in pluralist form, that is, as divided and competitive, in order to impose limits upon it. On the other hand, for liberals, power – especially in the form of the state – is necessary precisely to curb the selfish and aggressive instincts of the individuals within and under the state, as well as to mediate relations between states. So, on the one hand, we have Lord Acton's classic dictum that *'Power tends to corrupt, and absolute power corrupts absolutely'*; and, on the other hand, one of the most liberal of all US presidents saying, with reference to foreign policy, *'Speak softly and carry a big stick'* (Theodore Roosevelt, speech, 1901).

In modern liberal democracies, a further central dispute about the exercise of power is whether it is genuinely pluralist or elitist. Critics of C. Wright Mills' theory of a single, self-serving power elite include liberals who argue that the power hierarchy comprises many diverse and truly competing elites who, between them, represent the diverse interests throughout society and are therefore a buttress of pluralist democracy. Mills' response would be that liberals focus on the apparent diversity of institutional power bases – economic, political, military etc. – but that they ignore the coalition of interests between these power groups and their consequent, common privileges and benefits of wealth, income, power and status. Marxists criticise Mills' theory for its focus on narrowly defined political elites rather than upon broader economic classes and interests. For Marxists, politicians are merely agents of an economic ruling class whose interests will always triumph until there is social revolution.

Liberal and socialist critics of power politics wish to see it replaced by considerations of international law, social justice or ethics in foreign policy. The UK's 'new' Labour government came to power in 1997 with a professed commitment to an ethical foreign policy, implying that economic and political profit and international power politics would take second place to considerations of right and wrong and international social justice. Opponents argue that, in areas such as arms sales, environmental policy, world poverty and pure international realpolitik – for example, in relation to Iraq – this has not happened.

Anarchists, Marxists and even some liberals argue that, as long as the world is divided into sovereign states, there is no alternative to power politics and it is, at best, self-deceiving – and, at worst, dishonest – to pretend otherwise.

Marxists and anarchists further argue that – especially in the modern era of mass society, mass media and mass socialisation – power can take the form of manipulation of minds and control of thought in the form of 'ideology'. This renders the concepts of power and authority virtually indistinguishable and inseparable, because it implies that we do not know and cannot recognise the difference between what we are compelled to do, what we are persuaded to do, what we think we want to do – and what we truly and autonomously desire. Odour Eaters, anyone?

Racialism/Racism

The Idea

THE PERCEPTION THAT HUMANS CAN MEANINGFULLY BE CATEGORISED INTO ETHNIC or biological castes and that these groups can be ranked in a hierarchy which has economic, political, social and/or psychological significance. Racial theories are perceived as 'right-wing' because they invariably advocate hierarchy. Textbooks and dictionaries differ on whether 'racialism' and 'racism' are conceptually different.

Development of the Idea

THE TERMS 'RACIALISM' AND 'RACISM' ARE OFTEN USED INTERCHANGEABLY AND, WHERE they are not, dictionaries and textbooks differ on their precise definitions. 'Racialism' usually suggests simple prejudice, not necessarily linked to any systematic theory. 'Racism' implies a developed theory of biological difference and hierarchy justifying patterned racial discrimination, separation, exile, extermination or genocide.

Thus it can range from simple prejudice against particular groups based on perceived ethnic characteristics and physiognomy, through active discrimination – whether informal and personal, or systematised and legalised throughout a political system – to political end goals such as racial separation (e.g. South African apartheid) or genocide (e.g. the 'final solution' of German Nazism). South Africa is the outstanding recent – that is, post-war – example of a state whose entire economic, legal, political and social relations were structured principally around perceived racial criteria.

Basic ethnic prejudice may be centuries old (see, for example, Shakespeare's *Othello*), but systematic theories of racism were first developed in the nineteenth century by, for example, self-styled 'Count' Arthur de Gobineau, and Houston Chamberlain, who perverted the biological theory of Darwinism to legitimise the era of European imperialism. Gobineau perceived three races – white, yellow and black – in descending order of cultural superiority. Chamberlain developed his anti-Semitic theories out of the anti-Judaism of Kant and Hegel. In the 1960s, psychologists such as Arthur Jensen took up their ideas and attempted (unsuccessfully) to establish a correlation between race and intelligence.

Racism is often assumed to be simply 'colour prejudice'; for example, one basic textbook defines it purely as the assertion of *the inferiority of black people in comparison to white people*' (Joyce 2001). However, this reflects the socialisation of the author more than anything else. For one thing, colour prejudice may, of course, be anti-white: for example, the 1960s' American Black Power movement: *'It's just like when you've got coffee that's too black, which means it's too strong. What do you do? You integrate it with cream, you make it weak . . . It used to wake you up, now it puts you to sleep.'* (Malcolm X, 1962).

Elements of Rastafarianism may also be racist against whites. Rastafarianism is a black religious and sociopolitical movement which originated in Jamaica in the 1930s as a form of anti-colonial nationalism. It regards its ultimate homeland as Ethiopia (Zion) and the former emperor of Ethiopia, Haile Selassie, as the divine Ras Tafari. Decadent white society is known as Babylon and ganja (cannabis) is used as a sacrament to achieve spiritual enlightenment. The more radical adherents of Rastafarianism advocate black separatism and may be virulently anti-white. The heritage of imperialism runs deep.

However, racism need not be based on skin colour at all – for example, the Nazi movement in Germany in the 1930s was essentially pro-Aryan and anti-Semitic, that is, anti-Jewish, regardless of colour or nationality.

Racism has long been used to justify and legitimise economic and political power and control by one group over others, often in the form of imperialism and conquest. The nineteenth and early twentieth centuries were characterised by capitalist imperialism, where the northern, white, European states rationalised their conquest of black African countries with reference to pseudo-scientific theories of social or racial Darwinism and to 'the white man's burden' – the assertion that superior whites had a missionary duty to civilise the blacks. The British poet, Rudyard Kipling (1899), put it most famously: *'Take up the White Man's burden – send forth the best ye breed – go bind your sons to exile to serve your captives' need; to wait in heavy harness, on fluttered folk and wild – your new-caught, sullen peoples, half-devil and half-child'.*

Even by the turn of the twentieth century, however, there were critics of such arguments: for example, Edward Morel, a British journalist in the Belgian Congo, who wrote in 1903, *'It is the Africans who carry the "black man's burden" . . . What the partial occupation of his soil by the white man has failed to do . . . what the Maxim and the rifle, the slave gang, labour in the bowels of the earth and the lash, have failed to do; what imported measles, smallpox and syphilis have failed to do; whatever the overseas slave trade failed to do, the power of modern capitalistic exploitation, assisted by modern engines of destruction, may yet succeed in accomplishing . . . It kills not the body merely, but the soul . . . This is a crime which transcends physical murder.'*

Contemporary examples of racism in Western Europe are usually variants of neo-Nazism – for example, Jean Marie Le Pen's National Front in France and the British National Party. They target any convenient ethnic minority such as blacks and Asians, but especially immigrants and asylum seekers, blaming them for crime, social unrest and indigenous unemployment (although the UK, for example, currently takes just 1.98 per cent of the world's refugees).

The concepts of racism and nationalism are sometimes seen as synonymous and used interchangeably – especially by racist groups such as those above, seeking to legitimise their ideas under the cloak of nationalism – but they are quite different concepts. Nationalism entails a sense of group identity based upon common culture, that is, external factors such as language, religion, customs and history – invariably with territorial claims; whereas racism is a perception of innate biological traits by which humans can be classified and ranked hierarchically. Nationalism need not entail any sense of superiority, and racism need have no territorial claims. According to the contemporary writer Anthony Smith, the two concepts diverged out of the common root concept of 'ethnicity' during the period of industrialisation, with the collapse of traditional village and tribal loyalties. The two concepts may overlap in practice. Smith (1986) posits a continuum from pure nationalism, such as the Welsh or the Basques; through racial-nationalism, such as Rastafarianism; and then national-racism, such as Japan in the 1930s; to pure racism, such as the Ku Klux Klan. Nationalism is much more flexible and adaptable, and therefore more prevalent, than is racism.

Evaluation of the Idea

RACISM IS WIDELY HELD TO BE A SOCIAL CONSTRUCTION; THAT IS, CENTURIES OF interbreeding mean that racial differences are slight in biological and genetic terms and there is no objective evidence that they form the basis for valid economic, political, social or psychological stratification. However, perceptions of racial difference matter insofar as they have significant economic, social and political consequences.

There is disagreement about the root causes of racism. It tends to develop most vigorously in a climate of economic recession, insecurity and instability when people may be in acute competition for jobs or may be searching for a scapegoat to blame for their economic ills. Marxist theory argues that capitalism generates racism, first, by encouraging immigration during periods of economic growth to provide unskilled and semi-skilled labour, and then by fomenting racial prejudice in times of economic decline to cut across and prevent the development of working class consciousness. Subsequent problems such as unemployment or low wages generate conflict within the working class between different ethnic groups and so hinder any sense of class solidarity against a common bourgeois enemy or economic system. Although this analysis still holds good today, the nineteenth century was the period most clearly characterised by capitalist imperialism, where the northern, white, European states rationalised their conquest of black African countries with reference to pseudo-scientific theories of racial Darwinism and to 'the white man's burden'. Other factors which may sustain racism include religion (e.g. anti-Islamic sentiment in the West is increasingly exhibiting racist traits, especially since the September 2001 attacks on America); populist right-wing politicians (e.g. in 2002, Conservative leader Iain Duncan Smith felt obliged to sack shadow frontbencher Ann Winterton for making a racist 'joke'); self-inflicted or forced ghettoism, that is, failure to assimilate; ignorance, lack of education and travel etc. Psychological explanations of racism focus on the human need for 'group identity' and the tendency for insecure personalities to develop a 'them and us' perspective to bolster their own self-esteem. The recurrent political impact and success of racism is largely due to its emotional simplicity and its inherent trait of blaming others for the economic, social and psychological failures of the self; hence its appeal to the resentful and insecure who feel ignored, excluded or disadvantaged by mainstream politics or wider society.

Liberal democracies such as the UK experience a profound conflict of values over the issue of racism. On the one hand, tolerance of diverse views – even (or perhaps especially) of those views abhorrent to liberal values – is a central liberal doctrine. On the other hand, liberals find racism so irrational and intolerant that it threatens the very foundations of liberal democratic society. *'Racial hatreds seem to be at the core of the most hideous expression of violent collective emotion'* (Berlin 1990). Thus, racism poses a central liberal dilemma: just how far to tolerate intolerance. No liberal endorses unlimited toleration, either in theory or practice. Most liberal democracies have legislated against racial discrimination (since 1965 in the UK), but their legal attempts to define race and specific races are often, themselves, politically arbitrary – for example, in UK law, Jews are currently deemed a race but Muslims are not. It is therefore still legal to erect a sign in a British public house or place of employment saying, 'No Muslims allowed'. The Labour government sought to prohibit anti-Islamic discrimination in its 2001 anti-terrorism legislation, but the House of Lords blocked it.

The concepts of race and racism are now probably too emotive to be treated with real scientific objectivity; and the recent resurgence of 'sociobiology' (especially in America) – which seeks to explain social behaviour in terms of the comparative biology of its human actors with that of other animals – has been widely attacked as just another form of racism masquerading as pseudo-science: *'A genetic justification of the status quo and of existing privileges for certain groups according to class, race, or sex. Historically, powerful countries or ruling groups within them have drawn support for the maintenance or extension of their power from these products of the scientific community . . . Such theories provided an important basis for the enactment of sterilisation laws and restrictive immigration laws by the United States between 1910 and 1930, and also for the eugenics policies which led to the establishment of gas chambers in Nazi Germany'* (Lewontin 1975).

Representation

❀

The Idea

T HE FEW SPEAKING FOR THE MANY; USUALLY, THE ELECTION OF A SMALL NUMBER OF politicians who will reflect the wishes, interests and/or social background of their voters. Now, most commonly, 'representation' is taken to mean that those elected will carry out the wishes of their voters; but this raises questions of both principle and practicality. Other, broader, interpretations are also still widely used.

Development of the Idea

T HERE ARE DIFFERENT TYPES AND DEGREES OF POLITICAL REPRESENTATION. TECHNI- cally, it means a process whereby the interests or views of many are 'represented' to – argued for and given a platform before – a decision-making body by one or a few people speaking on behalf of the many. It need not mean that the representatives have any decision-making power themselves. Anyone can make representations to a decision maker; for example, many schools and universities have student representa- tives who speak for the students to the ruling educational bodies, but those represen- tatives have little or no decision-making power themselves.

The strongest interpretation of the concept of representative is that of a delegate: an elected power-holder who should act as instructed by his or her voters, thus reflecting, representing and implementing the voters' wishes on every issue. The eighteenth- century political philosopher Rousseau (1762) argued that, if direct democracy was impossible, the next best thing – indeed, the only 'democratic' alternative – was a system of delegates: *'Thus deputies of the people are not, and cannot be, its representa- tives; they are merely its agents, and can make no final decisions. Any law which the people have not ratified in person is null, is not a law'*.

Many trade unions – for example, the National Union of Railwaymen in the UK – send delegates to the Labour party conference who are instructed – 'mandated' – in advance on how to vote on every resolution by the majority votes of their branch members. British MPs, however, do not refer back to their constituents before every vote in the House of Commons; they are not representatives in this sense of the word. In purely practical terms, it is difficult to see how they could be.

A second interpretation of a representative is one who, once elected, serves the interests – rather than the wishes – of the whole nation, as the representative perceives those interests according to his/her own judgement and conscience. This was the proper role of the British MP according to Edmund Burke (1774), eighteenth-century politician, writer and exponent of the philosophy of traditional political conservatism: 'Your representative owes you, not his industry only, but his judgement; and he betrays, instead of serving you, if he sacrifices it to your opinion'.

This interpretation implies that a representative is not, and should not be, typical of the wider population, but that he should be better than them – wiser and more responsible in his political judgement. This is a feature of the traditional conservative theory of 'natural governors', and accords most people only the limited role of voting in their independent representatives. 'Democracy' by this view is not 'people power', but simply a method of selecting an MP or a government.

British MPs were representatives in this Burkean sense until the rise of the party system and the development of strong party discipline in the House of Commons. Nowadays, the opportunities for MPs to use their independent judgement, rather than merely toeing the party line, are rare.

Some argue that politicians should be representative of the people in the sense of being typical of the wider population, that is, from the same social background. In Britain in 2002 – where 60 per cent of MPs went to public school (compared with 5 per cent of the population), under 18 per cent of MPs are women (compared with 52 per cent of the population) and only 12 MPs (under 2 per cent) are black (compared with 7 per cent of the population) – MPs are obviously not representative in this, albeit limited, sense of the word.

Modern British MPs are not, therefore, strictly representative in any of the above senses. They are, of course, representative of the voters in that they are elected by them and hence, to some degree, responsive to their views. Also, since most people at elections vote for a party label and a broad package of party policies rather than for an independent individual, party loyalty by MPs may be an effective way of representing voters' wishes. This ties in with the 'doctrine of the mandate' – the theory that the electors give the government authority, via the ballot box, to implement its party manifesto promises and policies. This doctrine is, of course, only valid if the governing party does adhere to its manifesto promises.

Moreover, in Britain only the House of Commons, the regional assemblies and the local councils (and the British members of the EU Parliament) are directly elected; the government is not. It is indirectly appointed from within Parliament, and most political institutions – the monarchy, House of Lords, civil service, judiciary etc. – are not elected at all. This does not necessarily mean that that they are not representative of the people in any sense of the word – that remains to be discussed – but it is an obvious limitation on Britain's claim to democracy, even by its own, static, definition of the concept.

Evaluation of the Idea

'NO TAXATION WITHOUT REPRESENTATION' WAS THE PRINCIPAL SLOGAN OF THE American Revolution. As democracy came to be regarded as a valued principle and practice from the eighteenth century onwards, it was widely felt that tax-payers should have a voice in politics and a say on how their money was spent. Direct democracy is widely held to be impractical in today's large and complex nation states, and therefore representation through indirect democracy is an alternative method by which public opinion can be involved in political decision making. Representation need not even involve election; traditional conservatives used to favour what they called 'virtual representation', where politicians – including peers in the House of Lords – sought to reflect and protect the interests of the wider society, whether they were elected or not.

In contemporary liberal democracies, however, representation specifically refers to the processes whereby elected politicians reflect the views and interests of their voters, thereby providing a link between government and the governed. The basis of this representation is usually geographical; in the UK, for example, Westminster MPs are elected to represent territorial constituencies, while councillors are elected to represent wards, boroughs and counties. An alternative system is 'functional representation', where legislators (law makers) are elected to represent specific interests. This may take the form of representation through pressure groups rather than parties, where members of promotional (cause) or protective (sectional) groups are chosen and elected into the legislature to represent those interests in Parliament. The Irish Seanad is chosen in this way, and Winston Churchill advocated this form of representation for the second chamber in the UK to replace the House of Lords. However, it raises the question of which of many thousands of such groups should be chosen for representa-tion; and it may be argued that some interest groups – especially the economic ones – are sufficiently powerful and well represented in other ways already.

A key issue is just how representative – in any sense – are our politicians today. The first problem lies in the nature of electoral systems and rules. In the UK, for example, the first-past-the-post electoral system (where a candidate can win a seat on just a simple majority of the votes cast) expects a single MP to represent a whole constituency, although the majority of electors in that constituency may well have voted against him or her. This produces a government which usually has an absolute majority – over 50 per cent – of the seats in the House of Commons, on the votes of perhaps one-third of the total electorate (and, since the 2001 general election, just 24 per cent of the total electorate). Strong party loyalty and party discipline allow this unrepresentative executive to push through laws which may be very unpopular – a situation described by Lord Hailsham in the 1970s as 'elective dictatorship'. The present Labour govern-ment has 63 per cent of the seats in the Commons on just 41 per cent of the votes cast in the 2001 general election – which, with a turnout of only 59 per cent, represents well under one-third of the eligible electorate. In America, the election of George W. Bush as president in 2000 was the result of the very dubious application of flawed electoral mechanisms and laws in the crucial state of Florida.

The second problem relates to the whole doctrine of representation. We often assume that our elected representatives are chosen to implement our views and wishes, but there is no reliable mechanism in place whereby MPs, once elected, can ascertain the views and wishes of their voters. Doubtless those views are, anyway, often changing, diverse and conflicting; how can an MP in a farming constituency reflect the different views of the farmers, farm workers, retailers and consumers within that constituency? Nor can today's MPs be the independent-minded, free agents famously advocated by Burke in the eighteenth century. As Disraeli instructed his MPs a century later, '*Damn your principles! Stick to your party.*' Effectively, voters today are choosing a party label rather than a person (with very rare exceptions, such as the election of independent MP Richard Taylor in the 2001 general election).

The 'doctrine of the mandate' therefore becomes a crucial principle of representative government in modern party politics. A mandate, strictly, is the assent and authority, or even duty, given to the government by the electors to govern along the policy lines indicated in their party manifesto. The doctrine of the mandate thus seeks to ensure that the policies of the government reflect the views of the electorate through the party system. However, voters often do not read manifestos; compressed summaries in the media may not be comprehensive or accurate. More importantly, in casting their vote for a party label, voters cannot pick and choose between specific manifesto policies but must accept them as a 'job lot'; the poll tax, for example, was clearly specified in the Conservative party's 1987 manifesto, but was, equally clearly, deeply unpopular. No government has won 50 per cent of the votes cast since the 1930s and, anyway, governments often do not adhere to their manifestos. They may claim a 'doctor's mandate' to do as they see fit in changing circumstances. The doctrine of the mandate is therefore said by some academic writers to be a myth (Marshall 1971).

This begs the question of what kind of representatives our MPs are, if they are not delegates, nor free agents, nor socio-economically typical of their voters, and if the principle of representation through party is so fluid and flawed. Election seems to be neither a necessary nor a sufficient basis for valid claims to democratic representation. The virtue of election is, rather, that it provides a means by which politicians can be held accountable and, if necessary, replaced periodically, while allowing voters to absolve themselves of responsibility for making daily political decisions.

Rights

The Idea

RIGHTS ARE ENTITLEMENTS. FOR A PHILOSOPHY SUCH AS SOCIALISM, THIS IMPLIES entitlements to various forms of equality. For a philosophy such as liberalism, this implies entitlements to various forms of freedom. For philosophers such as Hobbes, this implies neither equality nor freedom, but security. Rights may therefore be associated with a very strong state, a limited state or a stateless society, and with both left- and right-wing philosophies.

Development of the Idea

RIGHTS ARE ENTITLEMENTS – WHETHER TO ACT IN A CERTAIN WAY OR TO BE TREATED in a certain way. Natural, inalienable or human rights are those to which, according to various philosophers, we are entitled simply by virtue of being human, regardless of the state, society or culture in which we live. Such natural rights are perceived as God-given and are, in effect, pre-legal rights assumed to exist before the sovereign state came into being. The classical liberal John Locke identified the key human rights as 'life, liberty and property'; he intended the concept of natural rights to deny the divine right of kings or the claim of any absolute, arbitrary, political power over individuals, but also to legitimise bourgeois property rights against the masses, who were to be denied even the right to vote.

The early nineteenth-century American President, Thomas Jefferson, a century after Locke, asserted 'life, liberty and the pursuit of happiness' as natural rights; he was also responsible for the celebrated statement of human rights in the American Declaration of Independence (1776): *'We hold these truths to be self-evident, that all men are created equal; that they are endowed by their Creator with certain unalienable rights . . .'*. Jefferson was influenced by the English radical, Thomas Paine, who advocated a republican democracy, popular sovereignty and substantial redistribution of wealth. Paine's widely read *Rights of Man* (1791) defended the aims of the French revolution against Burke's celebrated attack.

Mary Wollstonecraft (1759–97) was the first significant thinker to point out that all such liberal philosophers' references to the 'rights of man' were deliberate and denied women their natural rights and hence, in effect, their membership of humanity. Thus was 'first wave' feminism born. It sought to reduce sexual discrimination primarily through a campaign for equal suffrage. Wollstonecraft argued that women were, like men, essentially rational beings and therefore as capable of self-determination and as deserving of liberty, rights, the vote and, above all, education. Diverse theories of natural rights are, therefore, apparently selective and value-laden; philosophers do not agree about what our natural rights are or to whom they should apply (for example, John Locke supported slavery and a limited electoral suffrage); and, since the concept of natural rights is anyway a purely abstract and metaphysical one, the utilitarian philosopher Jeremy Bentham (1748–1832) famously dismissed it as *'nonsense on stilts'*.

Civil or legal rights are those which are granted and enshrined in law – or at least not prohibited by law – by a particular state at a particular time. They are usually based upon a society's broad philosophical concept of natural rights, and they vary widely from one country and culture to another. Liberal philosophers like Jeremy Bentham and John Stuart Mill asserted the need for individuals to have legal guarantees of protection for certain interests and entitlements. These should (for liberals) preferably be incorporated in a Bill of Rights, that is, a document enshrining in law citizens' entitlements in relation to each other and to the state.

Most contemporary interpretations of rights can broadly be associated with some concept of freedom, or some concept of equality. Liberals stress freedom, while social-ists stress equality.

Freedom, according to the nineteenth-century liberal philosopher T.H. Green, can be classified as either negative or positive. Negative freedom implies freedom from external constraints or barriers, that is, one is simply left alone to succeed or fail on one's own merits. New Right philosophy advocates negative freedom, especially from state help or hindrance, in the economic sphere, that is, a laissez-faire, free market economic system with minimal state intervention. The obvious implication of this is that individuals start out unequally, are equally unhindered in their efforts, and end up unequally according to their merits. Green rejected this concept of negative freedom as merely the potential freedom to be left to starve in the gutter, and instead argued for positive freedom – the actualised capacity to fulfil one's true potential – with state help if necessary.

Similarly, the concept of equality has different dimensions – economic, political, legal and social, or simply the concept of equality of opportunity – and all of these, in turn, have different sub-strands and degrees of interpretation. Western liberal democracies have tended to stress freedom over, or even at the expense of, equality – for example, the freedom to choose between private and state schooling at the expense of equality of educational access and opportunity – which puts them at odds with the more egali-tarian and collectivist, socialist, interpretations of citizenship rights.

For the seventeenth-century philosopher Thomas Hobbes, however, the role of the state was not to provide either freedom or equality, but personal security. He believed that humans were essentially selfish, competitive and aggressive creatures who posed a constant threat to each other – and hence the danger of a *'war of all against all'* – by their pursuit of rampant individualism. Hobbes' solution – unusually for an individualist theorist – was an absolute, sovereign state whose sole authority was to protect the individuals under it. If the state itself threatened any individual citizen's fundamental right of self-preservation – for example, by condemning a criminal to death – then that individual had the absolute right to resist the state. Clearly, however, the theoretical right of resistance is not the same as the actual capacity to resist, especially against such a strong state as Hobbes advocated.

Evaluation of the Idea

WHY ARE HUMANS DESERVING OF RIGHTS? THEORISTS OF NATURAL LAW SUCH AS John Locke maintained that we are all God's creatures and therefore subject to certain constraints in the way that we treat each other, and that these constraints are the basis of our natural and mutual rights. In other words, rights imply duties: first, the duty to respect and protect others' natural rights as much as our own; and secondly, the duty to strive, thrive and make the best of ourselves with the rights we are given.

The idea of rights – usually arising out of the notion of a social contract between citizen and state – used to be mainly a liberal preserve, but nowadays almost all political philosophies espouse some idea of human (or even broader, animal) rights. The main debates, therefore, arise over what rights should be primary and what are their implications, notably for the role of the state. The idea of negative rights – like that of negative freedom – implies that the state (and others) should simply leave us alone to pursue entitlements such as freedom of movement and freedom of speech unconstrained by external restrictions. Positive rights, however, require state intervention and action in the provision of resources such as education or welfare. Social and welfare rights are positive rights, and are most favoured by parliamentary socialists, whereas liberals – especially classical liberals – lean more to the idea of negative rights.

Classical liberals and New Right conservatives criticise notions of positive rights because these imply 'big government' – an interventionist state which is liable to foster a dependency culture, to be costly and restrictive of individuals' personal freedoms, especially the freedom to spend their money as they choose rather than to surrender it in taxes. Socialists, conversely, criticise the idea of negative rights because the end result is likely to be extensive inequality and social injustice.

Liberals and socialists also disagree over the primacy of individual versus collective rights, with socialists favouring community, working class and trade union rights over individual rights. The relatively modern philosophy of nationalism also favours the idea of collective rights, in the form of national self-determination.

Some philosophies, however, reject the very concept of rights, at least in any liberal or parliamentary socialist sense. Utilitarians regard natural rights as abstract, untestable and, therefore, pointless notions. Marxists regard the idea of individual rights within and against the capitalist state as a prime example of bourgeois ideology and false consciousness; there can be no true freedom in an exploitative and alienating economic system. Anarchists, similarly, believe that any notion of rights against any form of coercive state is delusional at best, bogus at worst. Organic theories such as traditional conservatism and fascism largely reject any concept of rights (except property rights), not as untenable, but as undesirable; they favour alternative concepts such as obedience and duty. All of the above, as collectivist philosophies, regard the idea of individual rights as especially dangerous, fostering selfish egoism and under-mining community spirit, solidarity and the common good.

This is a hard concept for liberal democrats to grasp, but even the idea of democracy is not wholly compatible with that of rights. Democracy – literally, 'people power' – is a collectivist concept where the majority may decide to ride roughshod over the rights of individuals and minorities. Conversely, in some countries such as the USA, a Bill of Rights imposes constraints upon the decisions which the majority of the people and their representatives may make. The concept of 'liberal democracy' seeks to reconcile majoritarian rule with the protection of individual rights, but they are not always comfortable bedfellows. For example, is racial discrimination an individual right or a social wrong?

Liberals also have to deal with the problem of conflicting individual rights: for example, a woman's right to choose abortion, versus the right to life of the foetus.

Although Britain claims to be a liberal democracy, historically, rights have not been particularly well protected. (Slavery, for example, was legally abolished only in 1834.) Most Western liberal democracies have a Bill of Rights – a legal safeguard of civil rights, usually entrenched within a codified constitution (as in the USA, where it was incorporated as Amendments 1–10 and overseen by the courts). Until recently, the UK had no such thing.

However, the UK has long been a signatory of the European Convention on Human Rights. This is nothing to do with the EU. It was agreed by the Council of Europe in 1950 (before the EU was even established) and has now been signed by 40 countries. The UK was the first country to ratify it in 1951. The European Court of Human Rights (ECHR) in Strasbourg has ruled against successive British governments on phone tapping by government agencies, corporal punishment in state schools, torture of prisoners in Northern Ireland, press censorship, discrimination against women and ethnic minorities, lengthy detention without charge of prisoners under the anti-terrorism laws, the killing of three unarmed IRA suspects in Gibraltar by the SAS in 1988, discrimination against gays on the age of consent (1997) and many other matters. The 1997 Labour government was first ruled illegal by the ECHR in 1998 for trying to prohibit pressure groups from leafletting the public about parliamentary candidates' personal views on abortion. However, its rulings are not formally binding in the way that EU law is: for example, in 1990 the ECHR ruled illegal the detention without charge of three men over four days under the Prevention of Terrorism Act, but the British government declared that it would simply ignore the ruling.

Therefore, until recently, in Britain few rights were guaranteed in law; such rights as UK citizens had tended to be negative, that is, they were allowed to do something if there was no law against it. However, the Human Rights Act 1998 incorporated the European Convention on Human Rights into UK law, and it came into force in 2000 after British judges had undergone relevant training. Lord Woolf promptly used it to challenge the automatic 'two strikes' life sentences incorporated in the Crime

(Sentences) Act 1997 and to return sentencing discretion to the judiciary. It was also used, for example, to protect the lifelong anonymity of the young killers of toddler Jamie Bulger upon their release from prison.

Given the UK Bill of Right's liberal democratic origins and its need for future bipartisan consensus – that is, its long-term survival depends upon its acceptance by both main parties – it is, necessarily, based upon political and legal, rather than upon social, rights – which the Conservative party would not endorse. British socialists have traditionally rejected the idea of a Bill of Rights for this very reason – because it entrenches individual and property rights against the principles of collectivism and egalitarianism – and also because they feared that it would vest too much power in the hands of unrepresentative and unaccountable judges. Socialists such as Tony Benn would prefer to strengthen the powers of the elected House of Commons to control the executive and to enact specific statutes on clearly defined entitlements for clearly defined groups such as ethnic minorities and the disabled. The fact that 'new' Labour introduced the Human Rights Act 1998 is one indicator of the Labour party's significant shift to the right and to a more liberal agenda since the mid-1990s.

However, there is one major difference between the UK Bill of Rights and that of most other liberal democracies such as the USA. In cases of conflict between the UK Bill of Rights and ordinary parliamentary statute, British judges are required to enforce statute law (to maintain the concept of parliamentary sovereignty); they can only point out any such conflicts to Parliament for possible action – or not. It is therefore much weaker than, for example, the US Bill of Rights, and was easily overridden by Parliament to legislate in 2001 for the indefinite internment, without charge or trial, of suspected foreign terrorists. The UK Bill of Rights also has sweeping exemptions 'In accordance with the law and the necessity for public safety, prevention of disorder or crime, protection of public health or morale or rights and the freedoms of others'. On the plus side, the UK Bill of Rights has prompted more 'rights awareness' in the drafting of laws, in judicial interpretation of those laws and, increasingly, among the general public.

Rule of Law

The Idea

A THEORY OF EQUALITY BEFORE THE LAW (DEVELOPED IN THE UK PARTICULARLY IN THE nineteenth century), implying also that the law should be fair, impartial, consistent and independent of politics. The rule of law is an ideal principle asserting that no-one – not even government and state – should be above the law, which, at the very least, implies an independent and impartial judiciary. It also implies equal access to a fair body of law with no economic or social barriers.

Development of the Idea

THE RULE OF LAW IS A PRINCIPLE OF WESTERN THOUGHT WHICH SEEKS TO EQUATE LAW and justice: everyone should be equally subject to the same, fair, laws. There should be a clear statement of people's legal rights and duties, fair and consistent trial and sentencing, and no arbitrary law or government. There should be formalised procedures that should only be applied when citizens have knowingly broken the law. Justice should be an end in itself and always impartial. Judges should be independent of the wider political system and defendants should be regarded as innocent until proven guilty. These principles should apply equally to governments.

Broadly, the stress is on the generality and neutrality of the rules of state. The rule of law assumes a liberal concept of foundational equality, that humans are of equal moral worth and are thus deserving of equal basic rights and legal treatment.

The rule of law is sometimes asserted as a fact of Western legal systems: liberal jurisprudence tends to claim that the law is a fair, equal, neutral and rational institution which defends individual freedoms equally. Sometimes this assertion is extended to argue that, since fair and equal law is a fact, we all have a moral obligation to obey the law. This includes governments themselves, and therefore embraces the liberal principle of constitutional government.

In the context of the UK, the renowned nineteenth-century Oxford professor of law A.V. Dicey is widely regarded as the high priest of orthodox constitutional thought. He was the first to apply the methodology of legal positivism to the study of English constitutional law. In his *Law of the Constitution* (1885) he asserted three major and beneficial principles which, in his view, underpinned the British constitution: 'regular law' as opposed to the discretionary or arbitrary fiat of officials; proper court jurisdiction of disputes between citizen and state; and citizens' rights protected by ordinary law rather than by a written and rigid constitution.

However, since even these assertions of either fact or desirability are debatable (never mind the more recent and more sweeping interpretations of the rule of law), the concept is best seen as an ideal or statement of principles to which many legal systems, especially liberal ones, may seek to aspire.

Aristotle, in his *Politics*, was probably the first to assert that judicial decisions in particular cases should be based upon previously fixed and general rules to avoid partiality and injustice, that is, to ensure fairness and equity. The rule of law contrasts with the personal whim of a decision-maker – whether judge or dictator, whether benign or despotic – and with arbitrary power as may be practised in a police state. It is explicitly demanded in the American constitution which calls for '*the rule of law and not of men*'. In the UK it is largely grounded in common law.

The rule of law should ensure not only fairness in the treatment of citizens but effective and enforceable limits to the power of state and government. As such, it is a central principle of liberal theory.

Evaluation of the Idea

THE CHIEF ECONOMIC AND SOCIAL HURDLES TO THE MAIN PRINCIPLE OF THE RULE OF law – that is, legal equality – are widely perceived to be sheer cost (as Lord Justice Darling 1992, famously said, '*The law, like the Ritz hotel, is open to all*'), and barriers of class, race and gender. One cynical writer has referred to '*the majestic egalitarianism of the law, which forbids rich and poor alike to sleep under bridges, to beg in the streets and to steal bread*' (France 1927). In the UK, for example, the monarch, MPs and diplomats are exempt from some or all laws; the government's control of the legislative processes in Parliament may effectively put it above the law; judicial or police bias is sometimes alleged (for example, in the Stephen Lawrence case); and stringent limits to legal aid make the cost of litigation prohibitive for many people.

Feminist jurisprudence asserts that the body of law, or at least legal practice, in societies such as the UK and USA, is fundamentally patriarchal and, therefore, that it systematically discriminates against women. To give women genuine – as opposed to nominal – equal rights, either legal practice must be reformed to remove even unconscious bias and injustice or, more fundamentally, the whole body of law must be restructured and rewritten to remove inherent male norms.

The rule of law requires no arbitrary law or government. However, as Machiavelli noted long ago, the rule of law must protect itself from those who would seek to subvert or overthrow it, and it must therefore allow for laws against sedition, treason and terror which – especially in conditions of social instability – tend to be arbitrary, oppressive and violent (in application, if not in writing) – and such laws therefore subvert the rule of law in themselves. The draconian anti-terrorist legislation currently in force in the UK is one obvious example: in 2002, the Court of Appeal upheld the government's right under that law to detain, indefinitely, suspected foreign terrorists without charge or trial. Lord Woolf, the Lord Chief Justice, said that in certain national security situations the government was better able than a court to make decisions about suspects. *'When doing so in the particular context in which this challenge arises, namely a state of public emergency, the court must also recognise that the executive is in a better position than a court to assess both the situation and the action which is necessary to address it.'*

Also, since the constitution and executive power in the UK are based substantially upon convention rather than law, the scope for arbitrary government is especially substantial, in liberal democratic terms.

The rule of law further implies legal certainty – that the law should be clear, knowable and consistent. However, the sheer quantity of law, its many diverse sources in the UK (Westminster, the devolved assemblies, Europe, case law and common law) and its frequent ambiguity, make for much legal uncertainty and even contradiction.

Trial by fair and independent judges and courts of law is another key principle of the rule of law. It assumes a separation of powers which is undermined in the UK by overlaps between the judiciary, legislature and executive – notably in the offices of the Lord Chancellor and the law lords. Thus, for example, the Conservative Lord Chancellor in 1994 pressured judges to cut employment tribunal appeals to save government money. The Labour Lord Chancellor, Lord Irvine, was involved in controversy in 2001 when he asked Labour-supporting lawyers to donate £200 or more to the party – the so-called 'cash for wigs' affair.

Even if they were structurally separate, in the end it is the executive through Parliament in the UK which controls the appointment and dismissal of judges and, indeed, makes, amends and repeals the laws themselves through Parliament, often on a highly partisan, political basis. Since the legislature is sovereign, the judges can only interpret and enforce the laws of Parliament as written, even if those laws are manifestly party political. Former senior judge Lord Denning was noted for his (purely) verbal challenges in court to the 1970s' Labour government's laws on, for example, comprehensive schooling and local government financing. Equally, of course, the judges themselves have sometimes been accused of bias, notably by the left-wing author John Griffith (1991). One example: in 1998, the Law Lords for the first time overruled themselves because of senior judge Lord Hoffman's undeclared Amnesty connection in the Pinochet extradition hearing. Whether this example illustrates or contradicts the traditional judicial stereotype is debatable.

Finally, the rule of law implies that no-one should be subject to legal penalty unless he or she has clearly broken the law – that is, innocent until proven guilty. In the UK, this principle is breached by the practice of remand before trial, the laws of suspicion, the effective removal of the right to silence in the Criminal Justice Act 1994, and 'trial by media' (e.g. the *Daily Mail* in 1997 printing the names and pictures of five unconvicted men as the 'murderers' of black teenager Stephen Lawrence; or the public naming in 2002 of a television celebrity as an alleged rapist of media personality Ulrika Jonsson and others before any evidence or charges were advanced).

The rule of law is sometimes employed as a factual description of the basic fabric of Western liberal democracies or of the British constitution, but – since it clearly is not – it is best seen as a statement of an ideal. Explanations for breaches of the rule of law range from the purely practical (cost, inefficiency, occasional and unavoidable personal bias, structural flaws in the political and legal systems, justified exemptions etc.), to the ideological (e.g. the Marxist analysis of law as part of the superstructure of an exploitative capitalist system).

Even if the principles of the rule of law were practised to the full, they could not, of themselves, guarantee justice; but – at least from a liberal perspective – they are a necessary precondition of it. The rule of law has often been a shorthand phrase in liberal thinking for the constitutional constraints designed to limit the power of state and government and to protect citizens' rights and freedoms. However, critical scrutiny even of its basic principles raises questions. For example, consistent, certain and clear laws and legal procedures may be quite compatible with legalised tyranny. Dicey even argued that the rule of law and parliamentary sovereignty were 'the twin pillars' of the British constitution; although a Parliament which is above the law fundamentally contradicts the basic principle of legal equality embodied in the rule of law.

Above all, the essence of the rule of law is inherently contradictory, since the state must, on the one hand, make and enforce the rules by which citizens may defend themselves from the state; and, on the other hand, in circumstances of social instability or terror, the state must be as powerful as those it seeks to control; implying that – in the face of, for example, 'terrorism' – it must abandon natural justice and the normal judicial procedures in order to protect itself and its people against the subversion of the rule of law itself. This is precisely the contradiction which liberal democracies such as the USA and UK face in devising new anti-terrorism laws in the twenty-first century.

How far legal systems such as that in the UK genuinely seek even to aspire to the ideals of the rule of law is also a matter of debate: theories such as Marxism would argue that the basic principle or goal of legal equality is a fiction in a capitalist economy, and anarchists would argue that 'just law', under every inherently oppressive state, is a contradiction in terms. Even liberal or conservative appeals to the rule of law, supposedly in good faith, may be political games for ideological ends.

In the international sphere, the concept of the rule of law is increasingly employed to assert that the behaviour of states should accord with a growing body of international law which is, in turn, enforced by a growing number of international courts. For example, the War Crimes Tribunal at The Hague was established in 1993 specifically to indict former Yugoslav President Slobodan Milosevic and other Yugoslav officials. However, when an International Criminal Court (ICC) was created in 2000, the United States was one of only seven countries – along with Libya, Iraq, and Israel – to vote against its establishment, while 120 nations voted yes. According to critics of the USA, Washington was determined to make sure that it would never be subject to the international rule of law. The USA insisted upon – and was granted – immunity from the new ICC after threatening to veto UN peacekeeping missions in Bosnia and elsewhere. Similarly, the USA has threatened to attack Iraq for breaking UN resolutions, but the prime violator of UN resolutions – Israel – is supported to the hilt by the

USA. The arbitrary practices of 'victor's justice' and of 'might is right' may seem to be operative here.

Therefore, it is debatable whether the true principles of the rule of law can ever, with best will, be approached in practice, or whether states such as the USA or UK even genuinely seek to approach them.

Socialism

The Idea

A VERY BROAD RANGE OF THEORIES EMBRACING VARIOUS DEGREES OF COLLECTIVISM, common economic ownership, equality, social justice and democracy. Narrowly, 'socialism' means collective (communal or state) ownership of the means of production and extensive equality of outcome. For Marxism and left-wing anarchism, this means a stateless society. More broadly, it means varying degrees of equality of opportunity and outcome, often through the state as economic owner, political administrator and/or social arbiter.

Development of the Idea

THE TERM 'SOCIALISM' WAS FIRST USED IN BRITAIN IN THE 1820s. HOWEVER, AS BERKI (1975) said, *'It is not a single thing, but a range, an area, an open texture'*.

'There is no point in searching the encyclopaedias for a definitive meaning of socialism; it has none, and never could' (Crosland 1956). Crosland's statement highlights the fact that socialism is perhaps the most wide ranging of all political philosophies. It can broadly be subdivided into revolutionary socialism (utopian or 'ethical' socialism; and Marxism or 'scientific' socialism), and evolutionary socialism – that is, parliamentary, gradualist, reformist, revisionist, 'democratic' socialism, such as the British Labour party. Marxism perceived 'socialism' – in the form of proletarian dictatorship – as the transitionary phase between capitalism and full communism.

Many parliamentary socialists, past and present, regard themselves as Christian socialists and have always rejected the revolutionary road – with its likely violence – on the grounds of religious principle. Tony Benn is one such.

Other evolutionary socialists have revised or abandoned the original, orthodox and fundamentalist revolutionary theory, and now seek gradual reform by the parliamentary road, that is, by the ballot box rather than by mass workers' uprising. They have therefore accepted the liberal framework of pluralist, parliamentary democracy, constitutionalism and consent. They see socialism as an end in itself rather than as a transitionary phase; they perceive it differently from the ways in which the revolutionaries perceived it; and their goals are invariably more limited and moderate than those of communism. They very rarely seek the wholesale abolition of classes, and no evolutionary socialists seek the disappearance of the state.

The traditional values and principles of evolutionary, parliamentary or democratic socialism throughout the twentieth century were, first: a view of human nature as essentially social, cooperative and altruistic – and where it is not, it is the fault of nurture rather than nature – that is, of the capitalist economic system which requires and creates a competitive, individualist, selfish instinct in man, which belies his basic altruism and can be overcome.

Secondly, collectivism: a belief that humans operate best in cooperative social groups and that such collaborative action is more efficient and harmonious than is selfish, competitive individualism. Broadly, collectivism is the belief that humans have a social core and that social groups – whether classes, nations, races or whatever – are the most meaningful entities. For socialists it means a belief in common ownership, working class solidarity and brotherhood, and trade union rights and activities, that is, precisely the French revolutionary ideals of liberty, fraternity and equality.

Thirdly, egalitarianism: a belief in far-reaching equality is the defining doctrine of socialism. Socialists believe that social and economic inequalities are much more the result of economic disadvantages, barriers and injustices rather than of personal inadequacies. They argue that equality of outcome – well beyond the liberal concepts of foundational and formal equality of worth, rights and opportunity – is the prerequisite of genuine freedom, democracy and social harmony.

However, parliamentary socialists – unlike revolutionary communists – very rarely aim for total collective ownership and the complete abolition of class. Also, the state is seen as a crucial mechanism of planning, administration and distribution which can work for the working class – quite different from the Marxist view which predicts the disappearance of the state. Parliamentary or democratic socialism is essentially about state collectivism, redistribution and welfarism.

All socialists also seek social justice: a fair and equitable distribution of resources and rewards. Socialists obviously interpret this in an egalitarian way, in accordance with needs (to varying degrees) rather than individual birthright, luck, talent, effort or wants.

Finally, socialists favour democracy: it was the English Chartists, in the 1830s and 40s, who created the first, mass working class movement for universal suffrage wedded to socialist ideas of equality and collectivism. Socialism should mean equality of 'people power' as well as of wealth, rights and opportunities. For example, former Labour leader Neil Kinnock has defined his interpretation of socialism as *'That determination to use democratic collective action and mutuality (some call it solidarity) as the instruments for ensuring liberty for the individual, which marks socialism out from all other political causes. There are several which favour freedom but no others which accept the*

complete interdependence between individual liberty and collective action and provision'
(quoted in Morgan 1995).

The history of democratic, or parliamentary, socialism throughout the twentieth
century has been characterised by 'revisionism', that is, a shift from left to right, away
from these traditional principles, with a watering down or even abandonment of many
of them.

In the UK, in the first half of the twentieth century, traditional, left-wing, 'Bennite',
democratic socialism was the dominant school of thought within parliamentary
socialism; in the post-war era of consensus politics, the more moderate philosophy of
social democracy predominated; and, since the mid-1990s, 'new' Labour has sought to
redefine the political landscape and to deny the 'left versus right' model of political
thought altogether.

The term 'new' Labour was publicly introduced by Tony Blair in 1994, in his first
speech as leader to Labour's annual conference; though it has never, yet, been adopted
as the official title of the British Labour party. Having lost four successive general
elections, the British Labour party in the mid-1990s decided to 'modernise' in response
to declining working-class numbers, economic globalisation, the collapse of communism and the discrediting of 'old fashioned' socialist ideas after almost 20 years of New
Right Conservative governments. Successive Labour leaders Neil Kinnock, then John
Smith and now Tony Blair (who was elected party leader in July 1994) therefore
pulled the party ever further to the right. Thus 'new' Labour was born, the most
symbolic turning point being the abandonment in 1995 of the party's historic, constitutional commitment to Clause Four – which expressed their nominal pursuit of collective ownership (and which used to be printed on every party membership card): *'To
secure for the workers by hand or by brain the full fruits of their industry and the most
equitable distribution thereof that may be possible upon the basis of the common ownership of the means of production, distribution and exchange, and the best obtainable
system of popular administration and control of each industry or service*'. Former Labour
leader Hugh Gaitskell had attempted to revise Clause Four as far back as 1959, but had
met a humiliating defeat at that year's party conference. Thirty-six years later, Labour's
traditional, manual working-class constituency had shrunk and Labour had been in
permanent opposition for 18 years. The motivation for change was far greater.

The new Clause Four, in 1995, committed the Labour Party to *'a dynamic economy, a
just society, an open democracy and a healthy environment*'.

Development of the Idea

A T ONE LEVEL, SOCIALISM MEANS ECONOMIC ARRANGEMENTS BASED UPON COMMON
or public ownership. At another, it refers to core values such as equality, collectivism, social justice and democracy. For traditional socialists, these different levels
were inseparably intertwined; 'modernisers', however, are much more pragmatic and
flexible about acceptable economic structures. Contemporary 'socialists' say that
they are using the language of equality, freedom, community and cooperation in a

pragmatic update of socialism for the twenty-first century. They argue that they are dogmatists about ends but pragmatists about means. For example, one 'new' Labour spokesman has drawn a distinction between 'socialism' and 'democratic socialism or social democracy': for him, socialism refers to *'the belief that a society is best ordered if a high level of public ownership of the means of production, distribution and exchange is achieved and maintained . . . [But] Democratic socialism or social democracy refers to the belief that, although the balance between private and public ownership is not of prime importance, all economic activity must be open to the influence and, in the last resort, control of a democratically elected government'* (Lord Kennett, quoted in Morgan 1995). This, however, is a far remove from socialism and even liberalism, towards sheer electoralism.

Arguably, of course, the British Labour party was never, actually, socialist: the old Clause Four was always more rhetoric than reality and, apart from a brief flurry of nationalisation after World War II, economic collectivism was never wholeheartedly pursued. It is, after all, the 'Labour' party, not the 'Socialist' party; it was founded primarily to give a voice in Parliament to the trade union movement and 'a fair day's pay for a fair day's work' to labourers within a capitalist economy, rather than to pursue radical socialist goals. It was always about labourism more than socialism. Now, even its links with the trade union movement are substantially weakened and the party's very label sounds rather anachronistic. Now, perhaps, it is more about 'social-ism': that is, still more communitarian than individualist, but no longer a party of the working class or the labour movement.

Since the nineteenth century, socialism of all sorts has primarily upheld the interests of the industrial working class against the perceived iniquities of capitalism. Some non-socialists argue that we now live in a 'post-industrial society', that the traditional working class is a dying breed, that globalised capitalism has triumphed and that socialism everywhere is therefore obsolete. The collapse of orthodox communism since 1989 has obviously added fuel to this argument. As journalist Peter Kellner has put it, the 'ism' of socialism has become a 'wasm'.

Is socialism still viable? Many critics argue that, in its revolutionary form, it was always a utopian impossibility and, since the traditional, manual, working class has diminished in numbers to a minority since the 1980s, even parliamentary socialism is now untenable and, Conservatives would say, undesirable, since it demands too much state planning, interventionism, bureaucracy and denial of individual freedom.

Certainly, there does now seem to be a widespread disillusionment with centralised state socialism; but there is also growing and active protest against globalised free market capitalism with its implications for third world poverty and debt, and first world pollution, militarism and neo-imperialism. Broader concepts of inequality (e.g. of race and gender) and broader arenas of exploitation (e.g. of the environment) are being addressed by these burgeoning 'anti-capitalist' movements of recent years. It may be that new forms of socialism – less statist and more genuinely egalitarian, humanist, liberating, democratic and internationalist – could yet emerge from such developments in the twenty-first century.

Sovereignty

The Idea

THE CONCEPT OF ULTIMATE POWER AND AUTHORITY OVER A GIVEN TERRITORY AND peoples. Most commonly associated with statehood, but sovereignty may be exercised above the level of states and, within a state, ultimate power may be exercised by a monarch, a legislature, a single or collective executive or – in direct democracy – by the people.

Development of the Idea

HISTORICALLY, THE CONCEPT OF SOVEREIGNTY HAS USUALLY BEEN LINKED TO THE concept of the state – and statehood itself is widely defined in terms of sovereignty. Indeed, it is often argued that sovereignty only emerged with the development of the modern state, which was defined most memorably by Max Weber (1948) as an institution with a monopoly of legitimate force for a particular territory. *'Every state is founded on force'*, he said, and *'that indeed is right'*. This notion of monopoly implies a single, absolute source of power: hence sovereignty is *'the idea that there is final and absolute authority in the political community'* (Hinsley 1986).

Some writers (e.g. James 1986) stress the external rather than internal dimension of sovereign statehood. By this view, a state is sovereign – regardless of the nature or degree of its control over its own people – if it has formal constitutional independence in the international arena, in relation to other states.

The concept of sovereignty is arguably multi-dimensional: like power, it may take different forms – for example, political, economic, legal or national. Within the UK, one key pillar of the constitution, according to Dicey (1885) is the legal sovereignty or supremacy of Parliament. This suggests that Parliament is the supreme law-making body in the UK, and that no institution in the country can override its laws. Thus no Parliament can bind its successors – that is, any future Parliament may amend or repeal any previous statute. Also, Parliament is not bound by its own statutes, but instead by a special body of law known as parliamentary privilege. This exempts MPs from much ordinary law; for example, they cannot be sued for slander for words spoken in Parliament. (Incidentally, the doctrine of the legal supremacy of Parliament is, itself, not law but mere convention; Parliament is sovereign because the UK courts and judges, by long-standing tradition, accept that it is so and defer to its overriding power and authority.) Ultimately, however, said Dicey, the legal supremacy of Parliament is constrained by the political sovereignty of the electorate, who choose the MPs in the House of Commons. This remained the formal, constitutional understanding of sovereignty in Britain until the UK joined the European Union in 1973. The EU is a supranational institution, that is, it is not just an international fraternity but a sovereign power over member states with a body of law that takes formal precedence over national law.

The main issue raised by the UK's membership of the EU since 1973 has been political sovereignty which, in turn, has two dimensions. The first is parliamentary sovereignty (said to be the linchpin of the British constitution since the English civil war in the mid-seventeenth century) which has been effectively negated by the primacy of EU laws and treaties. British courts are obliged by the European Communities Act 1972 to refuse to enforce Acts of Parliament which contravene European law (a principle established in the courts by the 1990 *Factortame* case about fishing rights in British waters). Even on entry in 1973, the British Parliament had to accept 43 volumes of existing EU legislation. Over 60 per cent of UK legislation now originates from the EU.

Secondly, however, domestic governments and many voters are generally more concerned about the loss of national sovereignty to the EU, that is, their ability to pursue their own policies without external interference. Until 1986, for example, any single member state could veto any EU directive. The Single European Act 1986 (agreed, ironically, by the Eurosceptic Margaret Thatcher) introduced qualified majority voting (QMV) by which several states had to combine to veto certain EU laws, the scope of which has since increased steadily. This has progressively diminished the sovereignty of individual member states.

Late in 2002, the skeleton of a draft EU constitution was published, suggesting such future possibilities as a potentially powerful post of EU president, dual citizenship of their home country and of the EU for everyone inside the union, a Congress containing both EU and national legislators, simplified rules, more openness and – for the first time – exit procedures for countries seeking to leave the EU. Eurosceptics promptly condemned it as presaging an all-powerful 'United States of Europe'.

A more positive view (Moravcsik 1993) argues that national governments benefit from EU membership, pooling sovereignty to achieve policy goals which would be unattainable alone; and that EU decision making helps to strengthen national governments by reducing the impact of both domestic and international constraints. A United States of Europe is untenable in the foreseeable future but – if it allows Europe to compete on the world stage on more equal terms with, for example, the United States of America – it may not, from this perspective, be wholly undesirable.

Economic sovereignty has become another important issue especially with the creation of the single European currency in 1999. However, this has actually long been undermined in the UK by foreign ownership and investment from Europe and elsewhere, and by Britain's dependence especially on the health of the American economy – apparently with little hostility from the traditional right-wing Eurosceptics. Moreover, the Labour government's granting to the Bank of England of independent control of interest rates (immediately after the 1997 general election) was a willing surrender of a key economic power which brought Britain into line with one of the conditions for joining the euro.

Evaluation of the Idea

SOME POLITICAL PHILOSOPHIES, SUCH AS TRADITIONAL CONSERVATISM AND FASCISM, favour a single, central, sovereign power; others, such as liberalism, favour dispersed power and, therefore, perhaps reject the very concept of sovereignty.

To say (as above) that sovereignty is multidimensional and may take different forms, implies the possibility of divided sovereignty (for example, Dicey's assertion that Parliament has legal sovereignty but the people have political sovereignty). However, 'divided sovereignty' seems a contradiction in terms – either there is one ultimate and overriding power, or there is not. For this reason, some constitutional academics (e.g. Hinsley 1986) deny that it exists at all as a political fact – only as an abstract concept.

Certainly, British parliamentary sovereignty is limited in practice, mainly by the EU whose laws have formal sovereignty over all member states – for example, fishing quotas and the 48-hour working week. There are also many other, informal, constraints on parliamentary sovereignty: for example, other international bodies, courts and laws, such as the UN or the European Court of Human Rights. Parliament is also influenced and constrained by pressure groups, business, the City and other economic power bodies, the media and, ultimately, said Dicey, by the political sovereignty of the electorate, who choose the MPs in the Commons.

Internally, the UK Parliament tends to be dominated by a single-party, majority seat government which, with strong party discipline and backbench support, can usually ensure that its legislative proposals are passed by Parliament. In his 1976 Dimbleby Lecture, Lord Hailsham therefore used the term 'elective dictatorship' to suggest that a majority government, in control of a sovereign Parliament, with a flexible constitution, could effectively change the constitution at will. This thesis gained renewed strength after the general elections of 1997 and 2001 when Labour won massive majorities of seats in the House of Commons (on a minority of the votes cast in the country) and seemed, to many critics, virtually unstoppable. Thus, for example, within its first year in office Labour had pushed through many unpopular policies which were not in its manifesto, such as lone parents' and disabled peoples' benefit cuts, students' tuition fees, completing the Millennium Dome, etc. The (rare) exceptions to this balance of power within Parliament are a backbench revolt, defeat by the House of Lords or a minority government. It is, therefore, often argued that parliamentary sovereignty is usually, in reality, executive sovereignty; or that *'the contradiction at the heart of the British constitution is the principle of parliamentary sovereignty being used by executives to minimise their accountability'* (Judge 1993) – that is, being used as a legitimising cloak for executive power. One example of this occurred in 1992 when the then Conservative government refused a public referendum on the Maastricht Treaty on the grounds that '*The British system is a parliamentary democracy: the government are accountable to Parliament and Parliament is accountable to the electorate . . . The government believes that is the right way to proceed in a parliamentary democracy*' (Britain in Europe, pamphlet published by the Foreign Office, 1992).

More generally, it is the association of sovereignty with statehood which has helped to generate some of the conceptual problems. If the modern state is perceived to be losing sovereignty – either to some power above it (such as the EU) or below it (such as federal bodies or the people themselves), there may be a perception that sovereignty itself is disappearing – rather than simply shifting or dispersing.

Moreover, governments and states have long sought to claim a monopoly of legitimate force for their territories, but that does not mean that they always possess it, in fact. If parents are legally allowed to smack their children, that is legitimate force. If reasonable force is allowed in court cases as a defence against assault, that, too, is legitimate. At the political level, a popular, even violent, rebel leader or group may have much more legitimacy – if not legality – both at home and abroad, than an oppressive state; consider Nelson Mandela and the ANC in apartheid South Africa, or the resistance fighters against the Nazis.

Modern states undoubtedly possess an exceptional concentration of power – but, perhaps, not as much today (either in economic or political terms) as that of some huge multinational corporations whose annual turnover could dwarf the gross domestic products of several small countries. The money markets also have enormous power: when they forced the British pound out of the European Exchange Rate Mechanism on 'black Wednesday' in September 1992, they destroyed the British government's entire economic policy in a single day. '*It has become unfashionable in the study of politics to refer to the power of private capitalism. On the foreign exchanges and in the money markets, however, "they couldn't give a Forex for anything else"*' (Ludlam 1994).

Further problems arise if sovereignty is externally defined as formal constitutional independence from other states – not least because such formal autonomy is only viable if it is backed by sufficient potential military strength to defend it from external aggression. Diverse examples over recent decades such as Bangladesh, Biafra, Palestine and Vietnam illustrate this point. Nor are most modern states legally autonomous, given globalisation and the plethora of international laws and courts.

In an increasingly interdependent world – currently dominated by just one political 'superpower' in the form of the USA – sovereign statehood is a very dubious concept. Nor, perhaps, is it a desirable concept, if it can be employed to ride roughshod over international law and ethical obligations.

Finally, the concept of the sovereign state – particularly when related to internal force – seems fundamentally to contradict the idea of democracy as people power. Liberalism, many forms of socialism and especially anarchism, have always divorced the concept of ultimate sovereignty from that of the state and have vested conclusive sovereignty in the people, whether individually or collectively.

State

The Idea

THE FORMAL, INDEPENDENT, SOVEREIGN POLITICAL POWER BODIES OVER A GIVEN territory, embracing legislative, executive and judicial functions. A distinction is commonly made between two roles of 'state' – that of imposing power or that of granting rights – against 'society': the former implying sovereign power and compulsory law, internationally recognised and with clear and accepted territorial boundaries; and the latter implying informal and fluid human groups and individuals protected by sovereign states.

Development of the Idea

EVEN THE EARLY DERIVATION OF THE WORD 'STATE' IS OBSCURE, BUT TODAY IT MEANS the formal political agents over a given territory, such as the executive, legislature and judiciary. The state is commonly distinguished from all other social institutions by its claim to exercise a monopoly of legitimate force (Weber, 1948). In the UK, for example, the state includes the monarchy, government, Commons, Lords, judges, civil service, devolved assemblies, local councils, police and army. It is, in some ways, easier to define what the state is not. It is not 'society' – the non-political people who live under and within the state, whether in neighbourhoods, families, schools, churches or clubs. The phrase 'civil society' refers to all of the autonomous groups and associations formed by private citizens which have no connection with government and state – for example, families, clubs, businesses etc. It is not, technically, even political parties, which is why a determined distinction is made in pluralist, liberal democracies between party and state funding and between the interests of the governing party and the state.

Further clarity may be gained by asking what is meant by a 'stateless' person or society; it implies an individual or group without legal membership of, or acceptance by, a territorial power, and therefore without rules of attachment or recognised rights and responsibilities between state and individual.

The concept of the state is widely attached to the concepts of country, nation and government, but is separable from all of them. The common features of the modern state are widely accepted as being sovereignty – in relation to both the people under the state and other, sovereign states in the international arena – territory, compulsory laws, more or less effective (not necessarily democratic) government and border defence. A state may include more than one country: for example, the United Kingdom includes England, Scotland, Wales and Northern Ireland, none of which are, in themselves, sovereign states. Similarly, a state may embrace many diverse nations – that is, many diverse groups of people who share a sense of common culture. The UK, USA, Russia and many other states are multicultural. The Scots, for example, may often feel a stronger sense of attachment to their national culture than to the wider UK state – hence devolution. True nation states, where the state houses one people who feel themselves to be a common cultural community, are actually quite rare. The government, finally, is the temporary agent of the state – that is, the political authority and personnel responsible for implementing the aims and functions of the state; it enforces the rulings of the state and acts under its authority. Thus a government, however established (with or without the consent of the people) is the agent and administrative organ of the state. Governments may change and their personnel may come and go, but the state is a permanent entity. All organisations, individuals and activities within a state are subordinate to it.

A recent analysis suggests that the form of the state has changed over the centuries, from the kingly states of the seventeenth century, through the territorial states of the eighteenth century and the later phase of nation states to today's market states which, it is argued, are defined by psychological and infrastructural (i.e. economic) rather than by territorial dimensions. Globalisation, therefore, simply marks another epochal transition in the form of the state (Bobbit 2002).

There are two key theories on the origins and role of the state. The first is the organic theory of the natural state, which likens the state to a living organism (such as a tree). Every part has its different place and function and is dependent on every other part. Since the parts (the people) are completely dependent on the whole (the state) for their continued survival, the whole is therefore more important than any group or individual within it. (The organic analogy is of the tree to the leaf.) The state is natural and prior to the individual and more important than the individual; and the individual exists to serve the state. There is a natural harmony and consensus within the organic unity, but also a natural hierarchy or inequality between its various parts (e.g. brain versus hand, rulers versus ruled). Examples of organic theory include traditional political conservatism (or Toryism) with its belief in social class and traditional hereditary institutions such as the monarchy; and fascism with its strong belief in elitism and the all-powerful state.

The second is the mechanistic theory of the artificial state, which likens the state to a machine, devised by man to serve man, with its parts (people) equal in social worth, autonomous and interchangeable. The individual is therefore more important than the group, society or whole state, and the state exists to serve the individual. Examples of mechanistic theory include liberalism, and New Right economic conservatism (or Thatcherism) which both assert the primacy of the individual.

Some political theories cannot be classified as either organic or mechanistic, because they seek the complete abolition of the state as a coercive political power over society. The main examples are Marxist theory and anarchism.

Philosophies which advocate a state may, therefore, be left wing or right wing, collectivist or individualist and they may seek a very strong or very limited state. Left-wing theories see the state as a means of increasing equality; individualist theories view it as a mechanism for enhancing freedom; while right-wing theories largely look to the state to promote order and security.

Evaluation of the Idea

THERE IS NO COMMONLY ACCEPTED DEFINITION OF THE STATE. IT MAY NOT ACCORD with the concept of sovereignty, since other bodies may have real power over it: for example, the European Union is a supranational body with formal, legal power over its member states; and other decision-making bodies, such as economic interest groups, may have real power over supposedly sovereign states (one notable example being the UK's forced exit from the European Exchange Rate Mechanism in 1992 by the currency speculators). Moreover, states have long sought to claim a monopoly of legitimate force for their territories, but that does not mean that they always possess it, in fact. A popular, even violent, rebel leader or group may have much more legitimacy – if not legality – both at home and abroad, than an oppressive state: for example, Nelson Mandela and the ANC in apartheid South Africa, or the resistance fighters against the Nazis. Anyway, in the twenty-first century, how valid is the concept of statehood as sovereignty, given the growing impact of globalisation and internationalism? Probably no state in the contemporary world – not even the USA as the only current 'superpower' – is genuinely autonomous and unrestrained by external economic, military, legal and political influences.

The idea of statehood may not even accord with the concept of territory, if a common body of law is the defining criterion: for example, Islamic law applies across a large number of states (and sometimes only within parts of them).

Very many political theorists have asked why states have been created. The dominant answer has been that human nature is imperfect or downright evil, and needs an ultimate power to control its baser instincts. Other theories postulate the dictates of economic and technological change, population pressures or war – but they do not seem to address the basic question of why social communities cannot solve those issues without recourse to some body of ultimate power and authority.

At one extreme is the belief in the need for an absolute state: *'The only way to erect such a common power as may be able to defend them from the invasion of foreigners and the injuries of one another . . . is to confer all their power and strength upon one man, or upon one assembly of men, that may reduce all their wills, by plurality of voices, unto one will . . . This is the generation of that great Leviathan, or rather (to speak more reverently), of that Mortal God, to which we owe under the Immortal God, our peace and defence'* (Hobbes 1651). This is the power theory of the state.

At some intermediate point: '*In a free society the state does not administer the affairs of men. It administers justice among men who conduct their own affairs.*' (Lippman 1955). From this viewpoint, the state is the neutral set of arbitrating political institutions and roles within and through which partisan conflict is confined and combined. The liberal view of the state is that it defends its citizens from internal and external aggression, protects their rights and provides health, educational and other social services to those in need. However, liberal thinking is deeply ambivalent as to whether the state is a dangerous bastion of power or a positive enhancer of freedom – or, potentially, both. Because of their fundamental stress on freedom, liberals are wary of power, especially state and government power. This reflects their belief that, although human nature is essentially rational, it is also self-interested and hence potentially corruptible. Therefore the role of the state should be positive but limited.

At the other extreme: '*So long as the state exists there is no freedom. When there is freedom there will be no state.*' (Lenin 1917). Revolutionary socialists and especially anarchists have long envisaged a future stateless society, because they believe that the state is an inherently oppressive and coercive force.

Marxism can, at least, explain the origin and duration of the state as the political agent of the economic ruling class throughout human history. However, a key weakness of the anarchist perspective is its failure to explain the origin (or duration) of the state, given the anarchists' belief in the perfectibility of human nature and the inherently evil, corrupting and oppressive nature of the state. If humans are, in origin and essence, perfect, how and why did the coercive state ever come to be? Are states merely superstructural – secondary – products of deterministic economic forces, as Marxism argues, or are they evil and oppressive agents of power who should be the primary target of opposition, as anarchists argue? Anarchist theories which perceive the state as the embodiment of power may neglect alternative sources of social power: for example, community, class, peer group or family. Liberal critics of anarchism fear that, in a stateless and lawless society, a tyranny of majority public opinion would prevail which could be deeply intolerant of minority rights and views. They point to the apparent need for state legislation against sexual and racial discrimination, apparent public support for capital punishment and so on. This suggests that, without the protective oversight of a state, a punitive form of social exclusion or coercion may prevail which could be crueller than most forms of retribution imposed by the state and its laws.

Most recent theorists of state power have rejected both the most negative and the most positive visions of the role of the state, and regard it simply as an agent of limited variants of freedom, equality and security. It may be that this will continue to be the case until other agents – individual, community or international powers – can step in and replace it.

However, this raises the final question: can we ever live without the state? Anarchists assert that, until some six thousand years ago – that is, for over four-fifths of our existence – all humans lived in stateless societies and, therefore, could readily do so again. To live without the state may not mean living without social rules, order and harmony – quite the contrary. The world seems currently threatened by nuclear, chemical or biological warfare, ecological catastrophe, and regional or religious conflicts – all dictated by people acting in the name of states who may, conceivably, be threatening the whole of humanity.

Given that the value of the state has been challenged since its inception, and that the very survival of the contemporary state is disputed by the impact of international agencies, international law and some theories of globalisation – perhaps the more telling question is, how much longer can we live with the state?

References

ACTON, LORD (1907) *The History of Freedom and Other Essays*, Macmillan, London.

ANDERSON, B. (1983) *Imagined Communities: Reflections on the Origins and Spread of Nationalism*, Verso, London.

ARENDT, A. (1968) What is Authority?, in *Between Past and Future*, Viking, New York.

ARISTOTLE (1946) *Politics* (trans. Barker, E.), Oxford University Press, Oxford.

BABEUF, F. (1976) *Manifesto of the Equals* (trans. Lukes, S., 1971), Methuen, London.

BAGEHOT, W. (1867) *The English Constitution*, Fontana, London.

BAKER, A.J. (1986) *Examining British Politics*, Hutchinson, London.

BAKUNIN, M. (1990) *Statism and Anarchy*, Cambridge University Press, Cambridge.

BARTLETT, J. (1992) *Familiar Quotations*, Little Brown, Boston.

BELL, D. (1962) *The End of Ideology*, Free Press, New York.

BELL, D. (1988) End of Ideology Revisited, *Government and Opposition*, 23.

BERKI, R.N. (1975) *Socialism*, Dent, London.

BERLIN, I. (1990) *The Crooked Timber of Humanity,* John Murray, London.

BLUNT, W.S. (2002) Britain's Imperial Destiny, 1896–1899, in *Internet Modern History Sourcebook*, http://www.fordham.edu/halsall/mod/mmodsbook.html.

BOBBIT, P. (2002) *The Shield of Achilles: War, Peace and the Course of History*, Allen Lane, London.

BULLOCK, A. AND SHOCK, M. (1967) *Liberal Tradition*, Oxford University Press, Oxford.

BUNTING, M. (2001) Intolerant Liberalism, *The Guardian*, 8 October.

BURKE, E. (1774) Letter to Constituents in Bristol, in *Edmund Burke: Selections from his Political Writings and Speeches*, T. Nelson and Sons, London.

BURKE, E. (1790) *Reflections on the Revolution in France* (ed. Hill, B.W.), Fontana, London.

CHAMBERLAIN, H.S. (1899) *Foundations of the Nineteenth Century*, John Lane, New York.

CLAUSEWITZ, C. VON (2000) *Book of War*, Random, New York.

CRICK, B. (1964) *In Defence of Politics*, Penguin, Harmondsworth.

CROSLAND, A. (1956) *The Future of Socialism*, Jonathan Cape, London.

DAHL, R. (1984) *Modern Political Analysis*, Prentice Hall, New Jersey.

DARLING, C.J. (1992) *Scintillae Juris*, Ibex/Heritage Book Group, Albert Park.

DARWIN, C. (1859) *On the Origin of Species*, Dent, London.

DEFOE, D. (1994) *Robinson Crusoe*, Penguin, Harmondsworth.

DE PAOR, L. (1977) *Divided Ulster*, Penguin, Harmondsworth.

DE TOCQUEVILLE, A. (1840) *Democracy in America*, Fontana, London.

DE TRACY, A.D. (1901) The Elements of Ideology, in Emmet, K. (1978) *A Philosophe in the Age of Revolution: Destutt de Tracy and the Origins of 'Ideology'*, American Philosophical Society, Philadelphia.

DICEY, A.V. (1885) *Law of the Constitution*, Macmillan, London.

DUPRE, J. (2002) *Human Nature and the Limits of Science*, Oxford University Press, Oxford.

DURKHEIM, E. (1902) *The Division of Labour in Society*, Free Press, New York.

ENGELS, F. (1884) *The Origins of the Family, Private Property and the State*, Lawrence and Wishart, London.

FEUCHTWANGER, E. (2002) *Bismarck (Routledge Historical Biographies)*, Routledge, London.

FIRESTONE, S. (1971) *The Dialectic of Sex*, Jonathan Cape, London.

FRANCE, A. (1927) *The Red Lily*, Grosset, New York.

FRIEDAN, B. (1963) *The Feminine Mystique*, Norton, New York.

FRIEDRICH, C.J. AND BRZEZINSKI, Z. (1963) *Totalitarian Dictatorships and Democracy*, Praeger, New York.

FROMM, E. (1941) *Escape to Freedom*, Avon, New York.

FUKUYAMA, F. (1989) The End of History, *National Interest*, Summer.

GAMBLE, A. (1988) *The Free Economy and the Strong State: The Politics of Thatcherism*, Macmillan, London.

GASSET, J. ORTEGA Y (1961) *The Revolt of the Masses*, Allen and Unwin, London.

GIDDENS, A. (1998) *The Third Way*, Polity Press, Cambridge.

GOBINEAU, J-A. (1855) Essay on the Inequality of Human Races, in Biddiss, M.D. (ed.) (1970) *Gobineau: Selected Political Writings*, Harper and Row, New York.

GODWIN, W. (1793) *Enquiry Concerning Political Justice*, Oxford University Press, Oxford.

GOLDING, W. (1997) *Lord of the Flies*, Faber and Faber, London.

GRAMSCI, A. (1971) *Selections from the Prison Notebooks* (ed. Hoare, Q. and Nowell-Smith, G.), Lawrence and Wishart, London.

GREEN, T.H. (1988) *Works* (ed. Nettleship, R.), Oxford University Press, Oxford.

GRIFFITH, J. (1991) *The Politics of the Judiciary*, Fontana, London.

HAILSHAM, Q. (1976) Elective Dictatorship: The Dimbleby Lecture, *The Listener*, 21 October.

HAYEK, F. (1944) *The Road to Serfdom*, RKP, London.

HEATER, D. (1975) *Contemporary Political Ideas*, Longman, London.

HEYWOOD, A. (1992) *Political Ideologies*, Macmillan, London.

HIMMELFARB, G. (1975) *On Liberty and Liberalism*, Secker, London.

HINSLEY, F.H. (1986) *Sovereignty*, Cambridge University Press, Cambridge.

HITLER, A. (1969) *Mein Kampf*, Hutchinson, London.

HOBBES, T. (1651) *Leviathan*, Penguin, Harmondsworth.

HOBSON, J.A. (1902) *Imperialism*, Routledge, London.

HOGG, Q. (1947) *The Case for Conservatism*, Penguin, Harmondsworth.

HOFFMAN, J. (1994) Human Nature, *Politics Review*, 3.3, February.

HOWARD, A. (1987) *Rab: The Life of R.A. Butler*, Jonathan Cape, London.

JAMES, A. (1986) *Sovereign Statehood*, Allen and Unwin, London.

JENSEN, A. (1969) *Environment, Heredity and Intelligence*, Harvard Educational Publishers, Massachusetts.

JOYCE, P. (2001) *101 Key Ideas: Politics*, Hodder and Stoughton, London.

JUDGE, D. (1993) *The Parliamentary State*, Sage, London.

KAUTSKY, K. (1915) *Die Neue Zeit*, S.A. Bloch, Chicago.

KEDOURIE, E. (1974) *Nationalism*, Hutchinson, London.

KELSEN, H. (1973) *Essays in Legal and Moral Philosophy*, Kluwer Academic Publishers, Boston.

KEYNES, J.M. (1936) *General Theory of Employment, Interest and Money*, Macmillan, London.

KIRK, R. (1982) *The Portable Conservative Reader*, Penguin, Harmondsworth.

KROPOTKIN, P. (1902) *The State: Its Historic Role*, Heinemann, London.

LASWELL, H.D. (1958) *Politics: Who Gets What, When, How*, Meridian, London.

LEFTWICH, A. (1983) *Redefining Politics: People, Resources and Power*, Methuen, London.

LENIN, V.I. (1915) *Imperialism as the Highest Stage of Capitalism*, Progress, Moscow.

LENIN, V.I. (1917) *The State and Revolution*, Progress, Moscow.

LENIN, V.I. (1973) *On Imperialism and Imperialists*, Progress, Moscow.

LEWONTIN, R. (1975) Letter from Sociobiology Study Group, *New York Review of Books*, 13 November.

LIPPMAN, W. (1955) *An Enquiry into the Principles of a Good Society*, Allen and Unwin, London.

LIPSET, S. (1969) *Political Man*, Heinemann, London.

LOCKE, J. (1962) *Two Treatises of Government*, Cambridge University Press, Cambridge.

LUDLAM. S. (1994) Parliamentary or Executive Sovereignty? The Ratification of the Maastricht Treaty, *Politics Review*, 3.4, April.

LUKES, S. (1974) *Power: A Radical View*, Macmillan, London.

MACHIAVELLI, N. (1972) *The Prince, Selections from the Discourses and Other Writings* (ed. Plamenatz, J.), Fontana, London.

MACMILLAN, H. (1927) *Industry and the State*, Macmillan, London.

MACMILLAN, H. (1938) *The Middle Way*, Macmillan, London.

MACPHERSON, C.B. (1962) *The Political Theory of Possessive Individualism: Hobbes to Locke*, Clarendon Press, Oxford.

MACPHERSON, C.B. (1966) *The Real World of Democracy*, Oxford University Press, Oxford.

MALCOLM X (1962) *Malcolm X Speaks*, Pathfinder, New York.

MANDELSON, P. (1996) *The Blair Revolution: Can New Labour Deliver?*, Faber and Faber, London.

MANNHEIM, K. (1960) *Ideology and Utopia*, Routledge & Kegan Paul, London.

MARCUSE, H. (1964) *One Dimensional Man*, Routledge, London.

MARSHALL, G.W. (1971) *Constitutional Theory*, Oxford University Press, Oxford.

MARSHALL, T.H. (1950) *Citizenship and Social Class*, Cambridge University Press, Cambridge.

MARX, K. (1843) *Critique of Hegel's Philosophy of Right*, Cambridge University Press, Cambridge.

MARX, K. AND ENGELS, F. (1848) *The Communist Manifesto*, Penguin, Harmondsworth.

MILIBAND, R. (1983) *The State in Capitalist Society*, Verso, London.

MILL, J.S. (1859) *On Liberty*, Penguin, Harmondsworth.

MILL, J.S. AND TAYLOR, H. (1869) *On the Subjection of Women*, Dent, London.

MILLER, D., COLEMAN, J., CONNOLLY, W. AND RYAN, A. (EDS.) (1991) *The Blackwell Encyclopaedia of Political Thought*, Blackwell, Oxford.

MILLS, C.W. (1956) *The Power Elite*, Oxford University Press, New York.

MIRZA, H.S. (ED.) (1988) *Black British Feminism*, Routledge, London.

MITCHELL, J. (1971) *Women's Estate*, Penguin, Harmondsworth.

MONTESQUIEU, C-L. (1748) *The Spirit of Laws*, Free Press, Illinois.

MORAVCSIK, A. (1993) Preferences and Power in the EC, *Journal of Common Market Studies*, 31(4).

MOREL, E. (2002) Quoted 1903. In *Internet Modern History Sourcebook*, http://www.fordham.edu/halsall/mod/mmodsbook.html.

MORGAN, I. (1995) The Labour Party and Socialism, *Politics Review*, 5.2, November.

MORRISON, R. (2002) The Englishing of Earth, *The Times*, 29 June.

NKRUMAH, K. (1965) *Neo-Colonialism, the Last Stage of Imperialism*, International Publishing Company, New York.

NOZICK, R. (1974) *Anarchy, State and Utopia*, Blackwell, Oxford.

OGDEN, J. (1969) *Isaac D'Israeli (Oxford English Monographs)*, Oxford University Press, Oxford.

O'SULLIVAN, N. (1976) *Conservatism*, Dent, London.

PAINE, T. (1791) *Rights of Man*, Penguin, Harmondsworth.

PONTON, G. AND GILL, P. (1982) *Introduction to Politics*, Blackwell, Oxford.

POPPER, K. (1945) *The Open Society and its Enemies*, Routledge & Kegan Paul, London.

RAWLS, J. (1970) *A Theory of Justice*, Oxford University Press, Oxford.

ROBERTS, J. (2000) *Joseph Goebbels: Nazi Propaganda Minister (Holocaust Biographies)*, Rosen Publishing Group, New York.

ROTHBARD, M. (1978) *For a New Liberty*, Collier Macmillan, New York.

ROUSSEAU, J-J. (1762) *The Social Contract and Discourse on the Origins of Inequality* (ed. Cole, G.D.H.), Dent, London.

SARTRE, J-P. (1974) *Existentialism and Humanism*, Methuen, London.

SCHAPIRO, L. (1972) *Totalitarianism*, Pall Mall Press, London.

SCHLESINGER, A. (1998) *Imperial Presidency*, Replica Books, New Jersey.

SCRUTON, R, (1982) *A Dictionary of Political Thought*, Pan, London.

SELIGER, M. (1976) *Politics and Ideology*, Allen and Unwin, London.

SIMPSON, B.D. (1996) *The Political Education of Henry Adams*, University of South Carolina Press, S.C.

SMILES, S. (1859) *Self-Help*, Penguin, Harmondsworth.

SMITH, A. (1976) *An Enquiry into the Nature and Causes of the Wealth of Nations*, University of Chicago Press, Chicago.

SMITH, A.D. (1979) *Nationalism in the Twentieth Century*, Australian National University, Canberra.

SMITH, A.D. (1986) *The Ethnic Origin of Nations*, Blackwell, Oxford.

SOREL, G. (1950) *Reflections on Violence*, Macmillan, New York.

STIRNER, M. (1843) *The Ego and His Own*, Jonathan Cape, London.

STRAUSS, L. (1959) *What is Political Philosophy?*, Free Press, New York.

SUMNER, W. (1884) *War and Other Essays*, New Haven, CN and London.

SWIFT, J. (1994) *Gulliver's Travels*, Penguin, Harmondsworth.

THACKERAY, W.M. (1982) *Letters*, Haskell House, USA.

TREVOR ROPER, H. (1947) *The Last Days of Hitler*, Macmillan, London.

WEBER, M (1948) *Essays in Sociology* (eds. Gerth, H.H. and Mills, C.W.), Routledge & Kegan Paul, London.

WHITE, R.J. (1964) *The Conservative Tradition*, Black, London.

WOLLSTONECRAFT, M. (1792) *Vindication of the Rights of Women*, Orion, London.

Index